CARTRIDGE DRAWINGS

Now and Then

From

The Pen of Ken

by

Ken J. Rutterford

Published 2007 by arima publishing

www.arimapublishing.com

ISBN 978-1-84549-213-7

© Ken J. Rutterford 2007

All rights reserved

This book is copyright. Subject to statutory exception and to provisions of relevant collective licensing agreements, no part of this publication may be reproduced, stored in a retrieval system, or transmitted in any form or by any means, without the prior written permission of the author.

Printed and bound in the United Kingdom

This book is sold subject to the conditions that it shall not, by way of trade or otherwise, be lent, re-sold, hired out, or otherwise circulated without the publisher's prior consent in any form of binding or cover other than that which it is published and without a similar condition including this condition being imposed on the subsequent purchaser.

arima publishing
ASK House, Northgate Avenue
Bury St Edmunds, Suffolk IP32 6BB
t: (+44) 01284 700321

www.arimapublishing.com

COPYRIGHT

All of the drawings in this book are of my own copyright. I do expect that cartridge collectors may wish to copy them so as to use in listing their own collections. Or the cutting out and sticking them on to the fronts of draws in cartridge cabinets, etc. What the publishers and I will not tolerate is having them copied and used for gain, or given away as a complete set. If one should wish to use them for any other genuine reason, then please be so kind as to seek my permission in writing via the publishers.

Ken J. Rutterford.

Many of my cartridge drawings are first drawn large and then reduced to correct size.   They are then stored for reuse.

DEDICATION

This book is dedicated in memory to a dear aunt, Miss Annie Millie Maria Rutterford. Also to her father, my grandfather, Mr Joseph Rutterford.

ACKNOWLEDGEMENTS

It is with thanks to so many people that has enabled me to have been able to make the many drawings and so to be able to compile this book. So many people have sent me sets of photographs even from as far away as Australia and the U.S.A. Then there are those kind collectors that have given me access to their prized collections. My thanks also to the many cartridge club members that have allowed me to take sets of photographs and foil rubbings from off of old rare cartridges. These they have brought along with them to club meetings so that others could have the pleasure to see them. By mentioning names, I invariably seem to leave some persons name out. As there has been so many of you, I have decided only to mention some names of those who have now moved on to pastures new. These people should not be forgotten. To all of you that have given me help I here thankyou very much. All that is now left for me to say is, please enjoy this book and it's drawings.

Known contributors who are no longer with us

D. Andrew;   G. Barrell;   G. Boothroyd;   T. Claridge;   D. Fleet;
A. Francis;   J. Glossop;   P. Harvey;   D. Hedlund;   G. Parker;
D. Stegall;   C. Twyman;   E. Wastie:

CONTENTS

COPYRIGHT	3
LARGE DRAWINGS	4
DEDICATION	5
ACKNOWLEDGEMENTS	6
THE PURPOSE OF THIS BOOK	8
INTRODUCTION	9
RESEARCHING OLD CARTRIDGE FIRMS	12
ON MAKING THE DRAWINGS	14
UNDERSTANDING THE DRAWINGS	17
THE CARTRIDGE DRAWINGS, Plate 21 to Plate 78	18
DRAWING HEADSTAMPINGS AND OVER-SHOT CARDS	79
UNDERSTANDING THE HEADSTAMP LIST	80
THE HEADSTAMPINGS	81
HEADSTAMPINGS, Pin Fire	83
HEADSTAMPINGS, Rim Fire	92
HEADSTAMPINGS, Central Fire	93
HEADSTAMPINGS BELATED ADDITIONS, Central Fire	174
THE SIDE ELEVATIONS	183
A DRAWING LARGE AND REDUCED	189
INDEX TO PLATES	190

PLEASE NOTE

That in this book all the Plate Numbers etc, have been kept within the page numbering sequence. Also that the Headstampings are listed by their gauge sizes and in a semi-alphabetical order. The Plate Cartridge Drawings are also listed semi-alphabetically.

THE PURPOSE OF THIS BOOK

Many good things come in threes. As I write this now I am hoping that this may hold good for this book. This is my third published book on shotgun cartridges. I was very pleased when I was to get my first book published, 'Collecting Shotgun Cartridges', but I was never happy with the end result. This then made me vow to have another go and to do better.

My second book, 'Cartridges of the British Isles' or, Great Great Granfer's Shotgun Fodder' was my attempt at doing something better and I now feel that with it I have at last succeeded. To obtain my desired results I then drew many line drawings of old shotgun cartridges. Maybe best described as flag type drawings. This then became a relaxing hobby for me. As a sufferer of osteo-arthritis I am now unable to do the many things that I once enjoyed doing in life. Due to this I now find that I have to pay other people to do many of these things. Sitting down making these cartridge drawings is one thing that I can enjoy doing and it has given me a great deal of pleasure. By making that second book it has enabled me to share my work with many other people and I now feel that my work will not be all wasted. It has also placed a lot of our past cartridge history on record.

Since then I have given thought to the many other cartridge drawings that I have made and for various reasons they could not be used in book number two. The thought then came to me, why not bunch them all up together in another book. By doing just that has created a companion to 'Cartridges of the British Isles' and at the same time it has recorded many more cartridges to history.

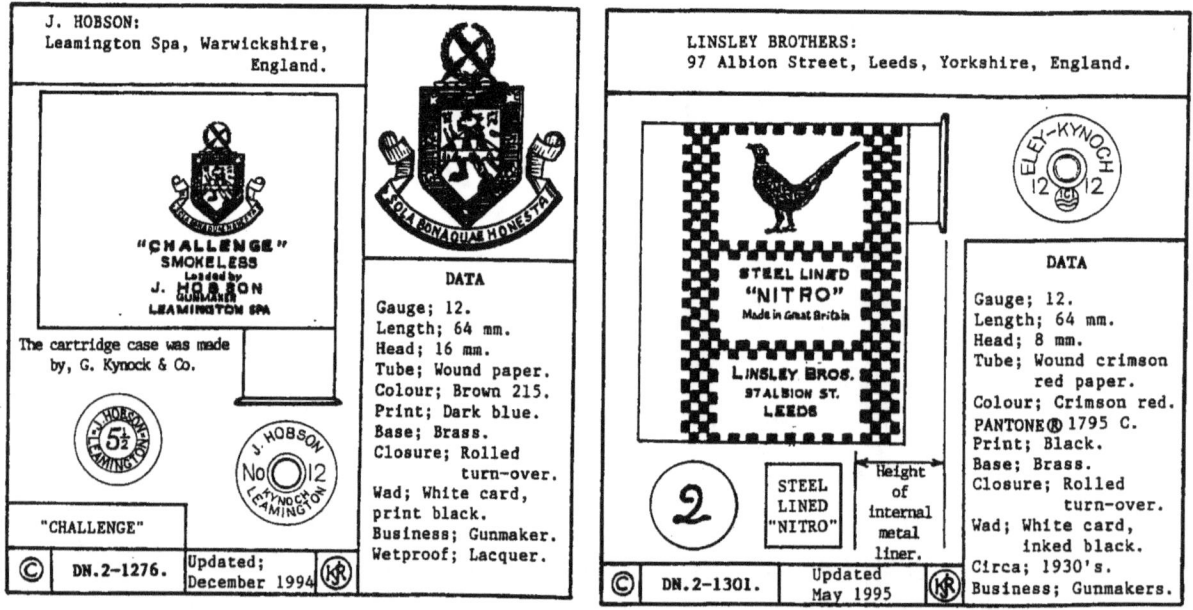

Two completed drawings at sixty-four percent reduction.

INTRODUCTION

Shotgun cartridges have always interested me right throughout my lifetime. I was born in a gamekeepers residence way down in Sarson Wood in the parish of Amport in Hampshire. The first six years of my life was a very lonely one. Each winter come the shooting season, the guns would stand to the front of our home and often with royalty amoung them. When they moved away to their next drive, they left the ground strewn with colourful empty cartridge cases. These then became my toys. That is how I became introduced to cartridges at a very early age.

I collected cartridge cases as a child, but in my later years I started to collect old cartridges more seriously. I well remember my father saying to me, 'What on earth do you want to collect those old things for'. He then said, 'Those old paper cartridges frightened me. When I first took your mother to make our home down in Sarson Wood, it was then that I saw all those empty cartridge cases rotting away on the ground from the previous shoot. It was only then that I realized the vast amount of pheasants that I was expected to rear and to hold on my beat.

Sarson Wood.

I have dedicated this book to my Aunt Annie and my Grandfather. This being so, I feel that it is most fitting to tell you a little bit about them. My aunt and father came from a very large family. Altogether there was six girls and six boys, but two of them died young. Grandfather was also a gamekeeper and a very good one at that. He had brought his new wife with him from Elvedon in Suffolk to work on the Highclere Estate in Hampshire. A new bungalow was built for him to move into. Painted all over in red oxide, the exterior was clad with sheets of corrugated iron. The interior was varnished matchboarding. Stove pipes went up through the roof and it is a wonder that it never burnt down. This timbered framed building still stands today, but all of it's outbuildings have long since been removed. Their old home'stead is at Easton Park, Crux Easton and today it serves as a place for shooting parties to get out of the weather and enjoy their lunches.

Captain deHavilland, later on to become Sir Geoffrey, became a friend of the Rutterford family. He had been known to have walked the woodlands with grandfather. On most weekends, the captain would fly one of his Moth aircraft from his factory to his country retreat at Crux Easton. I can well remember the times when my parents payed a visit and Aunt Annie would walk me to look at his aeroplane. It was always parked in an enclosure in the corner of a large field on Grandpa's pheasant beat. This field is still known locally as The deHavilland Field.

The Iron House.

Grandfather became known locally as 'Old Joe' and he was very much respected by all. Over the years I have been told several good stories about him. I feel that I must tell you some of them, and so here goes. Old Joe was on his way home from his local, 'The Three Legged Cross' and his dog was with him. It was a bright moonlit night and as he crossed what is known as The Lands, to the front of him was a giant of a fellow that was bending down. He then took this chap to be setting a snare and so he made after him. This fellow then glided off at a very fast pace. So much so that he could not keep up with him. He then realized that this chap was not leaving any footprints in the dew covered grass like he was doing. The story went on that his dog arrived home all of a shake with it's tail tight between it's back legs long before he did. I was told this story when I was staying there as a child. I did not sleep well that night.

Then there was the time when many gamekeepers had been given a clay shoot at Highclere Castle. The gentry had laid bets on their keepers. Old Joe had performed well. He was pushing his bike home as he had no front lamp. It is possible that he may have had a skin full as well. This was in the days when cycle lamps were fueled either by carbide or paraffin oil. He was then stopped by the police for having no light. This upset Grandpa and he became very angry. So much so that he walloped a policeman. When summond to court in Whitchurch, the judge on the case was a gent that had made himself some money by placing his bet on Old Joe. Due to that, grandfather turned up trumps.

Two boys were where they should not have been. They were up a tall tree. The one which had climbed up high then shouted down to his mate, 'Du yu know, you can see Old Joe's house from here'. A reply then came back from the ground, 'Oh yes, but can you see Old Joe'.

It was during a pheasant shoot when a gun pointed towards my grandparents home which was known as The Iron House. He then said to his loader, 'What is that place over there, it looks like a little factory'. His loader replied, 'You are quite right Sir, that's just what it is'.

Grandmother died through cancer when I was just four years old. Annie then gave her life to keeping home for the family and an apprentice keeper. She then continued to look after grandfather until he died. She then set herself up a home in a cottage. Then in 1964 we lost my mother, also through cancer. Annie then gave up her cottage home and came and made home with dad. She became a second grandmother to our children. Dad then passed on and Annie was left on her own. If she had got married she would have made some keeper a very good wife. A nicer person I have yet to meet.

It was always parked in an enclosure.
A deHavilland D.H.87B Hornet Moth.
Registered G-ADMT it was then the firm's demonstrator.

RESEARCHING OLD CARTRIDGE FIRMS

From time to time I have received letters or phone calls. Some person has unearthed some rare old cartridge and is desperate to know how old it is and what the firm that sold it did. It is not always possible to come up with an answer, but occasionally I have been able to do just that. The cartridge in question may have been by Joe Bloggs with an Eley stamping that had the place name of Neverworth. My answer might have been, 'He was once an ironmonger at 123 Whatsit Street and he was known to have been active between 1888 and 1908'. Fictitios I know, but that could have been a typical posed question.

Over the past three to four decades I have toured the mainland with two old Volkswagen campers. My latest camper I called 'Wandering Willie'. As my wife disapproved, I had to change her name to 'Wandering Williamina'. She is now going on for thirty-four years old and should have been classed as a historical vehicle having a free road tax. It was not to be, Mr Blair entered office and then struck a line through it. I soon took a dislike to that chap and his ways of running our country. This by the way they tackled the foot and mouth crisis. Woodland footpaths were closed while close by, sports games were being played on village recreation grounds. Worst still was the way dead carcases were piled up in heaps out in the open. This allowed the carrion to be easy pickings for animals and birds to then carry off for miles. When will they ever learn to understand the workings of the countryside ?. After all of this, the country then put them in for a second time. They now try to police the world and they are not capable of policing our own country. I must stop getting on about New Labour as you may be one of those persons that like them. I will get on with this chapter on the researching of old cartridge firms.

When ever we have been on tour with the VW, I have tried hard to visit many public record librarys. I have then undertaken research on the old gunshops and ironmonger stores. In most of the librarys that I have visited, for just 10p a time I have been able to make photo copys of pages from out of old county trade directorys. I would have liked to have coppied far more such as the agricultural firms, but my wife has always been waiting for me to move on. I now own a spring-back binder which is bulging with copies from these old directories. There are still many countys that I failed to cover. There are several reasons for this. One of them is because it is nearly always the larger towns who's librarys hold these old books. I have had my camper fitted with a high top. This is because I do not believe in raising the roof. She is seven feet and seven inches tall and refuses to be driven into multi-story parks. I have therefore made for open carparks by following the blue signs. Eventually the carpark is reached and sometimes down a one way street only to find that the council has erected a goal post across the entrance. This is a council disease that was started by one council and has since spread to many more. Often the ones in the large towns and citys. You have then got to the parking not knowing that you will not fit in. The next thing is that one cannot turn round as there is a row of cars right up your jacksy. This can also upset my Wandering Williamina.

Old cartridge boxes can sometimes yield some information that has not been printed on the cartridges. If you collect old advertisments, then do note the date from the magazine from which they were taken. To get to know the age of old cartridges is a thing that you have to gadually acquire. To get to know when certain headstampings were being used. When paper tubes were first rolled by using the same colour paper throughout. By studying old ammunition catalogues and advertisments. This is the only ways that you can get to know your subject. It cannot be done by judging the condition of a cartridge as some very old cartridges can still look as good as the day that they were produced if they have been stored well.

In researching old cartridges and their firms, one thing that you should not do is to take a lot of information from out of one book. To do that is known as copying. By taking information that is given in many books is called research.

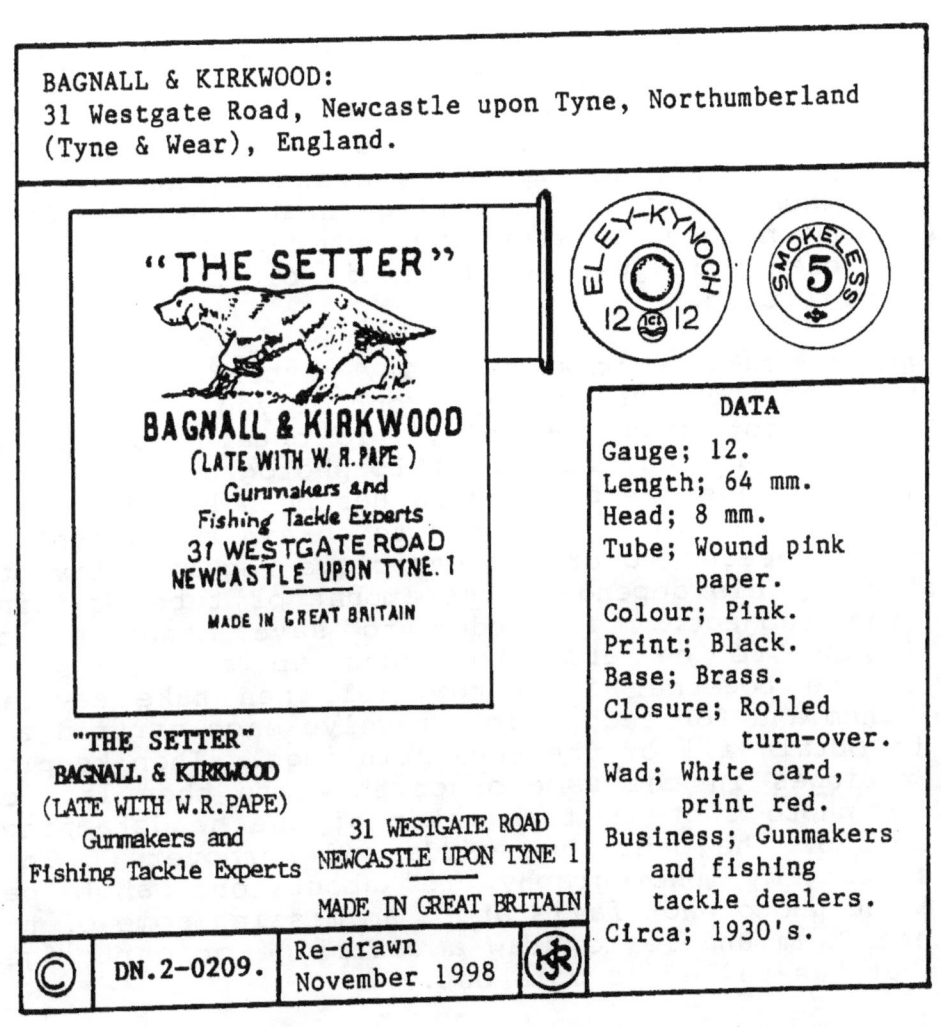

A completed drawing at full size.

ON MAKING THE DRAWINGS

The first things to have are the necessary materials to work with. I use a set of drawing pens with the sizes 1, 3, 5 and 7. Also some drawing pencils and the drawing paper. A steel ruler that can easily read. There has been a few times when tracing paper can be of use. If it is not used for anything else, it can help in obtaining the correct layout of the tube printings.

Over the years I have gone through an unlimited number of Pritt Stick adhesives containers. Also much use has been made of a Rolson cutting board and very many cutting knives as well. These items have been very much used as all of my cartridge drawings have been built up.

All of these drawings have been made to the cartridges actual size. Very much use of photo copying has been made in making my drawings. When ever I have shown any of them, then they have been reduced in size by sixty-four percent.

Prior to selling my large collection of shotgun cartridges, I could then take a round from out of my collection to draw it. Many of those cartridges got drawn, but not all of them. If I am unable to have the full details of a cartridge then I will not make an attempt at drawing it. I have been known to have broken this rule when a rare old cartridge head has been found with a stamping that no one has ever seen before. A provisional drawing has then been made just so that this old firm can then be recorded in my records.

The best way to make a drawing of any cartridge is to sit down quietly and have the cartridge in front of you. More often than not, this has not been possible. To obtain most of my needed information I have had to resort to photography. At one of our cartridge meetings, Peter McGowan has been heard to say, 'David Bailey is at it again'. In order to obtain the amount of information that is needed to draw a cartridge requires five to seven photo shots. This depending the amount of tube printing which is on the subject. In order to save money on my photography I like to be able to stand up six to seven cartridges up close together in a row. I then take several photo shots of them and for each shot I revolve each cartridge a little so as to obtain all of the tube printings. Then keeping all of the cartridges in the same order they are then laid on their sides. A photo shot is then taken of the headstampings and another shot of the over-shot cards and turnovers. This then averages out my photography to about one shot per cartridge. If one photo shot fails and I am missing some of the information then I am unable to draw a cartridge or cartridges depending on what has failed to come out.

As the tube printings come in various sizes, to draw these I make what I now call ladders. To make a ladder I cut several strips of thin card about 10 mm wide. These are then placed flat down with a gap between each which is just a little greater than the height of each line of tube printings. These strips of card are then all held together by a thin strip of masking tape down each side. These tapes then form the sides to a ladder. A drawing pen of the right size can then be used between what you might term as the rungs. Sometimes I have made several drawings of a line before I have become satisfied with one of them. The words and the line must be of the correct length. That chosen is then cut out and stuck on to the drawing in it's correct place using the Pritt Stick. Many times I have made parts of these drawings by using pencil, then when I consider it to be correct I have then inked it in. Any pencil lines remaining are then erased using a pencil rubber. All of these drawings can take time and patience which they say is a virtue. The more that one draws, the better one can become at it. I have never been beaten yet at drawing a cartridge. I have been beaten though when photographs have failed to show all of the relevant details. Each drawing becomes a challenge and many an old cartridge has been called just that. After a time one can pick up wrinkles of ways of overcoming things. If I can trace something which is not very often, then so what. My aim in drawing is to achieve accuracy. Well why not, Chas Hellis always spoke that his aim was Guaranteed accuracy.

I have not always carried a small magnet on me. When ever I have, I have used it by running it up the side of a cartridge. By doing this it has told me the height of any interior iron or steel reinforcings. It is only in later years that I have taken to doing this. Unfortunately many of my drawings do not show this added information. On some of the cartridges to be photographed, the headstampings are not always clear. By using an inch square of cooking foil and placing over the stamping it can then be rubbed either with your thumb or a pencil eraser. This rubbing can often give you perfect details to work from. If the stamping has been stamped lightly, then a qick sketch of the wordings can be made and then often a foil rubbing will give you a size or positioning of all of the lettering, etc.

The colourings of old cartridges that I have placed on my many drawings have not always been easy to describe. Sometimes it has been possible to use the named colours as to what their manufacturers have called them. Even so, different manufacturers have used different names in their catalogues for the same shades of a colour. When looking against most colour charts, you will find that most old paper tubed cartridges have colours what I can only describe as dirty. This is often due to their water resistant varnish lacquers. You may find that over the years many colours may have faded. Also some colours have changed due to varnish discolouring. This process is known as ageing.

A typical provisional drawing.

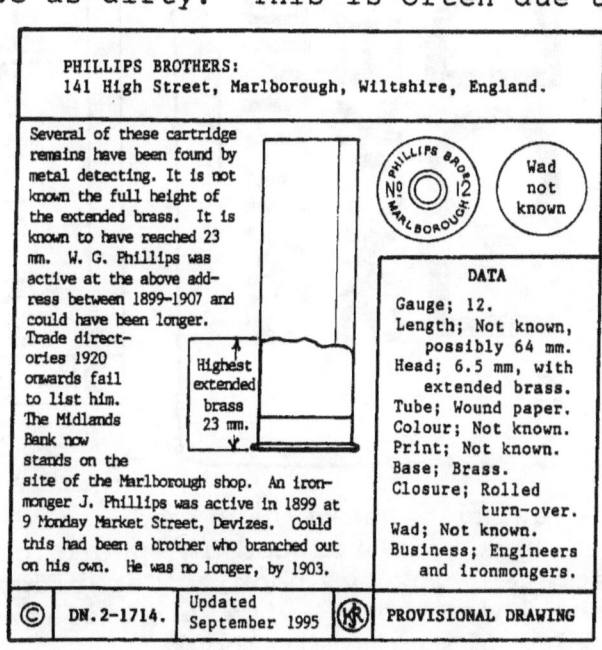

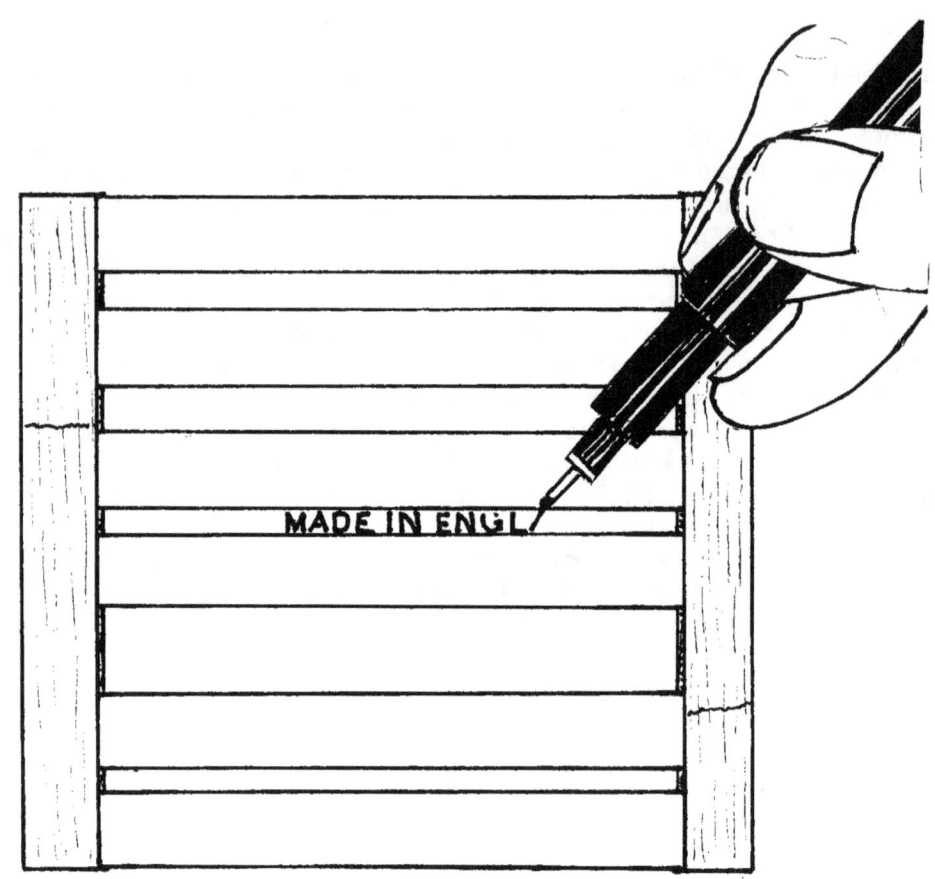

A typical ladder made from thin card and masking tape for use in drawing a cartridge.

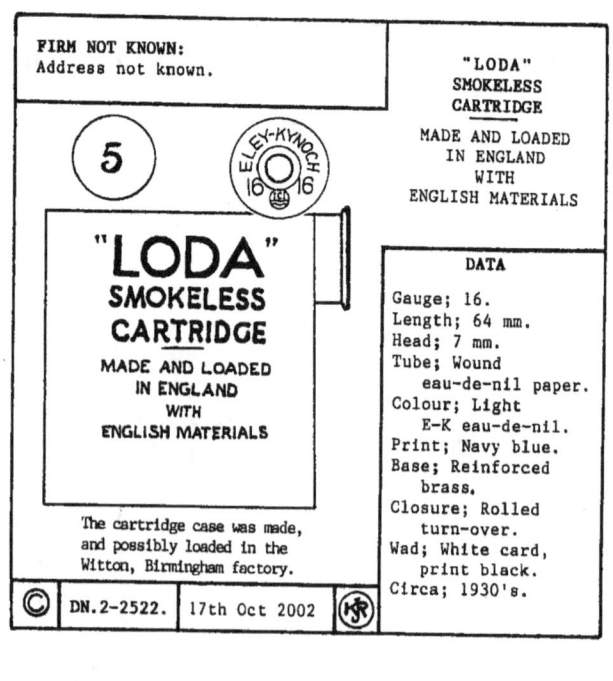

Some drawings that I have made were at double their full size. I then had them reduced by photo copy. The above drawing is illustrated in my book, 'Cartridges of the British Isles'. Compare this "Loda" with a similar which is shown on the last cartridge plate in this book.

UNDERSTANDING THE DRAWINGS

The drawings which illustrate this book have been made over a long period in time. Over the years my drawing has improved, well I like to think so. As more information has come my way, so I have updated several drawings so as to include any relevant fresh information. You will find that quite a number of these drawings are of foreign cartridges. As I can only speak English and this far from being perfect, is the reason why you may consider that many of these drawings lack their detailed information. Many continental cartridges are quite decorative and colourful and this has challenged me to want to draw them. Here in the United Kingdom they are not so sought after by collectors and this is a pity. The reason is, like me they do not understand what is written on them.

On some of the drawings you will find a reference to the Pantone® color formular guide 1000. This American firm, Pantone Inc, are based at, 590 Commerce Bouleyard, Carlstadt, New Jersey, U.S.A. They are the owners of this color chart and it's copyright. I sought their permission to use their formular color guide so that I could better describe the many colours of cartridges. They gave me their consent but I had first to submit copies of my drawings to them for their approval. This worked well for a while until another person took over the task of approving my work. He did not approve of several items which the other person had passed as being OK. It was because of this and also because collectors this side of the Atlantic Ocean were not keen enough to purchase their color formular that I gave up showing the Pantone® color numberings.

You will find that my drawings are placed in this book in a semi-alphabetical order usually starting with the first letter of the drawings heading. For an instance, I have shown the Earl of Carnarvon as being under Highclere so as to be situated close to two Highclere cartridges. It was on this large country estate that my grandfather and also my father had once keepered. I myself in younger days have bush-wacked nearly all over it. The last two plates of drawings are what I have termed as, Don't Kwows. Perhaps some of you that read this may know more about them than me.

Mixed in with these drawings is a handful of naughty funniess. The Lucking cartridge I was once told was first loaded for a fellow named Lucking. Over the years, several people have had print runs from it. Several people have layed claim to it. One thing that I do remember was being shown a mock-up of this cartridge in a gunshop in Wallingford. The Bang Bang Bugger cartridge I have shown under Raker. This because it is the only firms name on it. All the same, Raker may have loaded it under a contract for one of his customers. I drew this one also being shown as loaded. This because the shot load can be seen through the transparent case-wall. The name of this cartridge suggests to me that it will be part of a double miss. As the cartridge will have been seen to have had shot in it, then it would have to have gone somewhere. What an absurd name to have to finnish up with, 'Wanker'. I myself can think of far better names to call a cartridge, but then some people have been given a queer sence of humour.

When first drawn, all of my drawings had separate boxes for the data, etc. Also were the dates when drawn along with DN drawing numbers. In my wisdom, I have decided not to worry you with these in this book. By using so many photo copy machines over a period of time has made my range of drawings so that they refuse to line up with each other. Many have been thrown just enough to put them out of square. To combat this, I have now placed each drawing along with it's data altogether within a main frame. Each page of drawings I here refer to as a plate. Each plate has been given a number and to simplify, these numbers are a continuation of the page numbering, ie, page 20 has become plate 20. For the benefit of the Index to Drawings, each indivdual drawing is referred to as a letter. The letters on each plate run concurrently from A to F. From left to right, the top row, A and B. Centre row, C and D. Bottom row, E and F. An index example 30/E would be on Plate 30 and the referred drawing on the left of the bottom row. The 30 also keeping status with the page numbering.

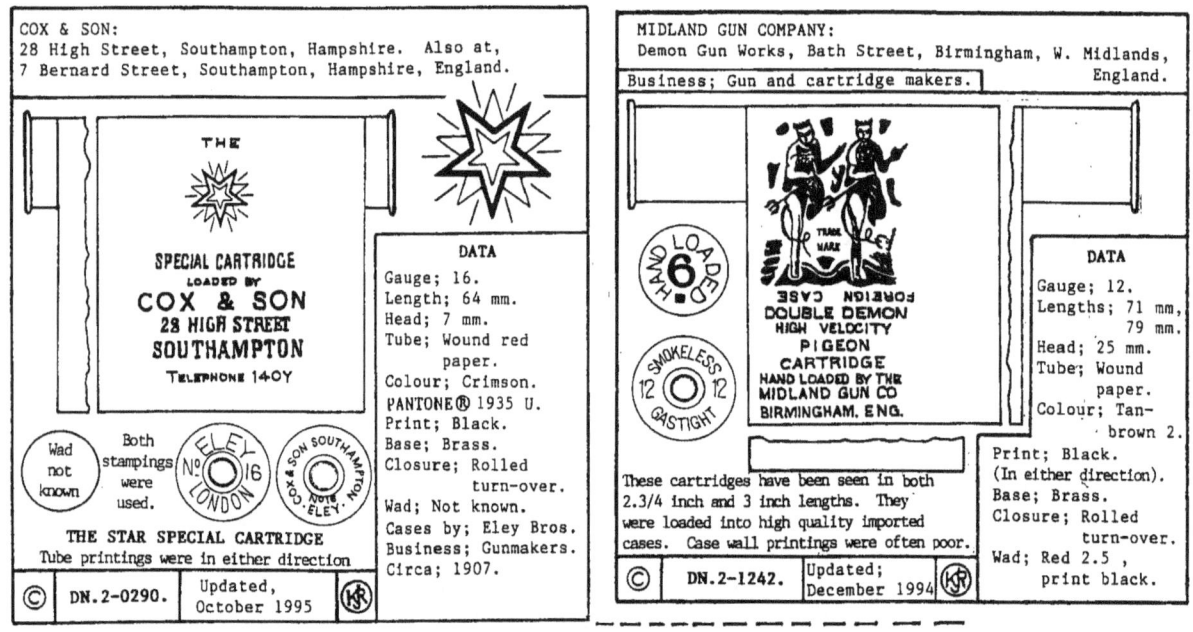

Illustrated above are two of my original drawings which refuse to line up with each other. The Cox & Son on the left is drawn showing a head on each side. This indicates that this cartridge has been seen with it's case-wall printings running both up and down it's paper tubes. The Midland Gun Company on the right also indicates that the tube printings have been seen running in both directions. This thing may have been true for some of the other cartridges drawn, but if I have not seen it, then I could not illustrate it. Also on the Midland Gun Company cartridge I have illustrated it as having been seen loaded for two different length chambered guns, 71 mm and 79 mm. The later being 3 inch. Both of these cartridges can be found in my book, 'Cartridges of the British Isles'.

The
Cartridge drawings

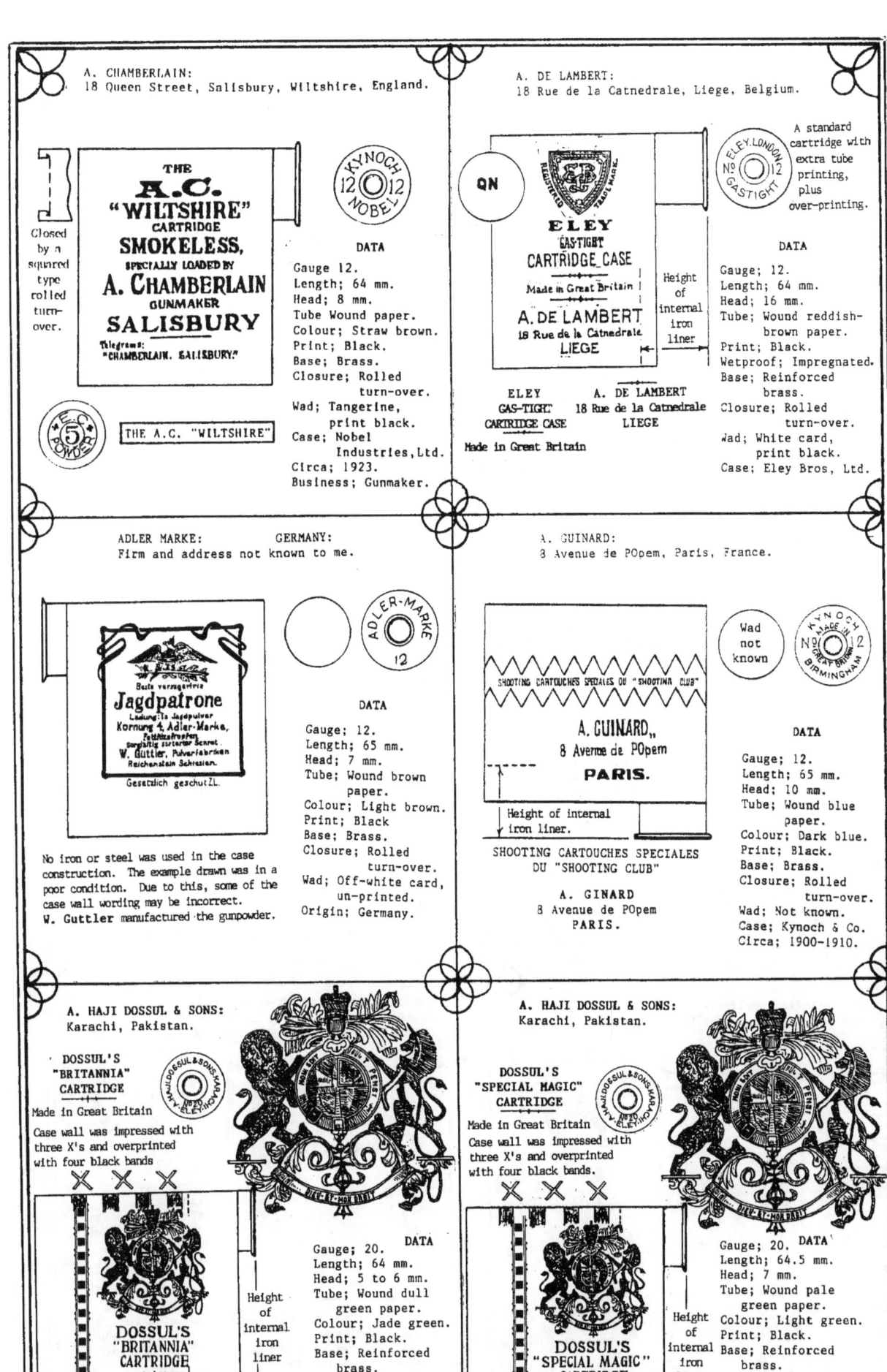

PLATE 21

ALAN EVILL & COMPANY:
Crossgates, Leeds, West Yorkshire. Also at,
High Street, Hungerford, Berkshire, England.

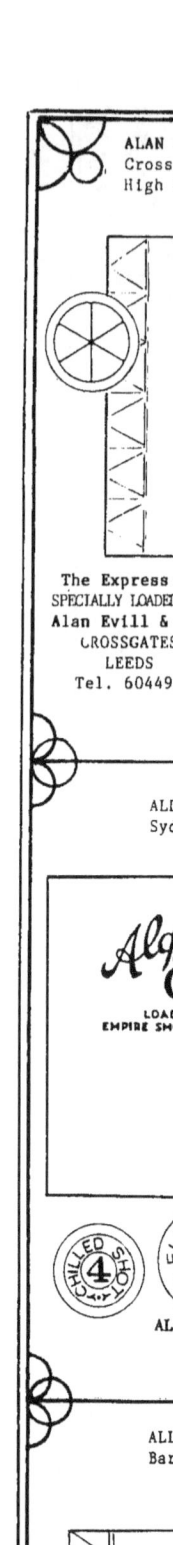

The Express 73
SPECIALLY LOADED FOR
Alan Evill & Co.
CROSSGATES
LEEDS
Tel. 604497

AND
FIELD SPORTS
HIGH STREET
HUNGERFORD

DATA
Gauge; 12.
Length; 69 mm.
Head; 7.5 mm.
Tube; Wound brown paper.
Colour; Poppy red.
Print; Black.
Base; Steel with brass coating.
Closure; Six fold crimp.
Business; Field sports stores.
Loading; Hull Cartridge Co. Ltd.
Case; Fiocchi, Italy.
Circa; 1973.

ALCOCK & PIERCE, PTY, LTD:
318 Little Collin's Street, Melbourne, Victoria, Australia.

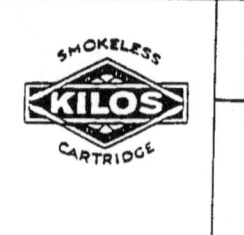

SMOKELESS
KILOS
CARTRIDGE

DATA
Gauge; 12.
Length; 64 mm.
Head; 8 mm.
Tube; Wound orange paper.
Colour; Orange.
Wetproof; Clear lacquered.
Base; Reinforced brass.
Closure; Rolled turn-over.
Wad; Light-brown, print blck.
Business; Field sports store.

ALDERSONS LIMITED:
Sydney, New South Wales, Australia.

Headstamp A had a greyish-green tube. Headstamp B had either red or cream-yellow tubes. These tubes were wound from the coloured papers. All case wall printings were in black.

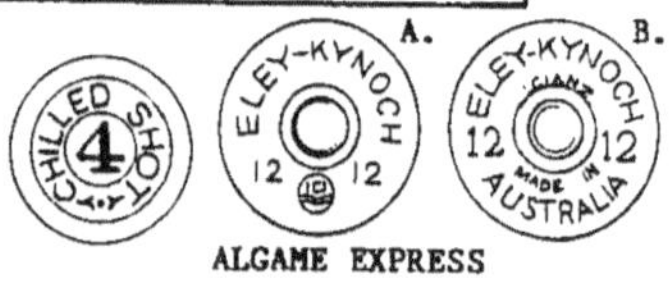

DATA
Gauge; 12.
Length; 64.5 mm.
Head; 8 mm.
Tubes; Wound coloured papers.
Colours; Greyish-green, Red or cream-yellow.
Prints; Black.
Wetproof; Clear lacquered.
Base; Brass.
Closure; Rolled turn-over.
Wad shown; Orange, black print.
Circa; 1930's.

ALGAME EXPRESS

ALDERSONS, LIMITED:
Sydney, New South Wales, Australia.

Algame Express
LOADED WITH
EMPIRE SMOKELESS POWDER

DATA
Gauge; 12.
Length; 64 mm.
Head; 8 mm.
Tube; Wound grey paper.
Colour; Grey.
Print; Black.
Base; Reinforced brass.
Closure; Rolled turn-over.
Wad; Orange card, print black.

ALLWELL & PHIPPS:
Barnstaple, Devonshire, England.

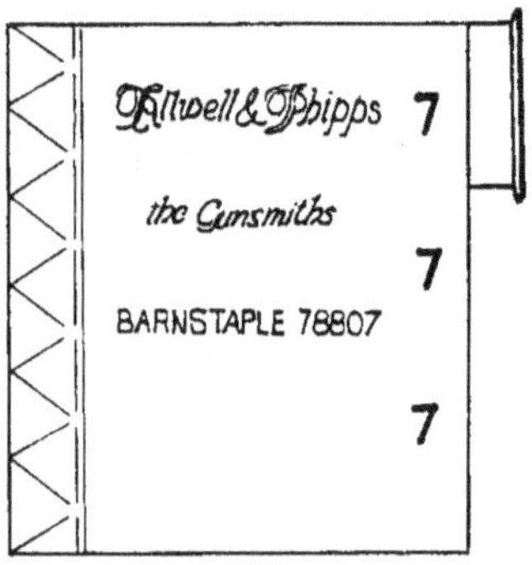

Allwell & Phipps
the Gunsmiths
BARNSTAPLE 78807

DATA
Gauge; 12.
Length; 68 mm.
Head; 8 mm.
Tube; Fine ribbed plastic.
Colour; Red 3.
Print; Black.
Base; Steel, brass coated.
Closure; Crimp, 6 fold.
Business; Gunsmiths.

AMERICAN AMMUNITION COMPANY:
Oak Park & Chicago, Illinois. Also at,
Muscatine, Iowa, United States of America.

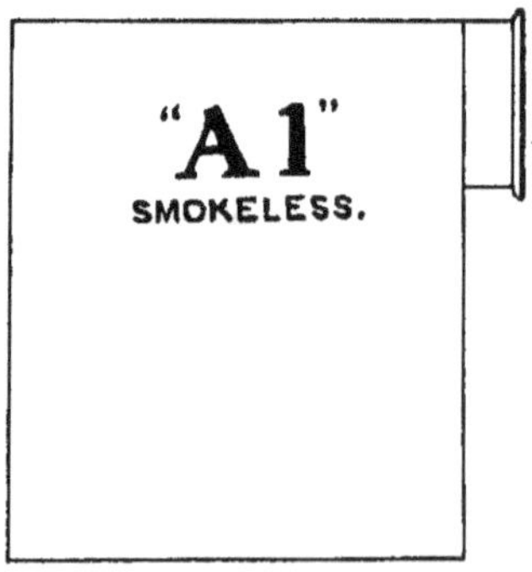

"A1"
SMOKELESS.

The American Ammunition Company were active for about twelve years. This was somewhere between 1910 and 1922.

DATA
Gauge; 12.
Length; 64 mm.
Head; 8 mm.
Tube; Wound paper.
Colour; Eau-de-nil.
Print; Crimson.
Base; Brass.
Closure; Rolled turn-over.
Wad; White card with red wording and black shot size.
Business; Ammo manufacturers.

PLATE 22

AMERICAN AMMUNITION COMPANY:
Oak Park, Illinois. Also at; Muscatine, Iowa, U.S.A.
Offices at; 40 Dearborn Street, Chicago, Illinois.
Later at, 180 Dearborn Street, Chicago, U.S.A.

Case originally for; CHARLES HELLIS & SONS;
119 Edgware Road, Hyde Park, London. W.2., England.

Closed by a squared turn-over

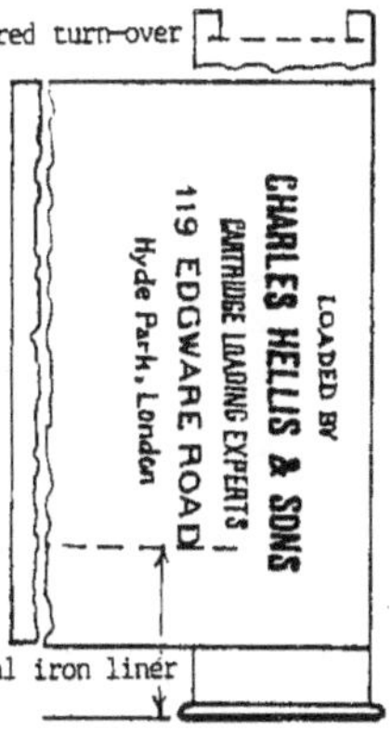

This cartridge was loaded in the U.S.A. by The American Ammunition Co.

Height of internal iron liner

DATA
Gauge; 12.
Length; 70 mm.
Head; 8 mm.
Tube; Wound paper.
Colour; Burgundy.
Print; White.
Base; Reinforced brass.
Closure; Rolled.
Wad; White card, printing red. shot size blue-black.
Business; Ammunition manufacturers.
Circa; 1910.

ANTHONY HORDERNS:
Brickfield Hill, Sydney. Later at, George Street, Sydney, New South Wales, Australia.

DATA
Gauge; 12.
Length; 64 mm.
Head; 8 mm.
Tube; Wound orange paper.
Colour; Brownish orange.
Print; Black.
Base; Reinforced brass.
Closure; Rolled turn-over.
Wad; Lime green, print black.
Case; Eley Bros, Ltd. England.

TREE BRAND
WHILE I LIVE I'LL GROW

A. P. WALSHE:
Johannesburg, South Africa (Republic of South Africa).

"WALSHE'S SPECIAL" CARTRIDGE

DATA
Gauge; 12.
Length; 64 mm.
Head; 16 mm.
Tube; Wound pink paper.
Colour; Pink.
Print; Dark blue.
Base; Brass.
Closure; Rolled turn-over.
Wad; Yellow card, print black.
Wetproof; Lacquered.
Circa; 1930's.
Business; Gunmaker.

ARMY & NAVY CO-OPERATIVE SOCIETY (GUNS DEPT):
8 Howick Place, Westminster, London. S.W., England.

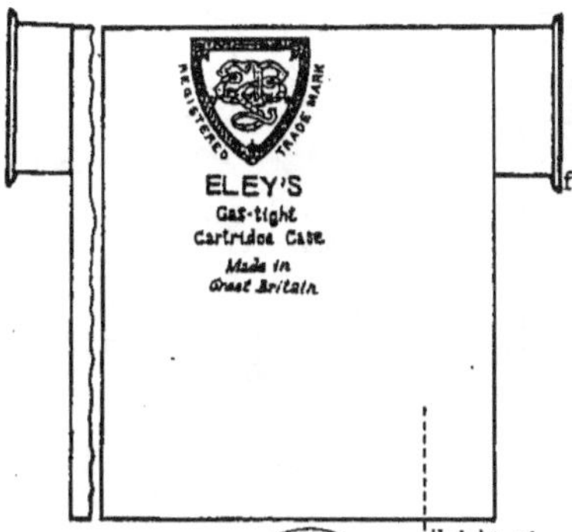

Manufactured by Messrs Eley Bros Ltd., the case walls were printed in either direction. This drawing was made from unused capped cases.

DATA
Gauge; 12.
Length; 65 mm.
Head; 10 mm.
Tube; Wound brown paper.
Colour; Dark green.
Print; Black.
Base; Brass.
Closure; Rolled turn-over.
Business; Stores and gunmakers.
Circa; Late 1800's.

Wad not known

Height of inner metal liner

ELEY'S GAS-TIGHT CARTRIDGE CASE

ARMY & NAVY CO-OPERATIVE SOCIETY, LIMITED:
Bombay, India. Also at, Howick Place, London S.W.1., England.

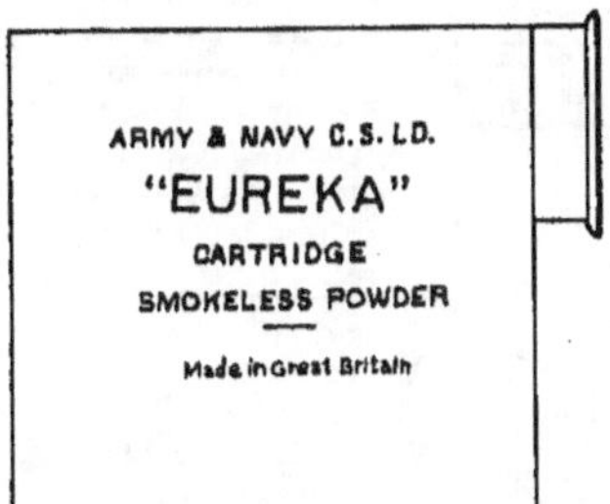

ARMY & NAVY C.S.LD.
"EUREKA"
CARTRIDGE
SMOKELESS POWDER
Made in Great Britain

DATA
Gauge; 12.
Length; 64 mm.
Head; 8 mm.
Tube; Wound maroon paper.
Colour; Maroon.
Print; Black.
Base; Brass.
Closure; Rolled turn-over.
Wad; White card, print red.
Business; Gunmakers and department stores.
Case; Kynoch, Ltd.

ARMY & NAVY C.S.LD.
"EUREKA"
CARTRIDGE
SMOKELESS CARTRIDGE
Made in Great Britain

ARMY & NAVY CO-OPERATIVE SOCIETY, LTD:
Bombay, India. Also a branch in London, England.

This cartridge case was loaded in The U.S.A. Liberty started loading circa 1911 and folded after 1917.

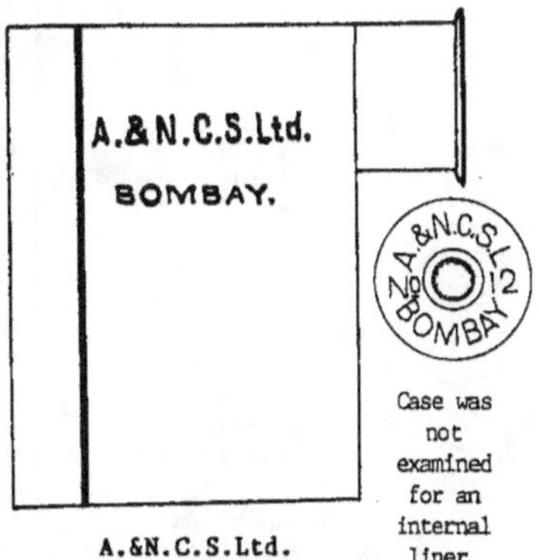

A.&N.C.S.Ltd.
BOMBAY.

Case was not examined for an internal liner.

Length; 64 mm.
Head; 16 mm.
Tube; Wound brown paper.
Print; Black. it includes the band around top of case. Most likely this was printed in U.S.A.
Base; Brass.
Closure; Rolled turn-over.
Business: Gunmakers and department stores.

PLATE 23

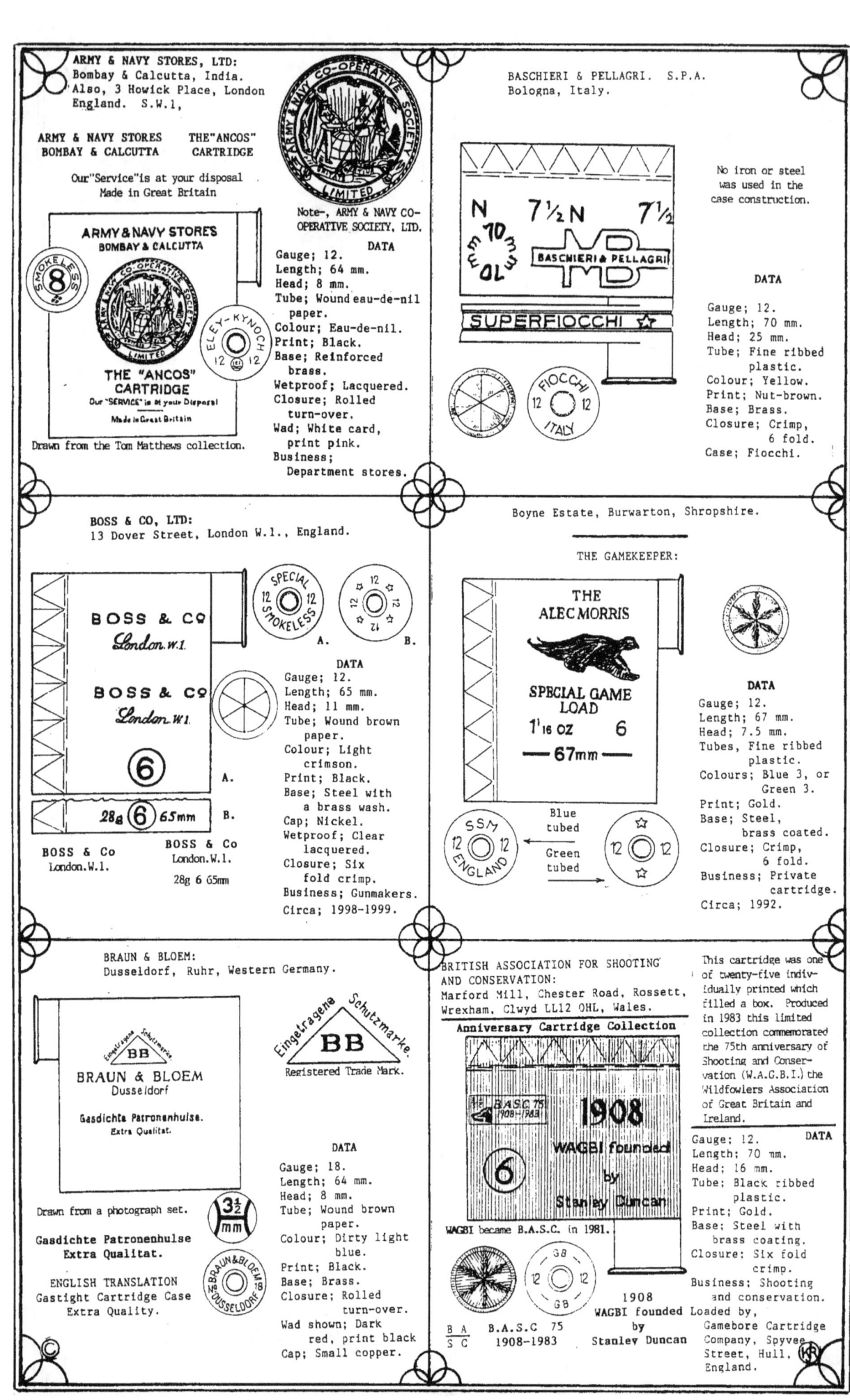

PLATE 24

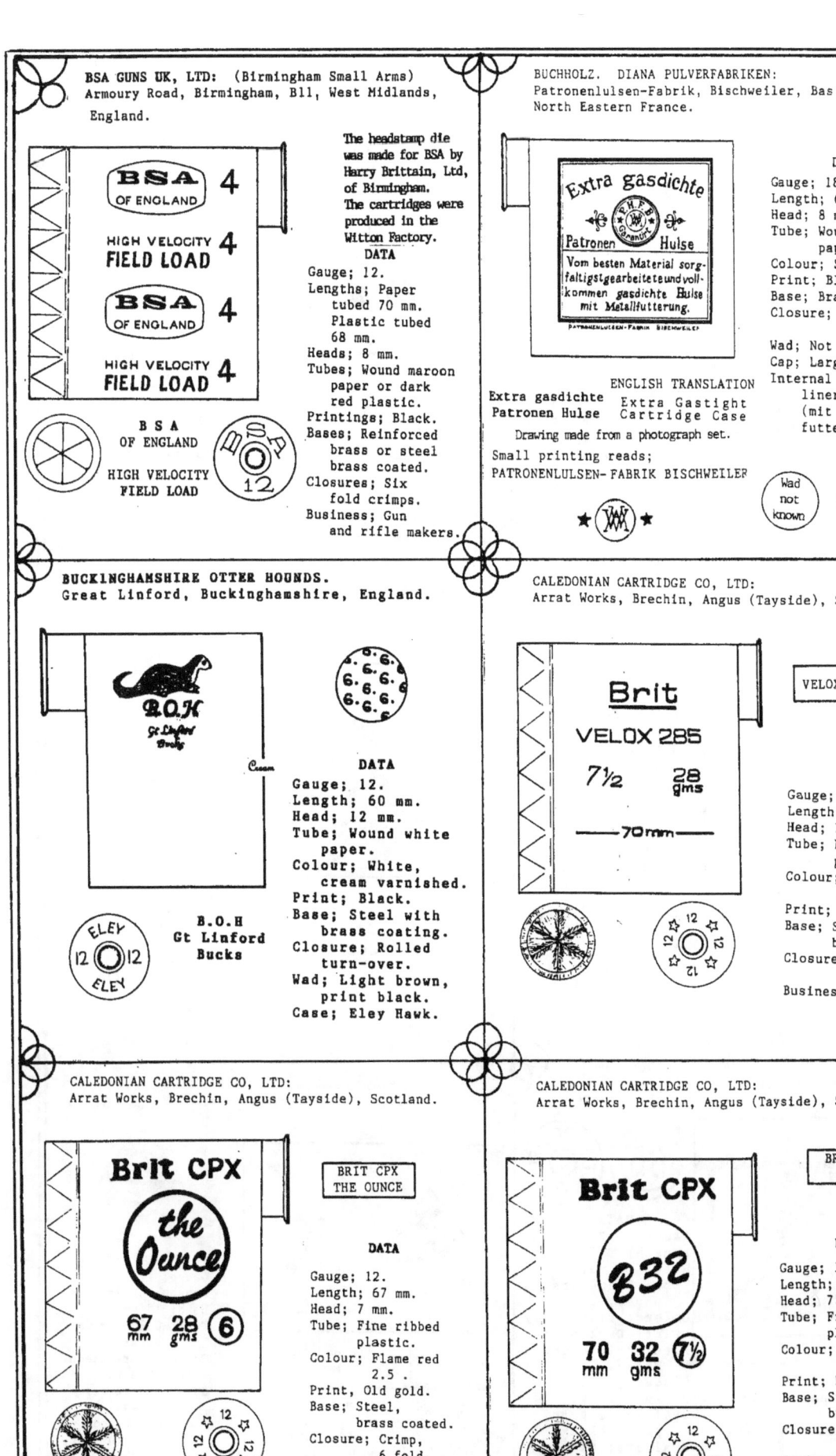

PLATE 25

CALEDONIAN CARTRIDGE CO, LTD:
Arrat Works, Brechin, Angus (Tayside), Scotland.

VELOX 285

DATA
Gauge; 12.
Length; 68 mm.
Head; 8.5 mm.
Tube; Fine ribbed
       plastic.
Colour, Deep blue
        3.5 .
Print; Black.
Base; Steel,
      brass coated.
Closure; Crimp,
         6 fold.
Business; Manu-
          facturers.

CALEDONIAN CARTRIDGE CO. LTD:
Arrat Works, Brechin, Tayside, Scotland.

DATA
Gauge; 12.
Length; 68 mm.
Head; 12 mm.
Tube; Fine ribbed
      plastic.
Colour; Dark-
        green 4.5 .
Print; Black.
Base; Steel,
      brass coated.
Closure; Crimp,
         6 fold.
Business; Cartridge
          manufac-
          turers.

Circa; 1994.

CALEDONIAN XL's

CANADIAN INDUSTRIES, LTD. THE DOMINION
CARTRIDGE COMPANY:
Montreal, Quebec, Canada.

"IMPERIAL"

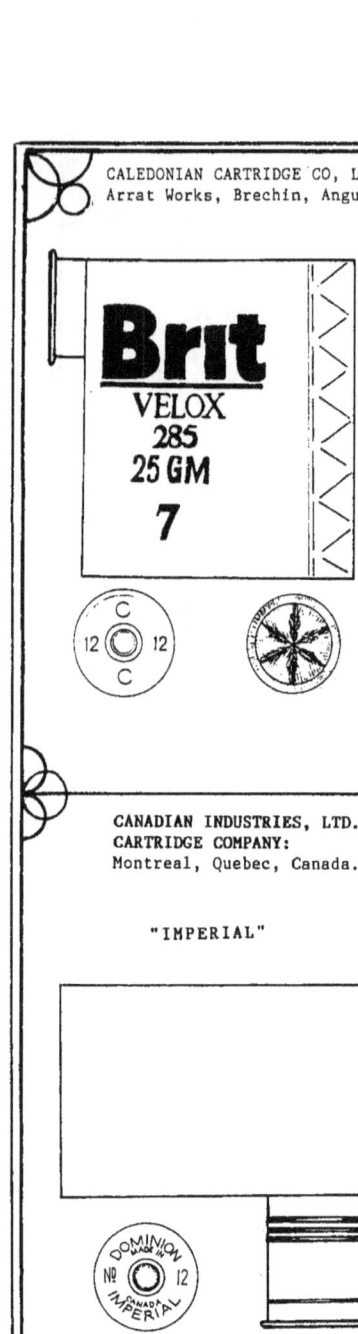

DATA
Gauge; 12.
Length; 70 mm.
Head; 27 mm.
Tube; Wound brown
      paper.
Colour; Purple.
Printings; Nil.
Base; Reinforced
      brass.
Closure; Rolled
         turn-over.
Wad; Mustard yellow,
     print black.
Business;
     Ammunition
     manufacturers.

CARTOUCHERIE FRANCAISE:
Address not known   ?, France.

DATA
Gauge; 20.
Length; 65 mm.
Head; 16 mm.
Tube; Wound paper.
Colour; Crimson
        red.
Print; Black.
Base; Brass.
Closure; Rolled
         turn-over.
Wad; Clear
     varnished over
     cork, print
     black.
Wetproof; Clear
          lacquered.
Case; France.

CARTOUCHERIE FRANCAISE.
8 et 10 Rue Bertin, Poiree, Paris 1, France.

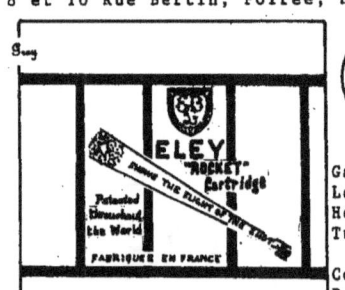

Height of metal
reinforcing
(Manufactured under licence)

ELEY "ROCKET" CARTRIDGE
SHOWS THE FLIGHT OF THE SHOT
Patented throughout the World
FABRIQUEE EN FRANCE

DATA
Gauge; 12.
Length; 64 mm.
Head; 8 mm.
Tube; Wound grey
      paper.
Colour; Light grey.
Print; Dark blue.
Base; Reinforced
      brass.
Closure; Rolled
         turn-over.
Wad; White card,
     print black.
Business; Cart-
     ridge manufac-
     turers.
Circa; 1930's.

CARTOUCHERIE FRANCAISE:
Address not known. France.

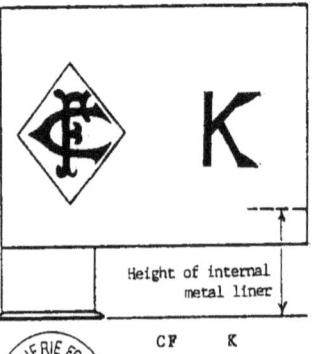

Height of internal
metal liner

CF   K
Has been seen
with or without
the letter K.

DATA
Gauge; 12.
Length; 64 mm.
Head; 15 mm.
Tube; Wound brown
      paper.
Colour; Dark green.
Print; Black.
Base; Reinforced
      brass.
Closure; Rolled
         turn-over.
Wad; Off-white
     card, print
     scarlet red.

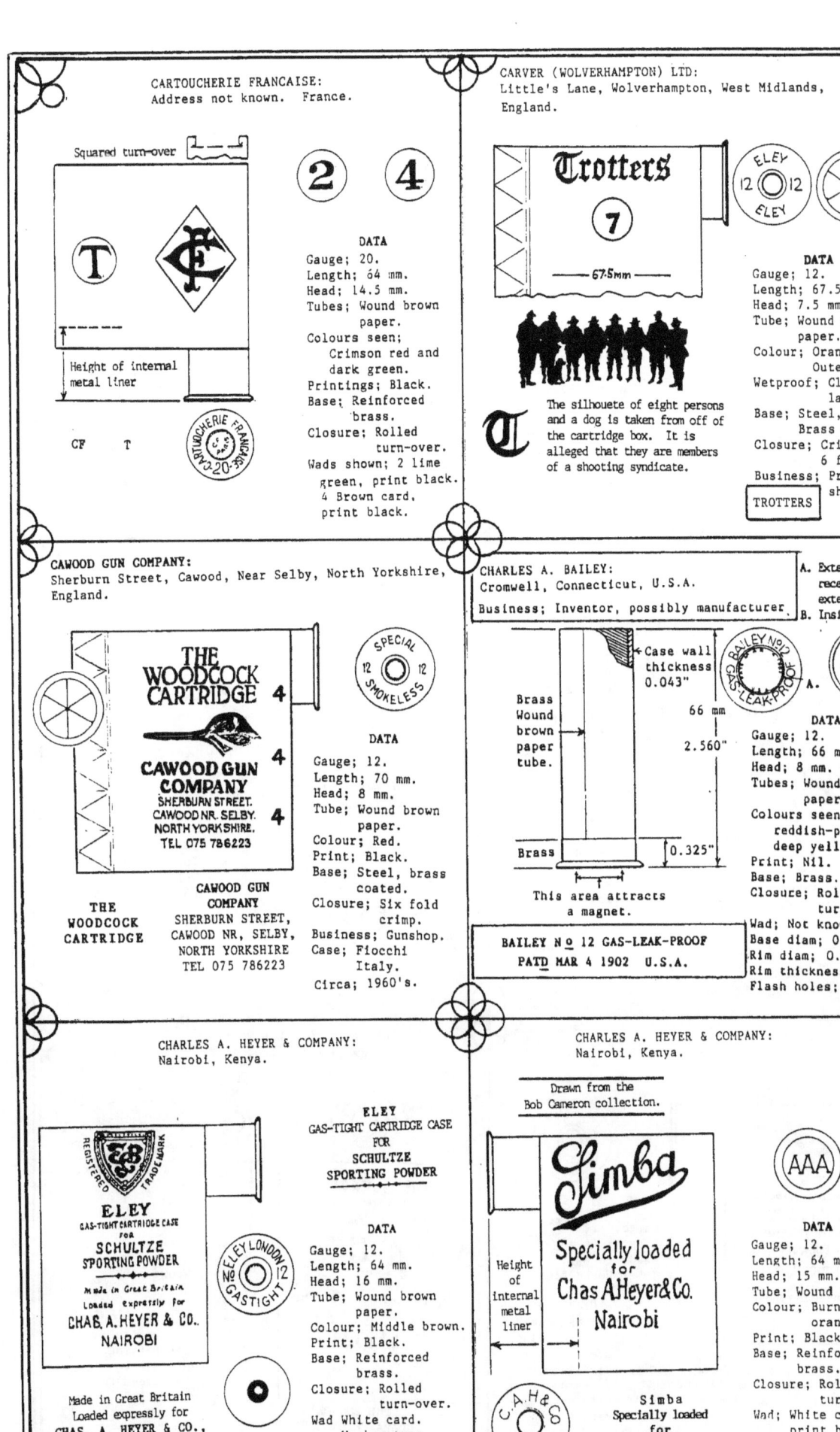

PLATE 27

CHARLES LANCASTER & CO. LTD:
99 Mount Street, London, England.

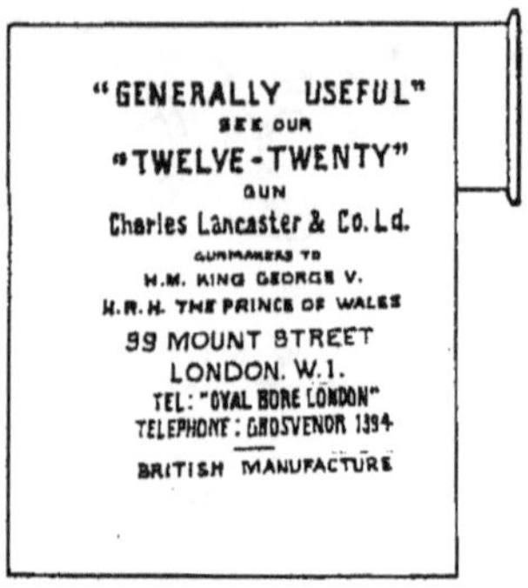

"GENERALLY USEFUL"
SEE OUR
"TWELVE-TWENTY"
GUN
Charles Lancaster & Co. Ld.
GUNMAKERS TO
H.M. KING GEORGE V.
H.R.H. THE PRINCE OF WALES
99 MOUNT STREET
LONDON. W.1.
TEL: "OVAL BORE LONDON"
TELEPHONE: GROSVENOR 1394
BRITISH MANUFACTURE

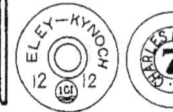

DATA
Gauge; 12.
Length; 64 mm.
Head; 8 mm.
Tube; Wound paper.
Colour; Orange 3.
Print; Black.
Base; Brass.
Closure; Rolled
 turn-over.
Wad; White card,
 print black.
Business; Gunmaker.
This drawing was made
from a live cartridge.

SEE OUR "TWELVE-TWENTY" GUN Charles Lancaster & Co.Ld. GUNMAKERS TO H.M. KING GEORGE V. H.R.H. THE PRINCE OF WALES 99 MOUNT STREET LONDON, W.1. TEL: "OVAL BORE LONDON" TELEPHONE: GROSVENOR 1394 ——— BRITISH MANUFACTURE

"GENERALLY USEFUL"

C.H. HAYGARTH & SONS.
The Cottage Gun Shop, Dunnet, Caithness, Scotland.

ECONOMAX
C.H.HAYGARTH
DUNNET CAITHNESS

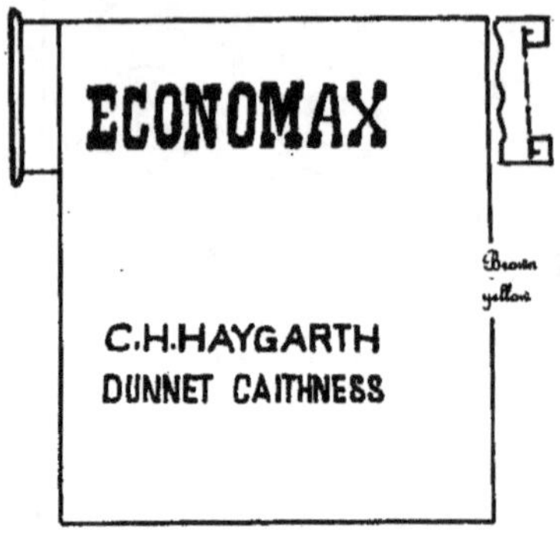

Brown yellow

DATA
Gauge; 12.
Length; 64 mm.
Head; 6 mm.
Tube; Wound paper.
Colour; Yellowish
 brown.
Print; Black.
Base; Steel with
 brass coating.
Cap; Large brass.
Closure; Squared
 turn-over.
Wad; Brown cork,
 print black.
Business;
 Gunmakers and
 cartridge
 loaders.

ECONOMAX
C.H.HAYGARTH
DUNNET CAITHNESS

C. H. HAYGARTH:
The Cottage Gun Shop,
Dunnet, Caithness,
Scotland.

Was produced in 12, 16 and 20 gauge sizes. 20 gauge is drawn here.

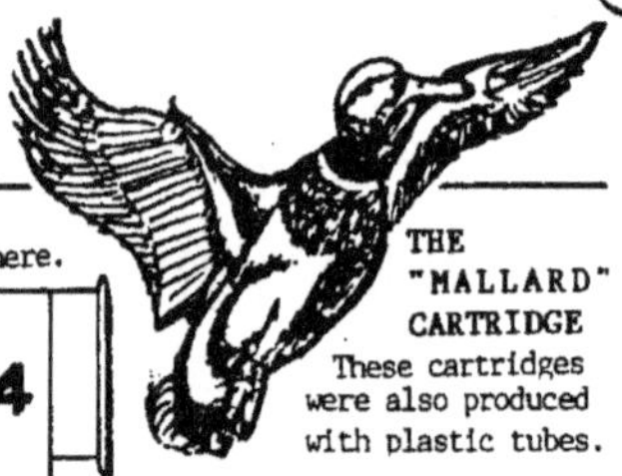

THE
"MALLARD"
CARTRIDGE
C.H. HAYGARTH
THE
COTTAGE GUN
SHOP
DUNNET

C. H. HAYGART
THE COTTAGE GUN SHOP   DUNNET

THE "MALLARD" CARTRIDGE
These cartridges were also produced with plastic tubes.

DATA
Length;
 20 gauge, 65 mm.
Heads; 20 gauge,
 7 mm.
 12 gauge,
 8 mm.
Tubes; Wound brown
 papers.
Colours; 20 buff-
 yellow; 16 blue;
 12 red.
Printings; Black.
Base; Brass finnished.
Closures; Six fold
 crimps.
Cases; Fiocchi, Italy.

CHARLES HELLIS & SONS:
119 Edgware Road, London, W.2., England.

Specially Loaded by
CHARLES HELLIS & SONS
Cartridge Experts
119 Edgware Road.
London W.2.

All three stampings shown were used on this cart- ridge.

Headstampings marked N.I., were those first used by Nobel Industries.

DATA
Gauge; 12.
Length; 64 mm.
Head; 16 mm.
Tube; Wound blue
 paper.
Colour; Middle blue;
Print; Black.
Base; Brass;
Inner liner; Nil.
Wetproof; Lacquered.
Wad; Blue 4, print
 black.
Case; Nobel
 Industries.
Circa; 1919-1924.
Business; Cart-
 ridge experts.

CHAS HELLIS & SONS, LTD:
121-3 Edgware Road, London, W.2., England.

SPECIALLY LOADED BY
CHAS. HELLIS & SONS LTD.
Cartridge Experts
121-3 EDGWARE ROAD
LONDON, W.2.
MADE IN GREAT BRITAIN

Made in Great Britain

Both versions of
'Made in Great Britain'
were used.

DATA
Gauge; 12.
Length; 64 mm.
Head; 16 mm.
Tube; Wound blue
 paper.
Colour; Middle blue.
Print; Either dark
 blue or black.
Base; Brass.
Closure; Rolled
 turn-over.
Wad; White card,
 print black.
Wetproof; Lacquered.
Circa; Late 1930's.
Business; Cartridge
 experts.

CHAS HELLIS & SONS LIMITED:
121-3 Edgware Road, London, W.2., England.

THE ECONOMIST
GUARANTEED ACCURACY
SPECIALLY HAND LOADED
BY
Hellis
LONDON   ENGLAND
Hellis

THE ECONOMIST
GUARANTEED ACCURACY

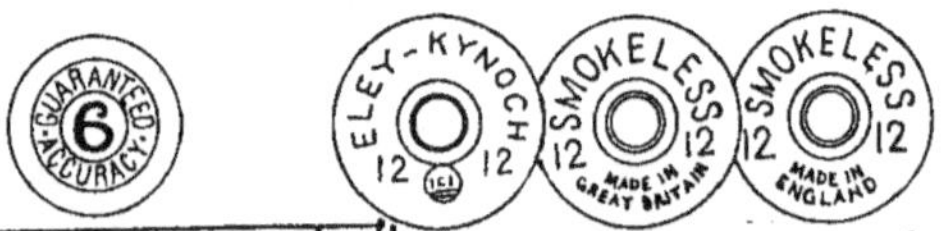

All three stampings were used.

DATA
Gauge; 12.
Length; 64 mm.
Head; 8 mm.
Tube; Wound pink
 paper.
PANTONE®198 C.
Print; Black.
Base; Brass with
 reinforcing.
Wetproof; Clear
 lacquered.
Closure; Rolled
 turn-over.
Wad; Deep orange,
 print black.
Business;
 Cartridge experts.

PLATE 28

CLARK & BUTCHER LTD:
Lion Mills, Soham, Ely, Cambridgeshire, England.

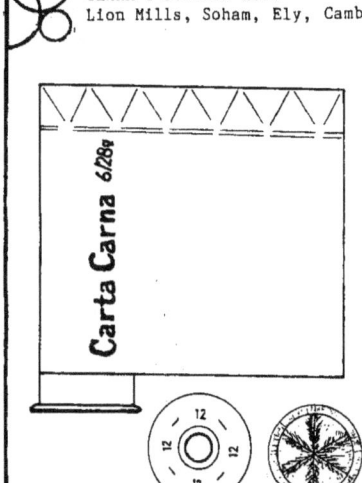

CARTA CARNA

DATA
Gauge; 12.
Length; 67 mm.
Head; 8 mm.
Tube; Fine ribbed plastic.
Colour; Blue 3
Print; Gold (heat embossed).
Base; Steel, brass coated.
Closure; Crimp, 6 fold.
Business; Game feed merchants.

CLARK & BUTCHER LTD:
Lion Mills, Soham, Ely, Cambridgeshire, England.

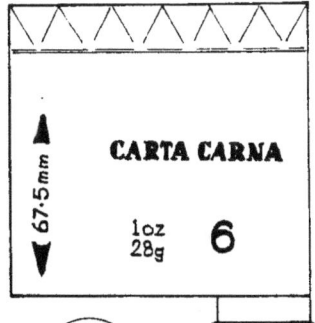

DATA
Gauge; 12.
Length; 67 mm.
Head; 7.5 mm.
Tube; Medium ribbed plastic.
Colour; Deep blue 3.5 .
Print; Silver.
Base; Steel, brass coated.
Closure; Crimp, 6 fold.
Business; Game feed merchants.

CARTA CARNA

CLARK & BUTCHER LTD:
Lion Mills, Soham, Ely, Cambridgeshire, England.

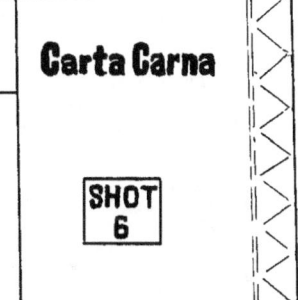

CARTA CARNA

DATA
Gauge; 12.
Length; 67 mm.
Head; 8 mm.
Tube; Fine ribbed plastic.
Colour; Blue 3 .
Print; Old gold.
Base; Steel, brass coated.
Closure; Crimp, 6 fold.
Business; Game feed manufacturers.

CLINTON CARTRIDGE COMPANY (C.C.Co.):
Illinois, U.S.A.

This drawing was made from an unused case.

DATA
Gauge; 12.
Length; 66 mm.
Head; 7 mm.
Tube; Wound off-white paper.
Colour; Off-white with brown tinge.
Print; Dark blue.
Base; Brass.
Closure; Rolled turn-over.
Wad; Not known.
Business; Cartridge manufacturers.

COGSWELL & HARRISON LIMITED:
141 New Bond Street. Also at, 226 The Strand,
And also at, Gillingham Street, Pimlico, London, England.

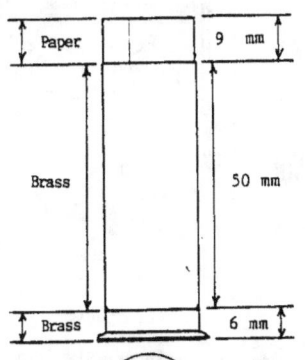

KYNOCH'S PATENT   GROUSE EJECTOR

DATA
Gauge; 12.
Length; 65 mm.
Head; 6 mm with extended brass to, 56 mm.
Tube; Wound brown paper.
Colour; Maroon.
Print; Nil.
Base and outer sleeve; Brass.
Closure; Rolled turn-over.
Wad; Not known.
Case; Kynoch & Co.
Business; Gunmakers and cartridge loaders.

COGSWELL & HARRISON, LTD:
141 New Bond Street. Also at, 226 The Strand,
Piccadilly, London, England.

The example drawn was not internally examined for metals.

THE COGSWELL & HARRISON GASTIGHT CARTRIDGE CASE

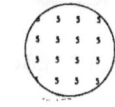

DATA
Gauge; 12.
Length; 64 mm.
Head; 12 mm.
Tube; Wound paper.
Colour; Jasmine yellow.
Print; Black.
Base; Brass.
Closure; Rolled turn-over.
Wad; White card, print black.
Business; Gun and cartridge makers.

PLATE 29

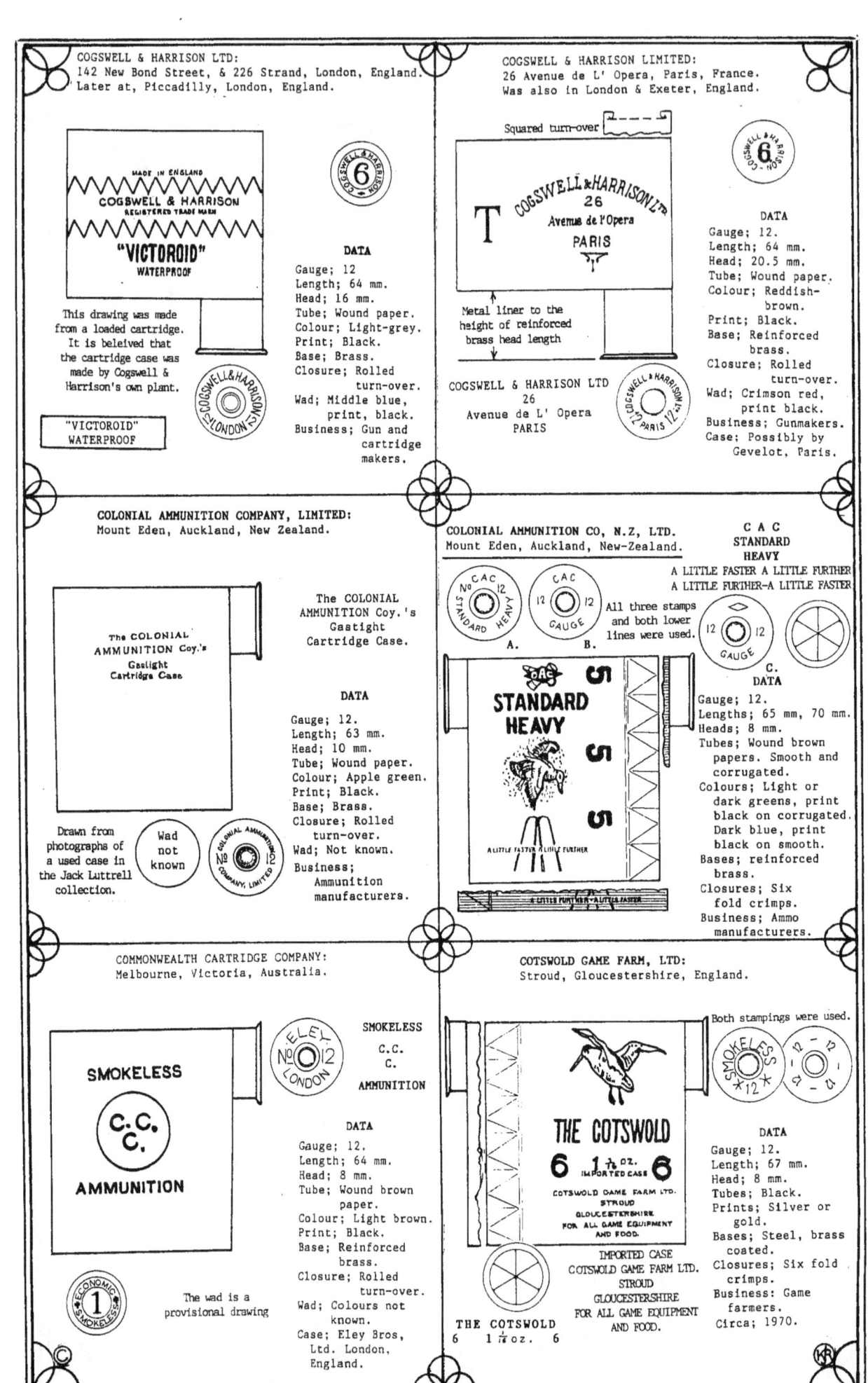

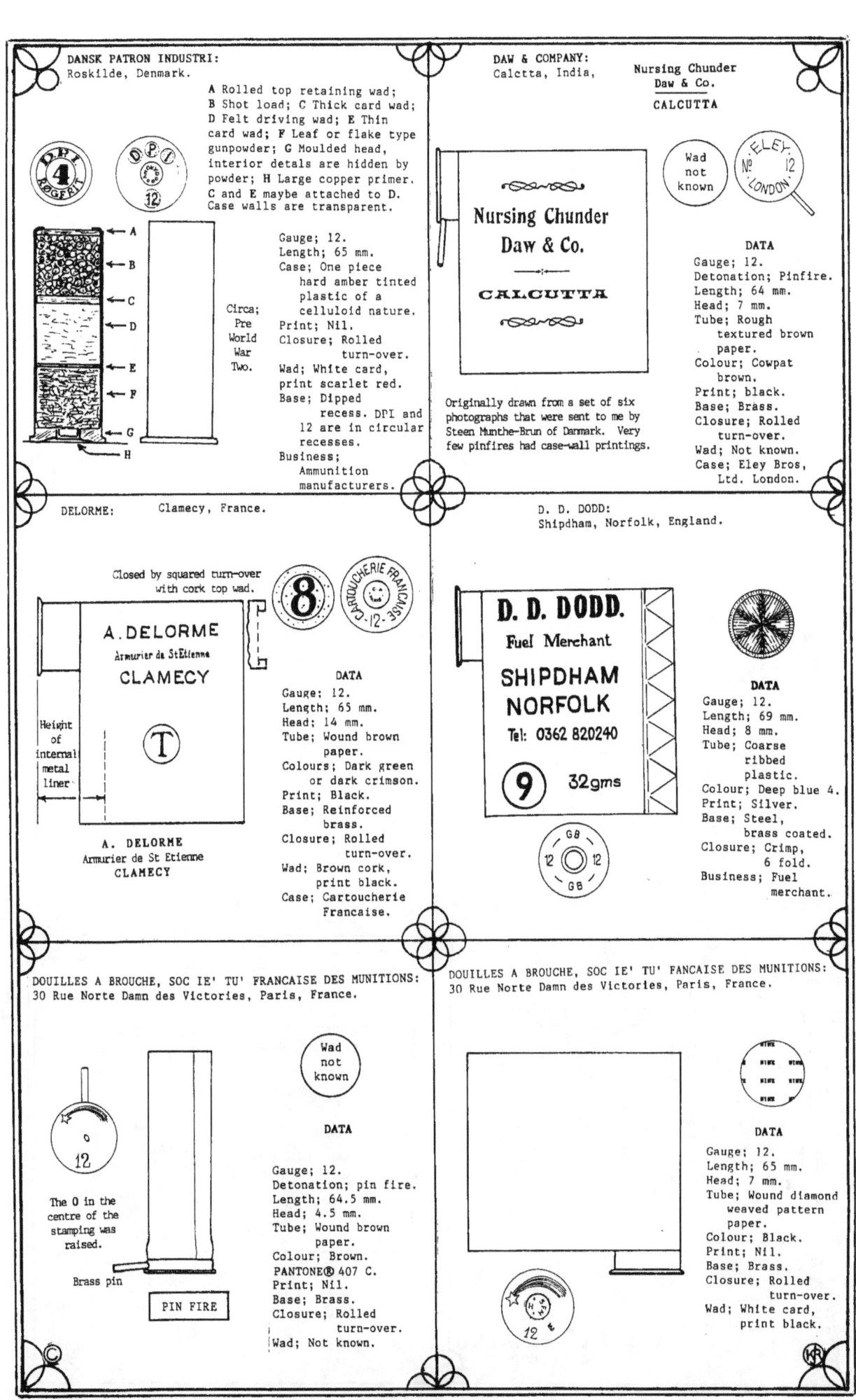

PLATE 31

DOUILLES EN ACIER ARMCO:
3 Av. Gourgaud, Paris 17, France.

A 18 mm. The grooves gripped the compression wadding.
B At grooves, 15 mm. This cartridge was also made in 12 gauge.
C 5 mm.
D 22 mm.
E Upper section, sleeve or tube.
F Lower section, base.

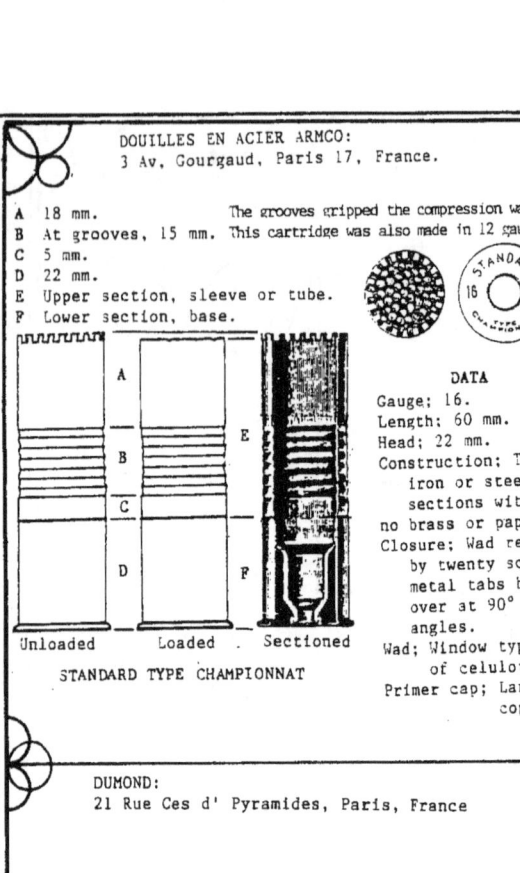

Unloaded   Loaded   Sectioned
STANDARD TYPE CHAMPIONNAT

DATA
Gauge; 16.
Length; 60 mm.
Head; 22 mm.
Construction; Two iron or steel sections with no brass or paper.
Closure; Wad retained by twenty squared metal tabs bent over at 90° angles.
Wad; Window type of celuloid.
Primer cap; Large copper.

DRETSE & COLLINSBUSCH:
Sommerda, Near Erfurt, East Germany.

20 Gauge cartridge. It was seen in the U.S.A. It has a similarity to C. Lancaster's cartridge. Outer layer of paper tube, dark green with no case wall printing.

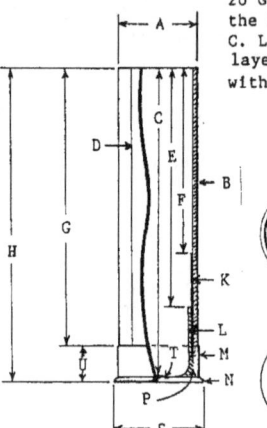

Headstamp

KEY TO DRAWING
A Tube diam. 0.679".
B Wall thickness, 0.030".
C 2.483".
D Wound brown paper.
E 1.950".
F 1.500".
G 2.286".
H 2.578".
K Metal liner with a copper wash.
L Base wad side.
M Brass head.
N Rim thickness 0.048".
P Undetected area.
S 0.751".
T Square flash holes.
U 0.292".

DUMOND:
21 Rue Ces d' Pyramides, Paris, France

This drawing has been made from a set of four photographs. These were sent to me from the U.S.A.

The small case wall wording is,
DÉPOSÉE
21 RUE CES PYRAMIDES PARIS.
Importé d' Angleterre

DATA
Gauge; 20.
Length; 63.5 mm.
Head; 24.5 mm.
Tube; Wound paper.
Colour; Crimson.
PANTONE® 193 C.
Print; Black.
Base; Brass.
Closure; Rolled turn-over.
Wad; Not known.

DUNMORE SHOOTING CENTRE:
Wooton Road, Abingdon, Oxfordshire. OX13 6BH.

There were variations in the size of the printings.

DATA
Gauge; 12.
Length; 69 mm.
Head; 8 mm.
Tube; fine ribbed plastic.
Colour; Maroon 3.
Print; Black, or grey 2.
Base; Steel, brass coated.
Closure; Crimp, 6 fold.
Business; Shooting centre. [tuition].

FRANK DYKE & CO, LTD:
10 Union Street, S.E.1. Later at, 1 - 7 Ernest Avenue, West Northwood, London N.W., England.

Crimped   Rolled turn-over

  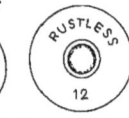

No iron or steel was used in the case.

"Yellow Wizard Rustless"
COOPALL POWDER
BRITISH HAND LOADED
FOREIGN MADE CASE

DATA
Gauges; 12.
Lengths; 65 mm with rolled turn-over.
70 mm with six fold crimp.
Heads; 8 mm.
Tubes; Wound light brown paper.
Colours; Dark yellow.
Printings; Black.
Bases; Brass.
Wad; Canary yellow, print black.
Cap; Nickel.
Business; Loadings.
Circa; 1960-1970.

EBRALL BROS:
Smithfield Road, Shrewsbury, Shropshire.

"COUNTRYMAN" CARTRIDGE
EBRALL BROS.
SMITHFIELD ROAD
SHREWSBURY
TELEPHONE 3048

DATA
Gauge; 12.
Length; 68 mm.
Head; 12 mm.
Tube; Fine ribbed plastic.
Colour; Red 3.
Print; Black.
Base; Steel, brass coated.
Closure; Crimp, 6 fold.
Business; Gunsmith.

PLATE 32

EDWARD CHAMBERLAIN:
1 Bridge Street, Andover, Hampshire, England.

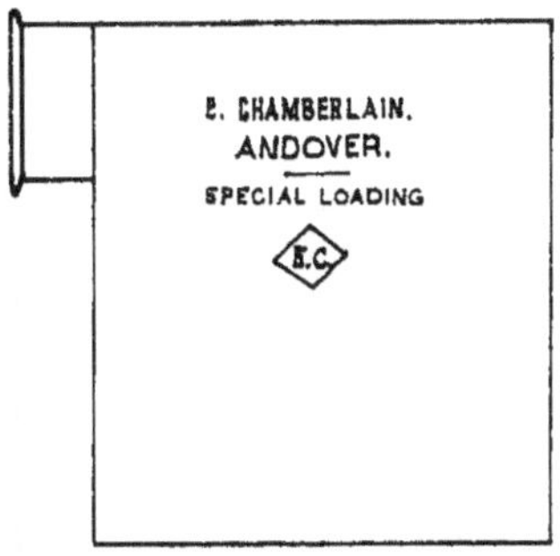

E. CHAMBERLAIN.
ANDOVER
SPECIAL LOADING
E.C.

Wad not known

DATA
Gauge: 16.
Length; 65 mm.
Head; 10 mm.
Tube wound orange paper.
Colour; Light house brick.
Print; Black.
Base; Brass.
Closure; Rolled turn-over.
Wad; Not known.
Business; Gunmaker.

Drawing made from an unused case.

EDWIN J. CHURCHILL.
8 Agar Street, The Strand. Later at, 39-42 Leicester Square, London, England.

The "UTILITY" CARTRIDGE
FOREIGN MADE CASE
BRITISH LOADED WITH
SPECIALLY SELECTED MATERIAL

Height of internal metal liner

DATA
Gauge; 16.
Length; 65 mm.
Head; 12 mm.
Tube; Wound paper.
Colour; Cambridge blue.
Print; Silver.
Base; Reinforced brass.
Closure; Rolled turn-over.
Wad; White card, print black.
Business; Gunmaker and cartridge loader.
Case; Foreign.

EICHEL:
FIRM NOT KNOWN:
Origin; Germany.

GERMAN
PRIMA PATRONENHULSE
MARKE   EICHEL

ENGLISH TRANSLATION
Excelent Cartridge Case.
Mark (Td Mk) Acorn (Acorn Brand).

No iron or steel was used in the case construction.

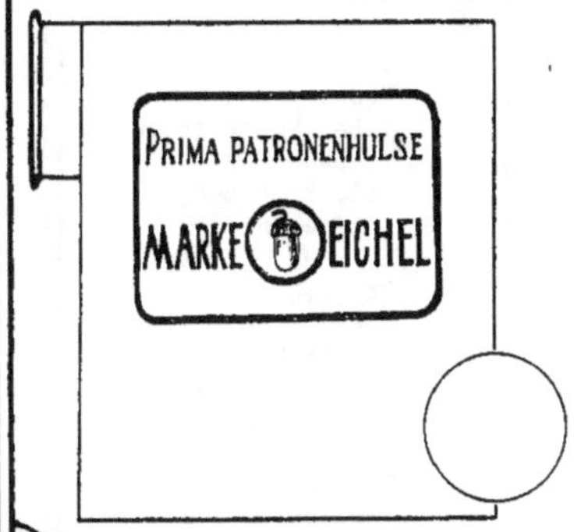

PRIMA PATRONENHULSE
MARKE EICHEL

DATA
Gauge; 12.
Length; 65 mm.
Head; 7 mm.
Tube; Wound brown paper.
Colour; Sand brown.
Print; Black.
Base; Brass.
Closure; Rolled turn-over.
Wad; Red card, blacked over.
Cap; Copper.

ELAHEE BUKSH & COY:
Meerut, Haryana, India.

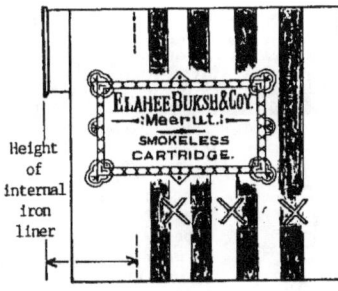

ELAHEE BUKSH & COY.
—:Meerut.:—
SMOKELESS CARTRIDGE

Height of internal iron liner

 X X X   Wad not known

The three X's.

Case wall was impressed with three X's and overprinted with four black bands.

DATA
Gauge; 20.
Length; 64 mm.
Head; 5 to 6 mm.
Tube; Wound dull green paper.
Colour; Jade green.
Print; Black.
Base; Reinforced brass.
Closure; Rolled turn-over.
Wad; Not known.
Circa; Post 1896.

ELAHEE BUKSH & COMPANY:
Delhi & Meerut, Northern India.

ELAHEE BUKSH & CO.
MEERUT & DELHI
KYNOCH
UNLINED NITRO QUALITY
LOADED WITH
Smokeless Diamond Powder
Made in Great Britain

ELAHEE BUKSH & CO.
MEERUT & DELHI
KYNOCH
UNLINED NITRO QUALITY
LOADED WITH
Smokeless Diamond Powder
Made in Great Britain

DATA
Gauge; 12.
Length; 64 mm.
Head; 8 mm.
Tube; Wound middle blue paper.
Nearest Pantone;
PANTONE® 322 C.
Print; Black.
Base; Brass with reinforcing.
Closure; Rolled turn-over.
Wad; White card, print black.
Circa; 1923.

ELEY BROTHERS, LIMITED:
254 Gray's Inn Road, London W.C.1., England.

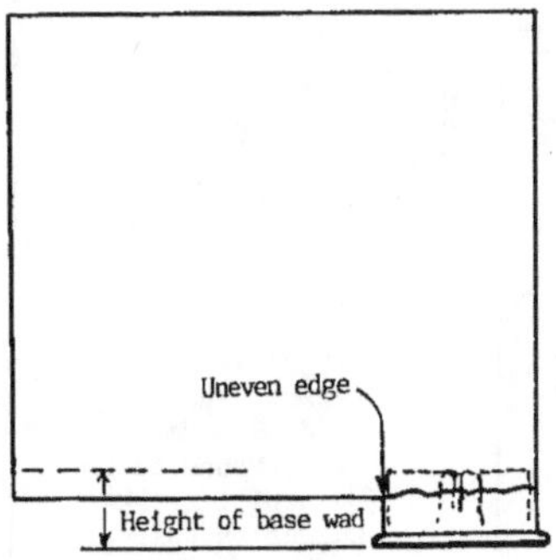

Wad not known

Uneven edge

Height of base wad

Drawing made from an unused case.
Some unanswered questions are;
What year was it made ?
Was it the first Eley case to carry a shield?
Was it a ceap or dear brand ?
Was it made for Eleys' by Gevelot ?
What was the 'G' for ?

DATA
Gauge; 12.
Length; 64 mm.
Head; 6-7 mm.
Tube; Wound rough textured (cowpat) brown paper.
Printings; Nil.
Base; Brass.
Headstamping; Raised.
Wad; Not known.
Business; Ammunition manufacturers.

PLATE 33

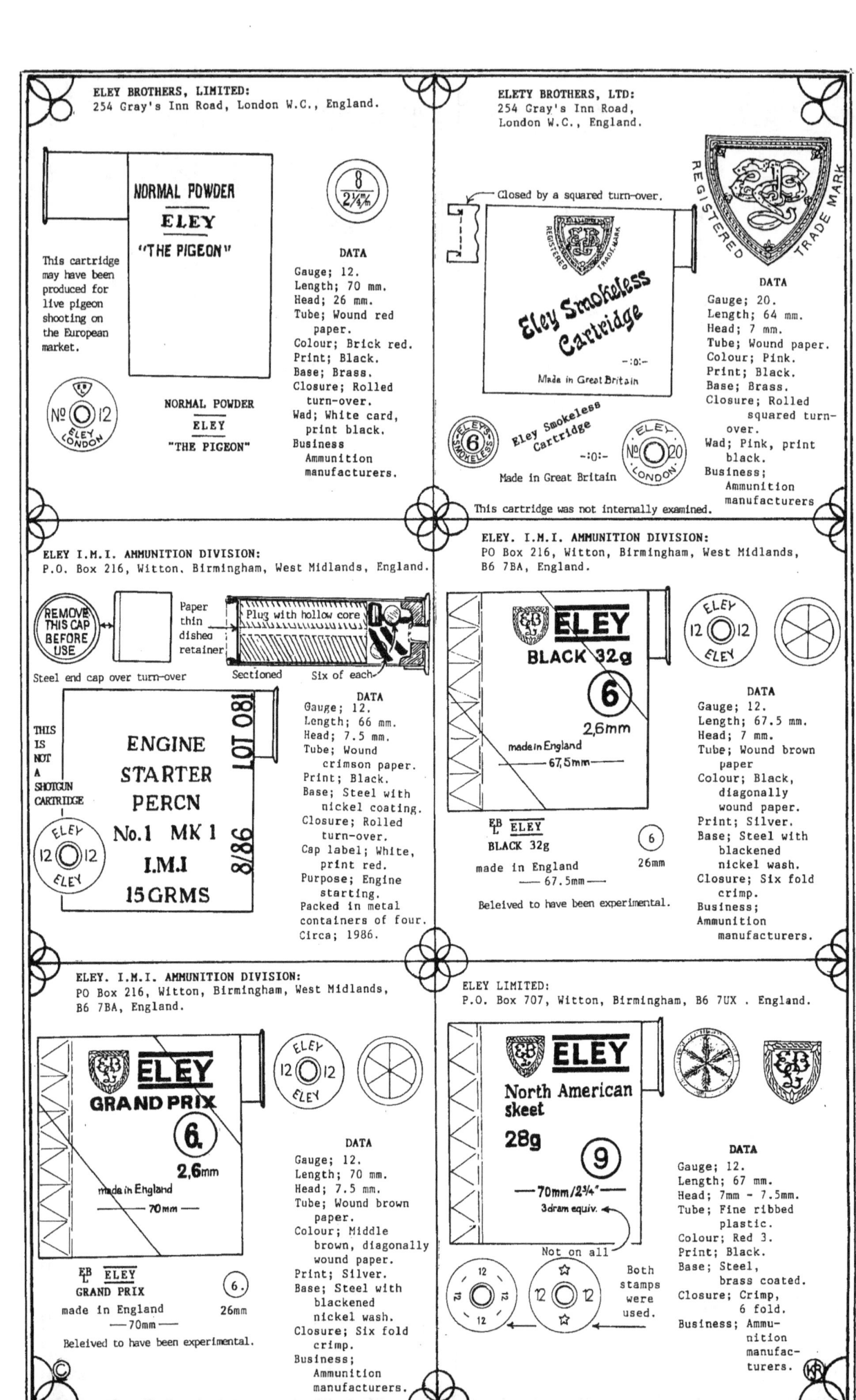

PLATE 34

ELEY LIMITED:
P.O. Box 707, Witton, Birmingham, B6 7UX. England.

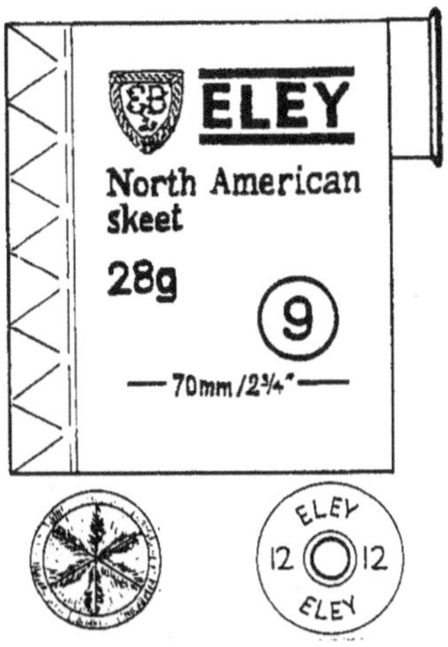

DATA
Gauge; 12.
Length; 67 mm.
Head; 8 mm.
Tube; Fine ribbed plastic.
Colour; Dark green 4.
Print; Silver.
Base; Steel, brass coated.
Closure; Crimp, 6 fold.
Business; Ammunition manufactures.

ELEY HAWK, LIMITED:
P.O. Box 707, Witton, Birmingham, B6 7UX, England.

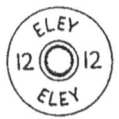

DATA
Gauge; 12.
Length; 67.5 mm.
Head; 16 mm.
Tube; Wound brown paper.
Colour; Dark green.
Print; Black or old gold.
Base; Steel with a brass wash coating.
Closure; Six fold crimp.
Business; Ammunition manufacturers.
Circa; 2001.

Made in England

Eley Classic Game 6cu 2.6 mm 67.5mm

ELEY HAWK LIMITED:
P.O. Box 707, Witton, Birmingham, West Midlands, England.

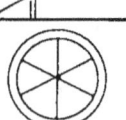

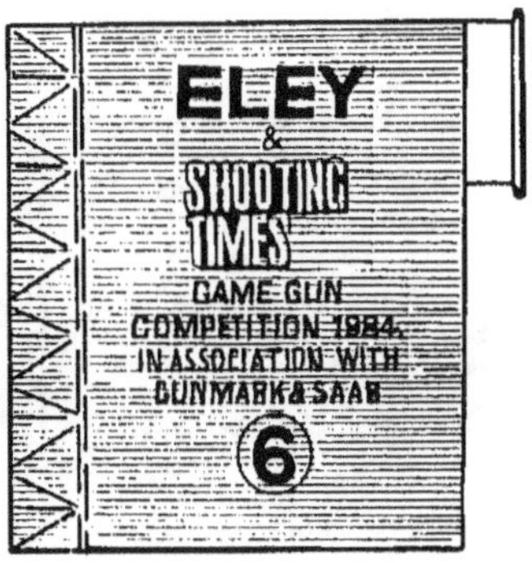

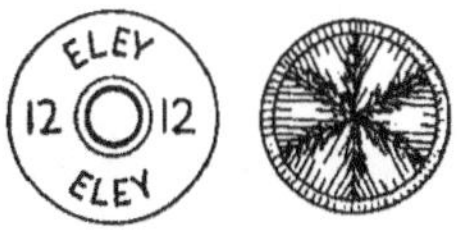

DATA
Gauge; 12.
Length; 68 mm.
Head; 8 mm.
Tube; Ribbed orange plastic.
Print; Black.
Base; Steel with a nickel wash.
Closure; Six fold crimp.
Business; Ammunition manufacturers (Eley Hawk, Ltd).
Circa; 1984.

ELEY & SHOOTING TIMES

GAME GUN COMPETITION 1984. IN ASSOCIATION WITH GUNMARK & SAAB

ELVEDEN ESTATE GUN CLUB:
Elveden Estate, Near Thetford, Norfolk/Suffolk. England.

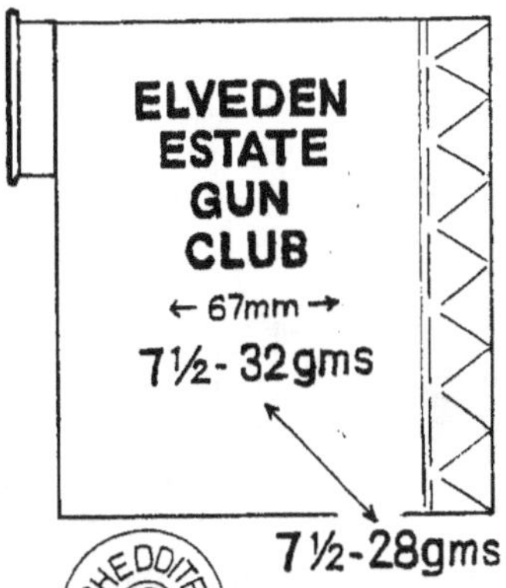

DATA
Gauge; 12.
Length; 67 mm.
Head; 7 mm.
Tube; Medium ribbed plastic.
Colours; Green 3, red 3, blue 4.
Print; Black.
Base; Steel, brass coated.
Closure; Crimp, 6 fold.
Business; Private gun club.

← 67mm →
7½ - 32gms
7½ - 28gms
Blue, 28gms.
Red, 28gms.
Green, 32gms.

ERRE:
Italy. Address not known.

I.G.I. EXPORT HIGH SPEED smokeless powder original loading Erre

DATA
Gauge; 12.
Length; 66 mm.
Head; 3 mm.
Tube; Smooth black plastic.
Colour; Black.
Print; Gold.
Base; Steel with a brass coating.
Closure; Rolled turn-over.
Wad; Not known.

Drawing was made from a used case.

EXPLOSIFS DE CLERMONT MULLER & CIE:
St. Kongensgade 57, Kobenhaven K, Sjelland, Denmark.

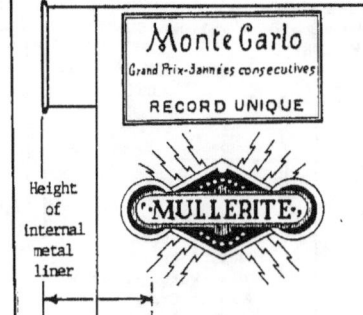

Height of internal metal liner

Monte Carlo
Grand Prix-3années consécutives
RECORD UNIQUE
'MULLERITE'

DATA
Gauge; 12.
Length; 64.5 mm.
Head; 12 mm.
Tube; Wound paper.
Colour; Brownish-orange.
Print; Black.
Base; Reinforced brass.
Closure; Rolled turn-over.
Wad; Brown-orange, print black.
Cap; Large copper.
Business; Powder and ammunition manufacturers.

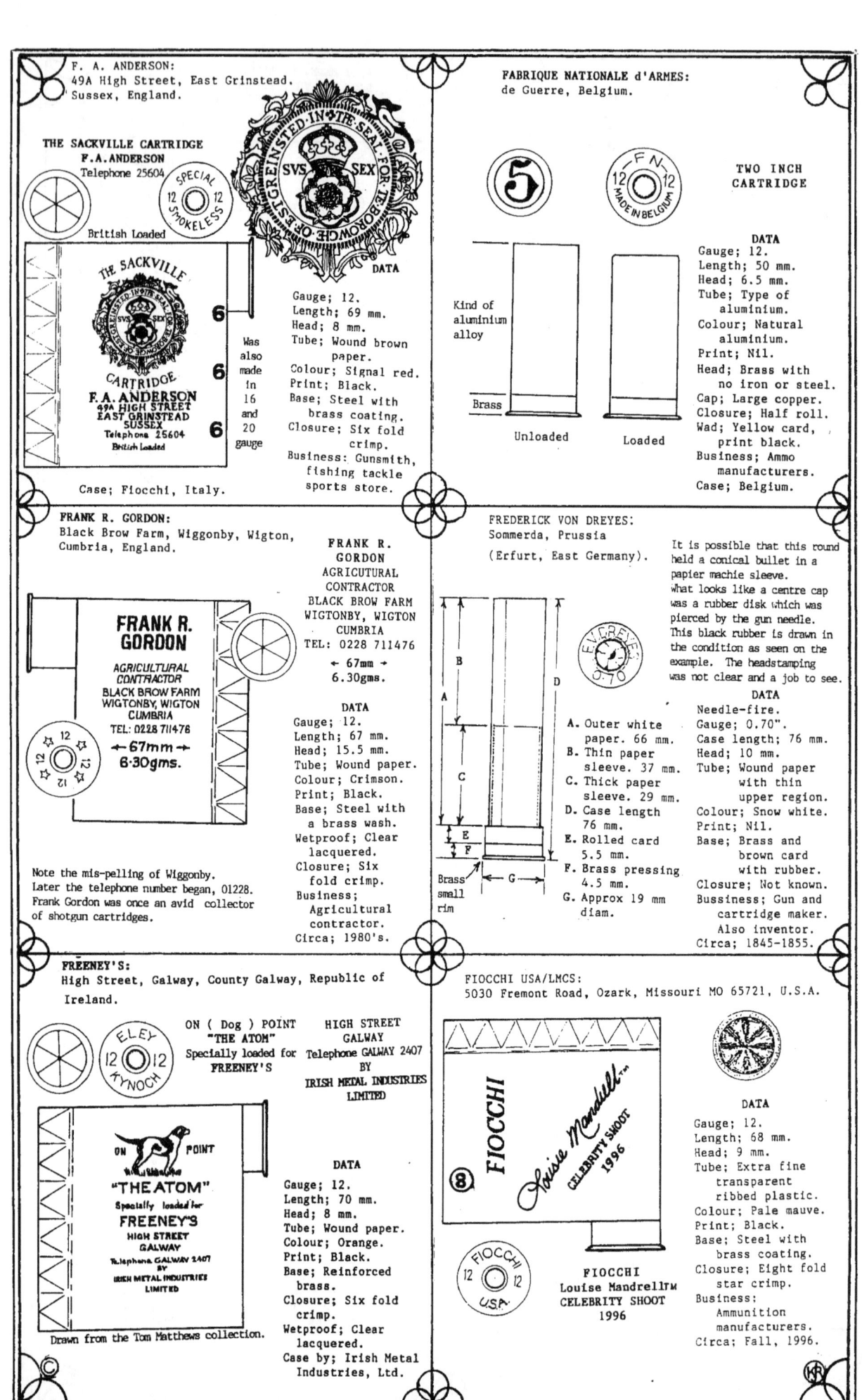

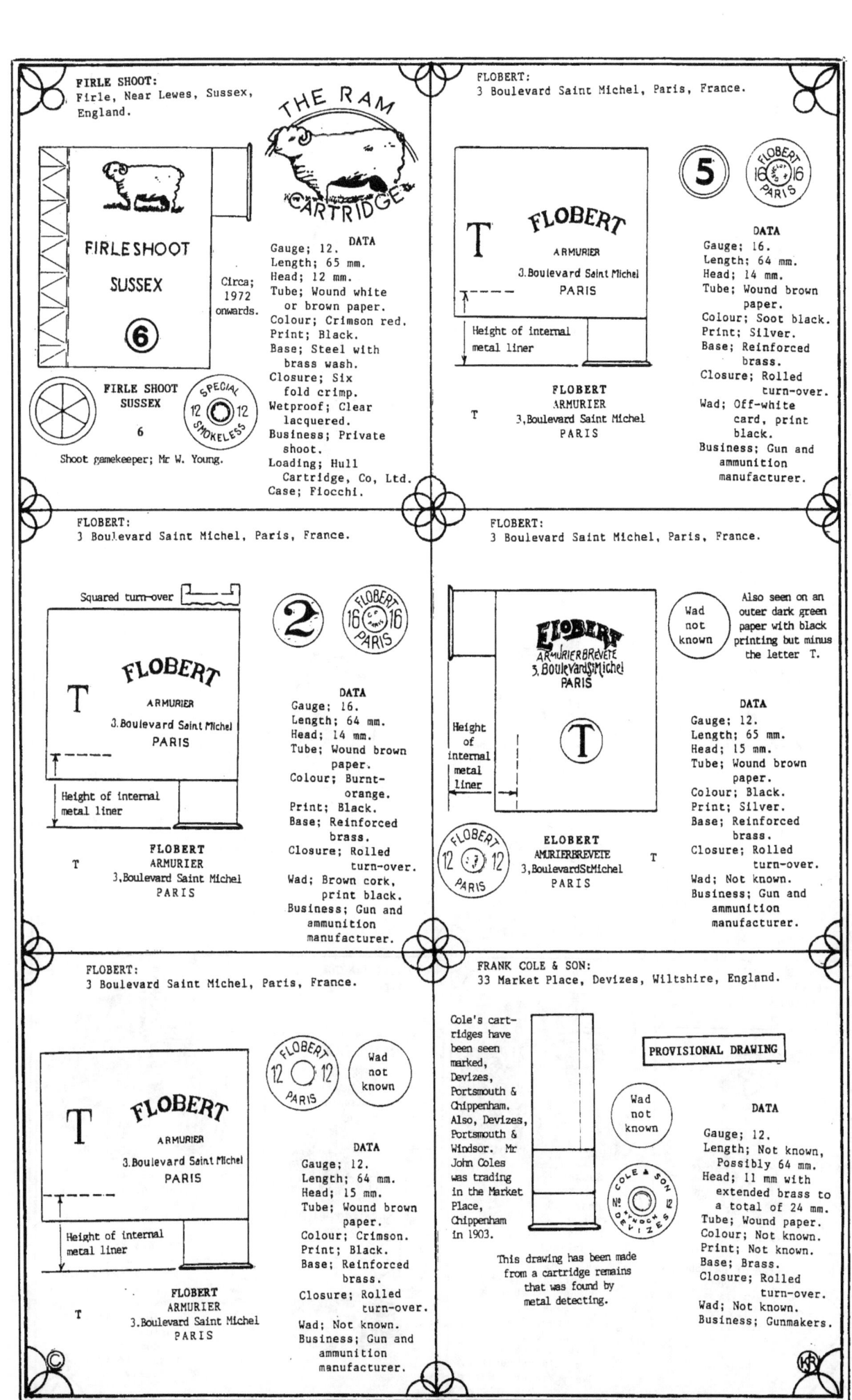

PLATE 37

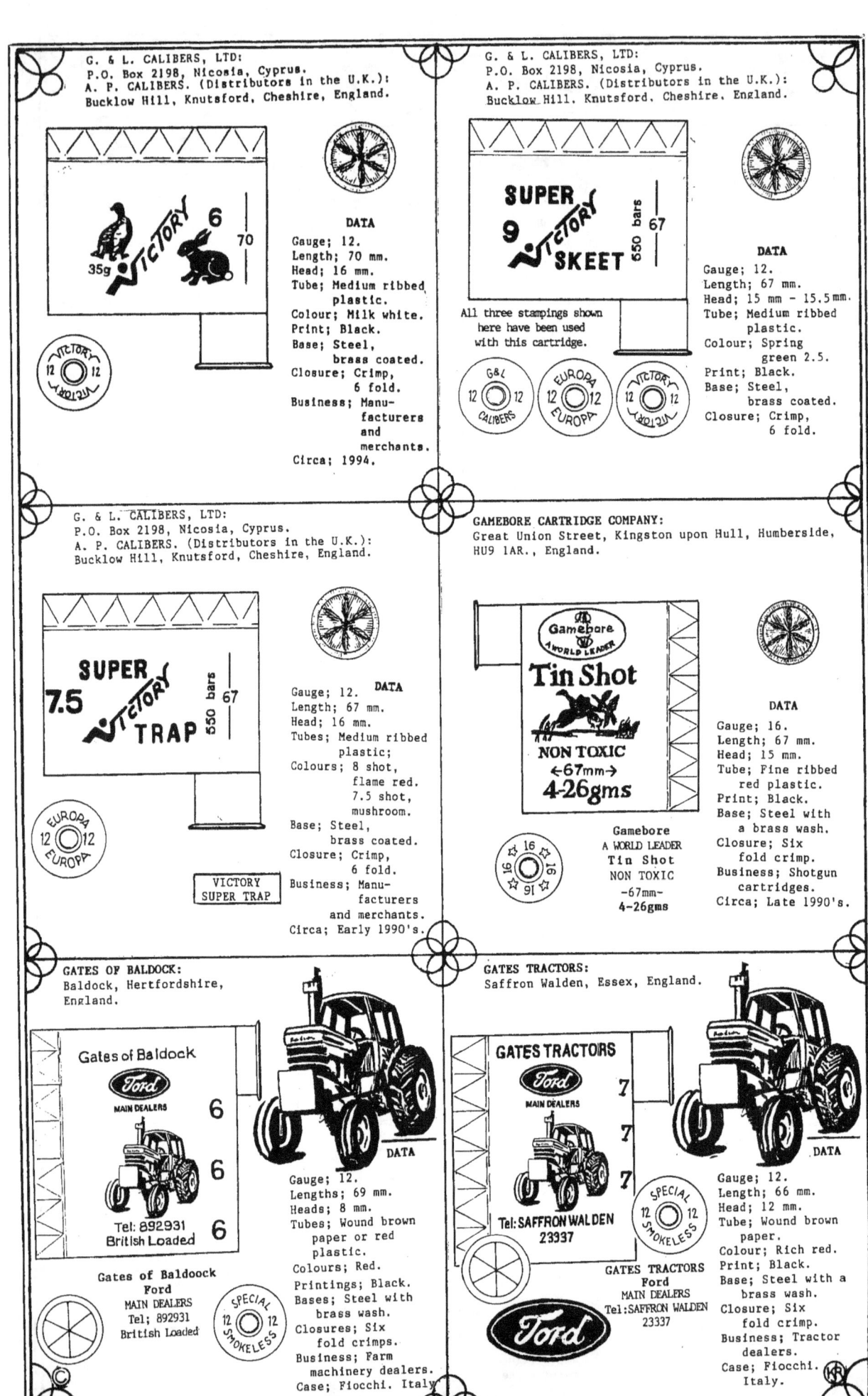

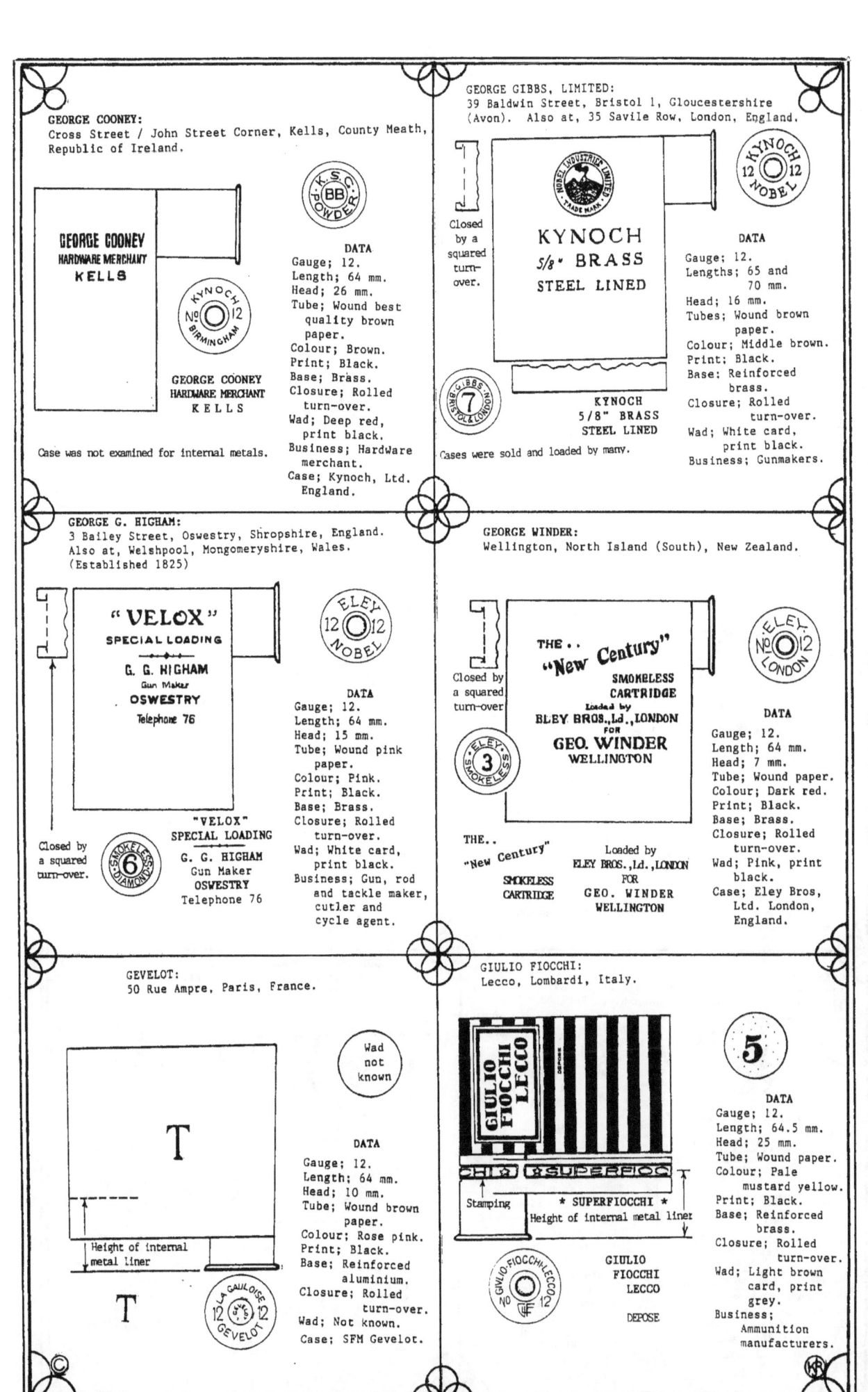

PLATE 39

GIULIO FIOCCHI:
Lecco, Lombardi, Italy.

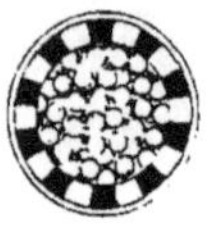

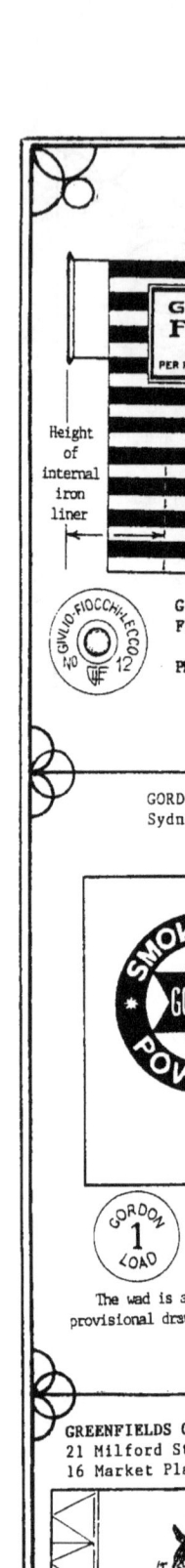

Top view of cartridge

DATA
Gauge; 12.
Length; 64 mm.
Head; 10 mm.
Tube; Wound paper.
Colour; Dark red.
Print; Black.
Base; Brass reinforced.
Closure; Rolled turn-over.
Wad; Transparent celluloid.
Business; Ammunition manufacturers.

GIULIO
FIOCCHI
LECCO
PER POLVERI VOLUMINOSE
DEPOSE

G. J. HANDY & CO., LTD:
120 Victoria Road, Old Town, Swindon, Wiltshire, England.

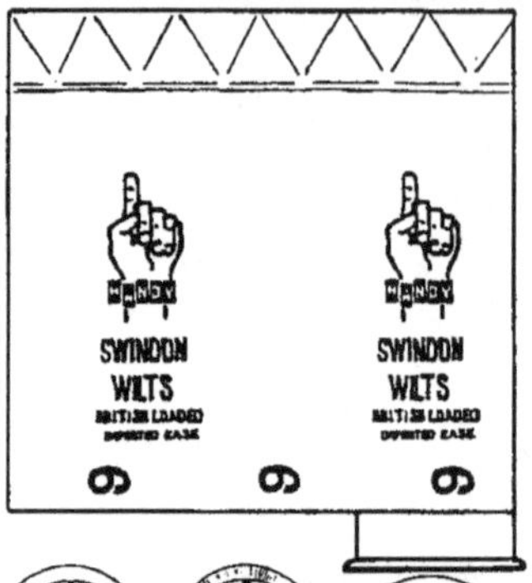

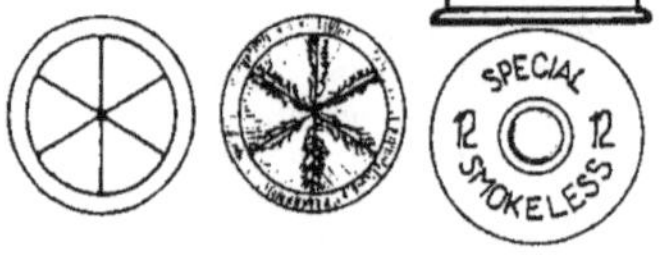

DATA
Gauge; 12.
Length; 70 mm.
Head; 8 mm.
Tubes; Either wound paper or fine ribbed plastic.
Colour; Red 3.
Print; Black.
Base; Steel, brass coated.
Closure; Crimp, 6 fold.
Business; Ironmongers.
Case; Fiocchi. Italy.
Loading; Hull Cartridge Co.

GORDON CARTRIDGE COMPANY:
Sydney, New South Wales, Australia.

DATA
Gauge; 12.
Length; 64 mm.
Head; 8 mm.
Tube; Wound orange paper.
Colour; Brownish-orange (unglossed).
Base; Reinforced brass.
Closure; Rolled turn-over.
Wad shown; Colours not known.
Case; Eley Bros, Ltd. England.

SMOKELESS
* GORDON *
POWDER
BULLS-EYE

The wad is a provisional drawing

GREENFIELD OF SALISBURY, LTD:
21 Milford Street, Salisbury, Wiltshire. Also later at, 16 Market Place, Ringwood, Hampshire, England.

DATA
Gauge; 16.
Length; 65 mm.
Head; 8 mm.
Tube; Fine ribbed dark blue plastic.
Print; Black.
Base; Steel with a brass wash.
Cap; Nickel.
Closure; Six fold crimp.
Business; Gunmakers.
Loading; Hull Cartridge Co, Ltd.
Case; Fiocchi, Italy.

THE 'WESSEX'
GREENFIELDS
(GUNMAKERS)
SALISBURY, WILTS.
RINGWOOD, HANTS.

GREENFIELDS OF SALISBURY, LTD:
21 Milford Street, Salisbury, Wiltshire. Also later at, 16 Market Place, Ringwood, Hampshire, England.

THE 'WESSEX'
GREENFIELDS
(GUNMAKERS)
SALISBURY, WILTS.
SALISBURY, WILTSHIRE

DATA
Gauge; 12.
Length; 70 mm.
Heads; 8 mm.
Tubes; Wound brown paper or fine ribbed red plastic.
Colours; red.
Printings; Black.
Bases; Steel with a brass wash.
Cap; Nickel.
Closures; Six fold crimp.
Business; Gunmakers.
Cases; Fiocchi. Italy.

Similar cartridges were possibly sold in 16 gauge dark blue and 20 gauge buff or light yellow. The words BRITISH LOADED and IMPORTED CASE were not always included on case walls.

GUNNERSIDE SHOOT:
Gunnerside, Swaledale, Richmond, North Yorkshire, England.

DATA
Gauge; 20.
Length; 67.5 mm.
Head; 8.5 mm.
Tube; Wound paper
Colour; Creamed-buff.
Print; Black.
Base; Steel with a brass wash.
Closure; six fold crimp.
Wetproof; Clear lacquered.
Business; Private shoot.
Circa; 2001.

GUNNERSIDE
(Grouse)
6
- 67.5 mm -

GUNNERSIDE SHOOT:
Gunnerside, Swaledale, Richmond, North Yorkshire, England.

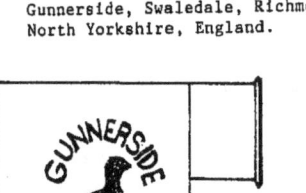

GUNNERSIDE
(Grouse)
6
- 67.5 mm -

DATA
Gauge; 12.
Length; 67.5 mm.
Head; 15.5 mm.
Tube; Wound paper.
Colour; Middle blue.
Print; Gold.
Base; Steel with a brass wash.
Closure; Six fold crimp.
Wetproof; Clear lacquered.
Business; Private shoot.
Circa; 2001.

HAERENS KRUDTVAERK:
Frederiksvaerk, Denmark.

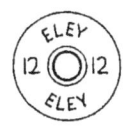

Haerens Krudtvaerk translated,
Army Powder Plant Krudtvaerk.
Rogfrit Jagtkrudt, Smokeless Sporting Powder.

DATA
Gauge; 12.
Length; 65 mm.
Head; 7 mm.
Tube; Wound brown paper.
Colour; Light blue.
Print; Black.
Base; Brass finnish.
Closure; Crimp, 6 fold.
Same; Gauge 16.
Business; Powder, ammunition manufacturers.

HAFIZ GHOUSE & COMPANY:
Meerut, India.

Wad not known

"SMOKELESS FIELD"

Height of steel or iron internal liner.

DATA
Gauge; 12.
Length; 65 mm.
Head; 8-9 mm.
Tube; Wound brown paper.
Colour; Dark green.
Print; Black.
Base; Brass.
Closure; Rolled turn-over.
Wad; Not known.
Case; Kynoch & Co.
Business; General merchants.
Words on crest ribbon; REGISTERED TRADE MARK.

HARRIS SCARFE, LIMITED:
Grenfell Street, Adelaide, South Australia, Australia.

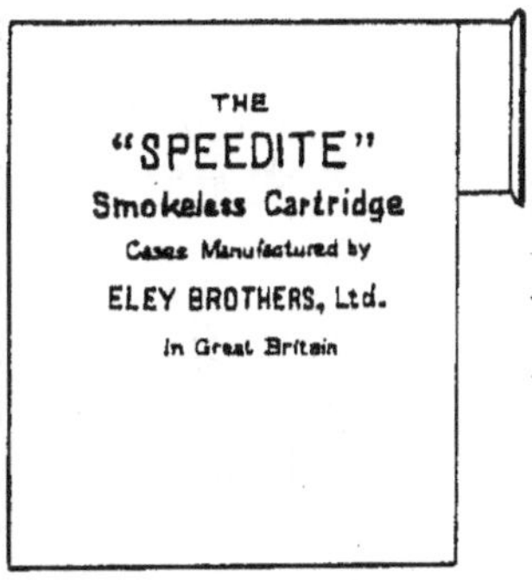

THE "SPEEDITE"
Smokeless Cartridge
Cases Manufactured by
ELEY BROTHERS, Ltd.
In Great Britain

DATA
Gauge; 12.
Length; 64 mm.
Head; 8 mm.
Tube; Wound orange paper.
Colour; Brownish-orange.
Print; Black.
Base; Reinforced brass.
Closure; Rolled turn-over.
Wad; Orange card, print black.
Case; Eley Bros, Ltd. England.

HARRIS SCARFE, LIMITED:
Grenfell Street, Adelaide, South Australia, Australia.

UNICORN
BLACK POWDER

DATA
Gauge; 12.
Length; 64 mm.
Head; 8 mm.
Tube; Wound brown paper.
Colour; Pale light brown.
Print; Black.
Base; Brass.
Closure; Rolled turn-over.
Wad; Yellow card, print black.
Case; Eley Bros, Ltd. London.

HARTLEY'S SPORT STORE:
Flinders Street, Melbourne, Victoria, Australia.

"Hartsport" Long Range

DATA
Gauge; 12.
Length; 64 mm.
Head; 8 mm.
Tube; Wound red paper.
Colour; Crimson.
Print; Black.
Base; Brass.
Closure; Rolled turn-over.
Wad; White card, print black.
Business; Sports stores.
Case; Eley-Kynoch I.C.I.

PLATE 41

HASHIM.S.HASHIM:
Wickham House, Wickham, Near Newbury, Berkshire, England.

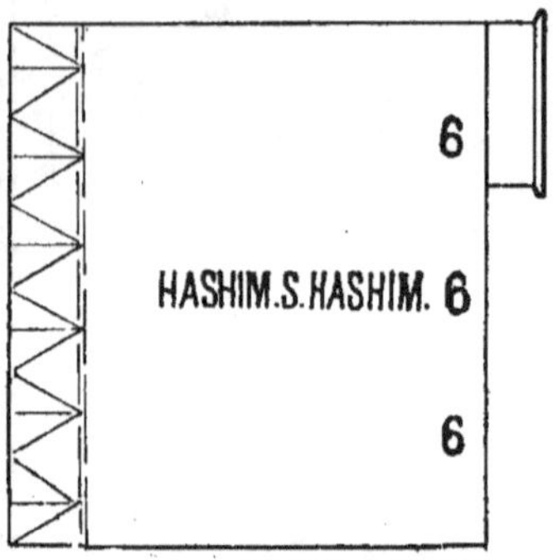

HASHIM.S.HASHIM. 6

HASHIM.S.HASHIM.
Private cartridge for Major General Hashim Said Hashim a former chief of the Saud Arabian Air Force. A keen shot.

DATA
Gauge; 12.
Length; 69 mm.
Head; 8 mm.
Tube; Wound brown paper.
Colour; Red.
Print; Black.
Base; Steel with a brass wash.
Closure; Six fold crimp.
Wetproof; Clear lacquered.
Loading; Hull Cartridge Co, Ltd.
Case; Fiocchi.
Circa; 1970's.

HARVEY SHAW SUCCESSORS:
560-6 Lonsdale Street, Melbourne, Victoria, Australia.

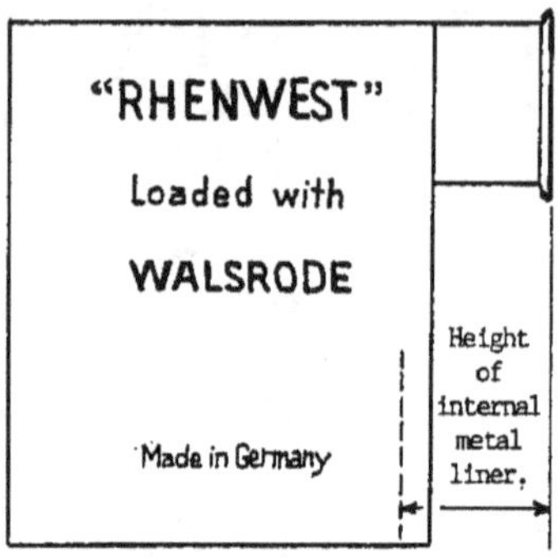

"RHENWEST"
Loaded with
WALSRODE
Made in Germany

Height of internal metal liner.

"RHENWEST"
Loaded with
WALSRODE
Made in Germany

DATA
Gauge; 12.
Length; 69 mm.
Head; 15 mm.
Tube; Wound brown paper.
Colour; Yellow.
Print; Black.
Base; Reinforced brass.
Closure; Rolled turn-over.
Wad; Orange card, print black.
Business; Stores and cartridge loaders.
Case; Germany.
Circa; 1930's.

HARVEY SHAW SUCCESSORS:
560 - 566 Longdale Street, Melbourne, Victoria, Australia.

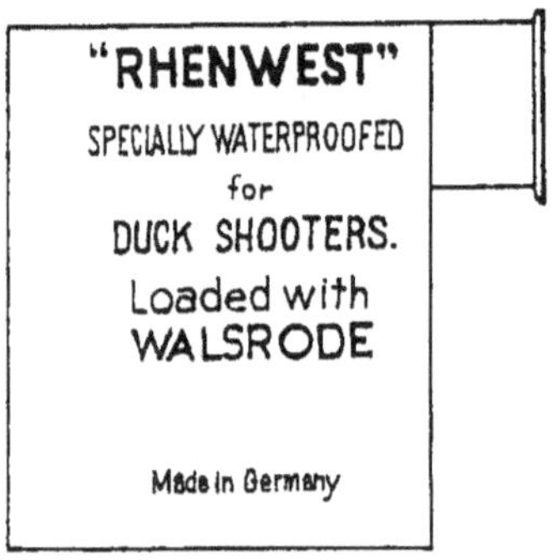

"RHENWEST"
SPECIALLY WATERPROOFED
for
DUCK SHOOTERS.
Loaded with
WALSRODE
Made in Germany

"RHENWEST"
SPECIALLY WATERPROOFED
for
DUCK SHOOTERS
LOADED WITH
WALSRODE
Made in Germany

DATA
Gauge; 12.
Length; 69 mm.
Head; 15 mm.
Tube; Wound red paper.
Colour; Ruby red.
Print; Black.
Base; Brass.
Closure; Rolled turn-over.
Wad; Orange, print black.
Business; Merchants and cartridge loaders.
Case; Germany

HAWKES BROTHERS:
Clare Street, Geelong, Victoria, Australia.

THE
"BARWON"
CARTRIDGE

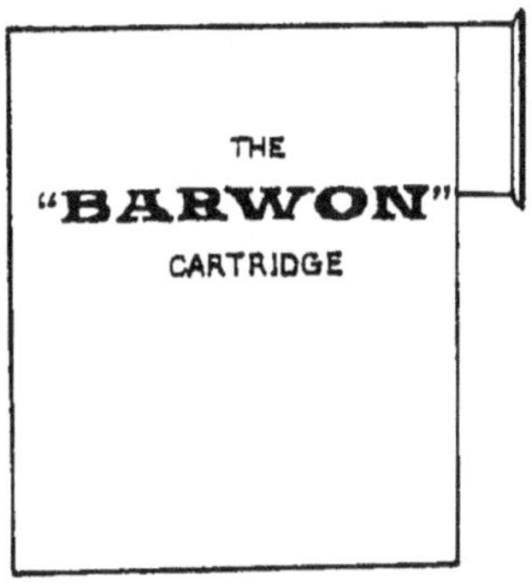

THE
"BARWON"
CARTRIDGE

DATA
Gauge; 12.
Length; 64 mm.
Head; 8 mm.
Tube; Wound grey paper.
Colour; Grey.
Print; Black.
Unglossed case.
Base; Reinforced brass.
Closure; Rolled turn-over.
Wad shown; White card, print black.
Case; Nobel Explosives Co, Ltd. Scotland.

HAWKES BROTHERS:
Clare Street, Geelong, Victoria, Australia.

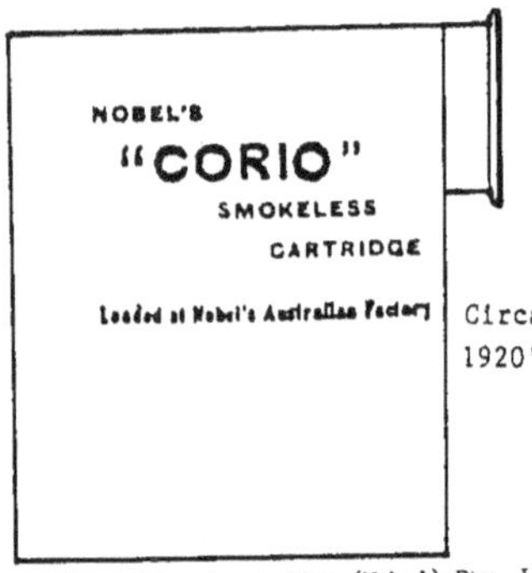

NOBEL'S
"CORIO"
SMOKELESS
CARTRIDGE
Loaded at Nobel's Australian Factory

Loaded by, Ammunition (Nobel) Pty, Ltd.
Deer Park, Melbourne.

NOBEL'S
"CORIO"
SMOKELESS
CARTRIDGE
Loaded at Nobel's Australian Factory

Circa; 1920's.

DATA
Gauge; 12.
Length; 64 mm.
Head; 7.5 mm.
Tube; Wound red paper.
Colour; Red.
Print; Black.
Base; Reinforced brass.
Closure; Rolled turn-over.
Wad shown; Light-yellow, print brown.
Case; Nobel Industries, Ltd, England.

HENRY ATKIN, LTD:
41 Jermyn Street, London S.W.1., England.

Specially Loaded by
HENRY ATKIN, Ld.
41 Jermyn Street
LONDON S.W.

Made in Great Britain
FROM
"PEGAMOID"
BRAND PAPER

Specially Loaded by
HENRY ATKIN, Ld.
41 Jermyn Street
LONDON S.W.

Made in Great Britain
FROM
"PEGAMOID"
BRAND PAPER

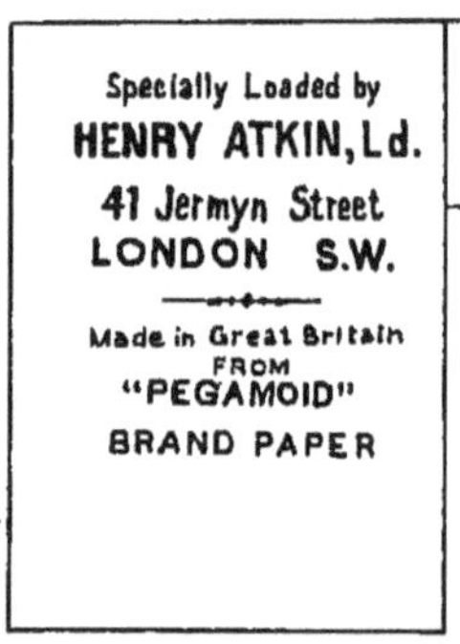

This cartridge was not examined for an internal metals.

Circa; 1908.

DATA
Gauge; 12.
Length; 64 mm.
Head; 16 mm.
Tube; Wound purple Pegamoid brand paper.
Colour; Purple.
Print; Black.
Base; Brass.
Closure; Rolled turn-over.
Wad; Red, print black.
Business; Gunmaker.
Case; Eley Bros, Ltd. London.

PLATE 42

HENRY CLARKE & SONS:
37½ Gallowtree Gate. Also at,
20 Humberstone Gate, Leicester,
Leicestershire, England.

The example was not examined for internal metals.

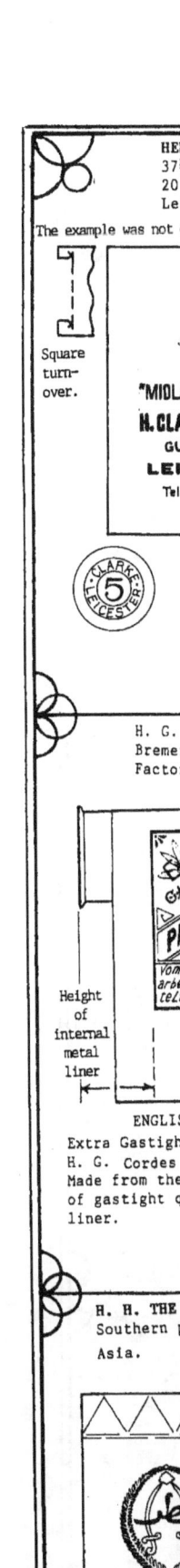

Square turn-over.

THE "MIDLAND" CARTRIDGE
H.CLARKE & SONS
GUNMAKERS
LEICESTER
Telephone 4122

DATA
Gauge; 12.
Length; 64 mm.
Head; 16 mm.
Tube; Wound pink paper.
Colour; Pink darkened by waterproofing.
Print; Black.
Base; Brass.
Closure; Rolled turn-over.
Wad; White card, print shocking pink.
Business; Gunmakers.
Circa; 1920's.

HENRY C. SQUIRES:
178 Broadway, New York, N.Y., United States of America.

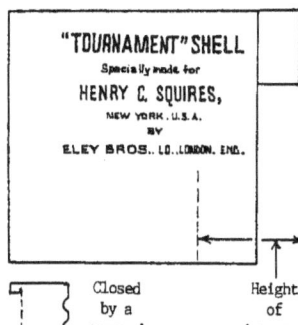

"TOURNAMENT" SHELL

Closed by a squared turn-over. Height of internal iron liner

DATA
Gauge; 28.
Length; 64 mm.
Head; 10 mm.
Tube; Wound brown paper.
Colour; Light brown.
PANTONE®471 U.
Print; Black.
Base; Copperish-brass.
Closure; Rolled turn-over.
Wad; White card, print nil.
English case.
Prior to; 1896.

H. G. CORDES:
Bremerhaven, Nieder Sachsen, West Germany.
Factory at; Bischweiler, West Germany.

Height of internal metal liner

ENGLISH TRANSLATION
Extra Gastight Cartridge case by H. G. Cordes of Bremerhaven. Made from the very best materials of gastight quality with a metal liner.

DATA
Gauge; 12.
Length; 65 mm.
Head; 8 mm.
Tube; Wound brown paper.
Colour; Old brown.
Print, Black.
Base; reinforced brass.
Closure; Rolled turn-over.
Wad; White card, print red. 0 shot size in black.
Cap; Small copper.

H. G. HOPKINS & SONS:
Sandbach, Cheshire.

H. G. HOPKINS & SONS
GUNMAKERS
Sandbach Cheshire
Tel: 0270 762404
— 67mm —
7½

DATA
Gauge; 12.
Length; 67 mm.
Head; 8 mm.
Tube; Fine ribbed plastic.
Colour; Maroon 3.
Print; Silver.
Base; Steel, brass coated.
Closure; Crimp, 6 fold.
Business; Gunmakers.

H. H. THE RULER OF QATAR:
Southern peninsula in, The Gulf, Asia.

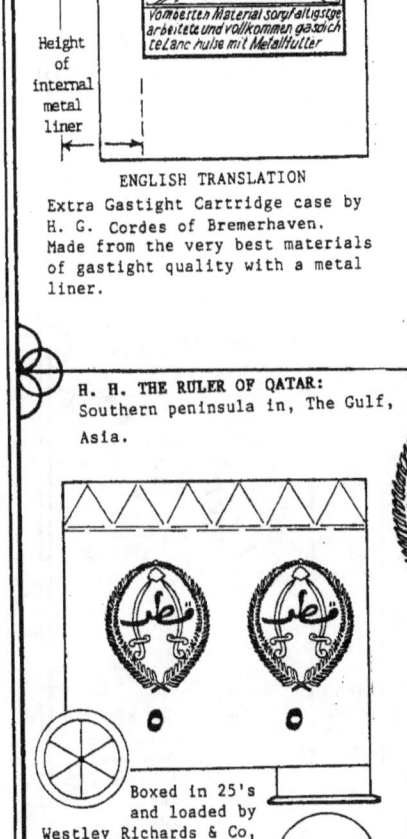

Boxed in 25's and loaded by Westley Richards & Co, in association with Holland & Holland, Ltd for H. H. The Ruler of Qatar, The Gulf, Asia.

DATA
Gauge; 12.
Length; 67 mm.
Head; 8 mm.
Tube; Wound off-white paper.
Colour; Off-white.
Print; Brown.
Base; Brass.
Closure; Six fold crimp.
Business; Private cartridge.

EARL OF CARNARVON:
Highclere Estate, Highclere, North Hampshire, England.

HIGHCLERE (shot size 6)

HIGHCLERE
6

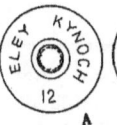 
A   B

Also loaded into an Italian case with the headstamp 'B'. This had a steel base with a brass wash. Its tube was made of fine ribbed red plastic, but no shot size was shown. Closure was a six fold crimp.

DATA
Gauge; 12.
Length; 65 mm.
Head; 8 mm.
Tube; Wound orange paper.
Colour; Orange.
Print; Black.
Wetproof; Clear lacquered.
Base; Steel with a nickel wash. Stamping 'A'.
Closure; Six fold crimp.
Business; Private cartridge.

HIGHCLERE ESTATE:
Highclere Park, Highclere, North Hampshire, England.

Head gamekeeper, Mr E. Hughes.

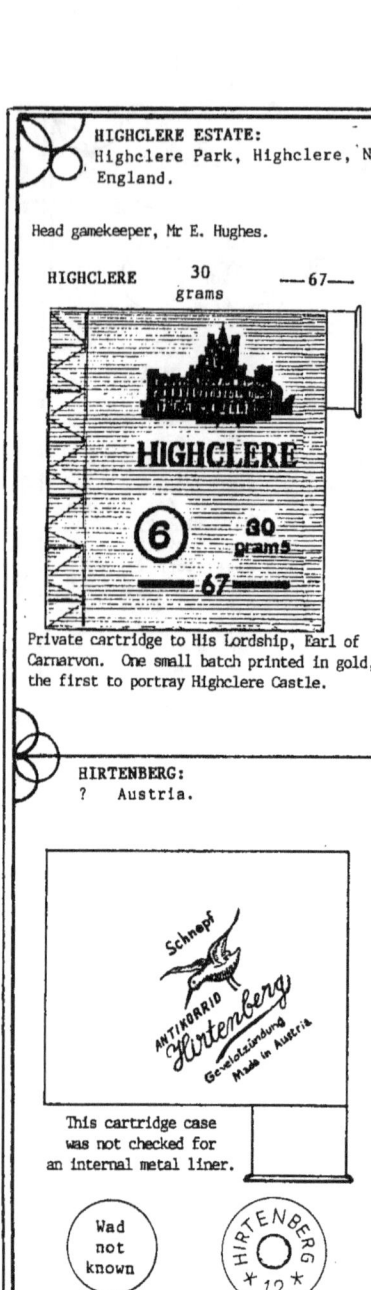

Private cartridge to His Lordship, Earl of Carnarvon. One small batch printed in gold, the first to portray Highclere Castle.

DATA
Gauge; 12.
Length; 67 mm.
Head; 8.5 mm.
Tube; flame red ribbed plastic.
Printing; As shown was in gold. Also black used but printed in other direction.
Head; Steel with a brass wash.
Closure; Six fold crimp.
Business; Private.
Case; Caledonian Cartridge Co.
Circa; 1992-1993.

HIGHCLERE ESTATE:
Hi ghclere Park, Highclere, North Hampshire, England.

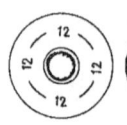 

Private cartridge to His Lordship, Earl of Carnarvon. Highclere Castle.
Head gamekeeper, Mr E. Hughes.

DATA
Gauge; 12.
Length; 67 mm.
Head; 12 mm.
Tube; Black ribbed plastic.
Printing; Gold.
Base; Steel with a brass wash.
Closure; Six fold crimp.
Business; Private estate.
Circa; 1993-1994.

HIRTENBERG:
? Austria.

Schnepf
ANTIKORRID
Hirtenberg
Gevelotzündung
Made in Austria

DATA
Gauge; 12.
Length; 68 mm.
Head; 16 mm.
Tube; Wound brown paper.
Colour; Soot black.
Print; Gold.
Base; Brass.
Closure; Rolled turn-over.
Wad; Not known.
Business; Ammunition manufacturers.
Case; Austria.

H. MAHILLON:
208 Rue Royale, Bruxelles, Belgium.

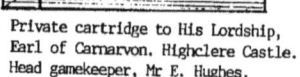

ACIENNE MAISON
H. MAHILLON
208 RUE ROYALE
BRUXELLES
ELEY
Regd.
GASTIGHT
CARTRIDGE CASE
Made in Great Britain

This drawing was made from unused cases that were brought back from Belgium.

DATA
Gauges; 12.
Lengths; 70 mm.
Heads; 15.5 mm.
Tubes; Wound coloured papers.
Colours; Either Brown, Crimson or Dark green.
Printings; Black.
Base; Reinforced brass.
Wetproof; Clear lacquered.
Closure; Rolled turn-over.
Case; British.

H. MAHILLON:
208 Rue Royale, Bruxelles, Belgium.

ANCIENNE MAISON
H. MAHILLON
208 RUE ROYALE
BRUXELLES
ELEY
Regd.
GASTIGHT
CARTRIDGE CASE
MADE IN GREAT BRITAIN

ANCIENNE MAISON
H. MAHILLON
208 RUE ROYALE
BRUXELLES

ELEY
Regd.
GASTIGHT
CARTRIDGE CASE
MADE IN GREAT BRITAIN

This drawing was made from an unused case that was brought back from Belgium.

DATA
Gauge; 12.
Length; 70 mm.
Head; 16 mm.
Tube; Wound red Gastight Quality paper.
Colour; Eley's brick brick red.
Print; Black.
Base; Reinforced brass.
Waterproofed; Clear lacqured.
Wad; Not known.
Case; Eley-Kynoch I.C.I.
Circa; 1930's.

H. MAHILLON:
208 Rue Royale, Bruxelles, Belgium.

ANCIENNE MAISON
H. MAHILLON
208 RUE ROYALE
BRUXELLES
ELEY
Regd.
GASTIGHT
CARTRIDGE CASE
Made in Great Britain

ACIENNE MAISON
H. MAHILLON
208 RUE ROYALE
BRUXELLES

ELEY
Regd.
GASTIGHT
CARTRIDGE CASE
Made in Great Britain

This drawing was made from an unused case that was brought back from Belgium.

DATA
Gauge; 16.
Length; 64 mm.
Head; 15 mm.
Tube; Wound blue paper.
Colour; Dark blue.
Print; Extra dark blue.
Base; Reinforced brass.
Closure; Rolled turn-over.
Wad; Not known.
Case; Eley-Kynoch I.C.I.
Circa; 1930's.

H. MAHILLON:
208 Rue Royale, Bruxelles, Belgium.

The example drawn was an unused ready capped case.

DATA
Gauge; 12.
Length; 64.5 mm.
Head; 7.5 mm.
Tube; Wound blue paper.
Colour; Middle blue. PANTONE® 285 C.
Print; Dark blue. PANTONE® 288 C.
Wetproof; Clear varnish.
Base; Brass.
Internal liner; Nil.
Closure; Rolled turn-over.
Wad; Not known.
Circa; 1930's.

ELEY Regd, GRAND PRIX CARTRIDGE CASE

Wad not known

H. MAHILLON:
208 Rue Royale, Bruxelles, Belgium.

The example drawn was an unused ready capped case.

DATA
Gauge; 16.
Length; 65 mm.
Head; 7 mm.
Tube; Wound red paper.
Colour; Crimson. PANTONE® 1935 C.
Print; Black.
Wetproof; Clear varnish.
Base; Brass.
Internal liner; Nil.
Closure; Rolled turn-over.
Wad; Not known.
Circa; 1930's.

ELEY Regd, GRAND PRIX CARTRIDGE CASE

Wad not known

H. MAHILLON:
208 Rue Royale, Bruxelles, Belgium.

The example drawn was an unused ready capped case.

DATA
Gauge; 20.
Length; 65 mm.
Head; 7.5 mm.
Tube; Wound buff paper.
Colour; Buff. PANTONE® 1555 C.
Print; Black.
Wetproof; Clear varnish.
Base; Brass.
Internal liner; Nil.
Closure; Rolled turn-over.
Wad; Not known.
Circa; 1930's.

ELEY Regd, 20 GAUGE CARTRIDGE CASE

 Wad not known

HOLLAND & HOLLAND LTD:
13 Bruton Street, London, W1X 8JS. England.

It has been pointed out to me that the scrolling after the dates reads as Sex. I would not think that Holland & Holland noticed this. Both stampings used. 12 gauge only.

DATA
Gauge; 12.
Length; 65 mm.
Head; 12 mm.
Tube; Wound brown paper.
Ext' colour; Gloss black.
Print; Gold.
Base; Steel, brass coated.
Closure; Crimp, 6 fold.
Cases; Fiocchi.
Business; Gunmakers.

150th ANIVERSARY CARTRIDGE 1835-1985

HOULLIER BLANCHARD. PIDAULT SUCC:
42 Rue del Arcade, Paris, France.

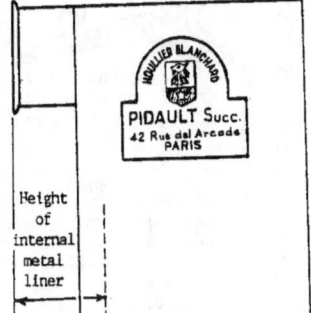

Height of internal metal liner

HOULLIER BLANCHARD
PIDAULT Succ.
42 Rue del Arcade
PARIS

Wad not known

DATA
Gauge; 12.
Length; 64 mm.
Head; 14 mm.
Tube; Wound brown paper.
Colour; Brownish-buff.
Print; Black.
Base; Reinforced brass.
Closure; Rolled turn-over.
Wad; Not known.

HUGH PARKER:
Port Elizabeth, Cape of Good Hope (Cape Province), Republic of South Africa.

"HUGH PARKER'S SPECIAL"
PORT ELIZABETH
MADE IN GREAT BRITAIN

Height of internal steel liner

"HUGH PARKER'S SPECIAL"
PORT ELIZABETH
MADE IN GREAT BRITAIN

DATA
Gauge; 12.
Length; 64 mm.
Head; 16 mm.
Tube; Wound red paper.
Colour; Eley's brick red.
Print; Black.
Base; Reinforced brass.
Closure; Rolled turn-over.
Wad; Brown card, print black.
Wetproof; Clear lacquered.
Circa; 1930's.

HULL CARTRIDGE COMPANY, LIMITED:
58 De Grey Street, Kingston-upon-Hull,
Yorkshire (Humberside), England.

THREE CROWNS
HULL CARTRIDGE
CO. LTD.
58 DE GREY STREET
HULL

DATA
Gauge; 12.
Length; 70 mm.
Head; 8 mm.
Tubes; Wound brown
   paper or fine
   ribbed red plastic.
Colours; Red.
Printings; Black.
Bases; Steel with a
   brass wash.
Cap; Nickel.
Closure; Six
   fold crimp.
Business; Shotgun
   cartridges.
Cases; Fiocchi,
   Italy.

Possibly also produced with a red plastic tube. Also in 16 gauge blue and 20 gauge buff or light yellow.
The address was not always on the case wall.

HULL CARTRIDGE COMPANY, LIMITED:
Bontoft Avenue, National Avenue, Kingston upon Hull,
Humberside, England.

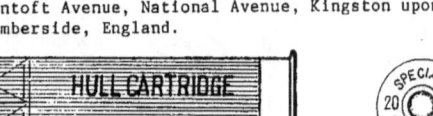
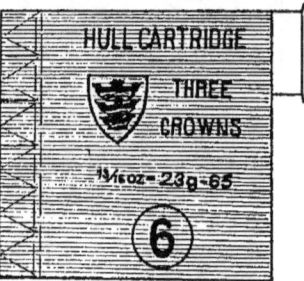

HULL CARTRIDGE
THREE
CROWNS
13/16oz-23g-65
6

DATA
Gauge; 20.
Length; 65 mm.
Head; 8 mm.
Tube; Lemon ribbed
   plastic.
Colour; Lemon yellow.
Print; Black.
Base; Steel with
   a brass wash.
Closure; Six
   fold crimp.
Business;
   Cartridge loading
   and merchants.
Case; Fiocchi,
   Italy.
Circa; 1993.

HUNGERFORD PARK ESTATE:
Near Hungerford Park, Hungerford, Berkshire,
England.

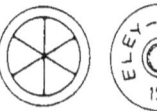

Both stampings shown were used.

HUNGERFORD
PARK ESTATE
1oz. GAME LOAD
Loaded by;
G.L. WOODS & SONS
Ovington, Norfolk.

DATA
Gauge; 12.
Length; 65 mm.
Head; 8 mm.
Tube; Wound paper.
Colour; Orange.
Print; Black.
Base; Steel, brass
   or nickel
   coated.
Closure; Six fold
   crimp.
Business; Private
   country estate.
Circa; 1970's.

HUTCHINSON:
Kendal, Westmorland (Cumbria), England.

NOBEL'S
"SPORTING BALLISTITE"
Special Cartridge
GUN MAKER
KENDAL

DATA
Gauge; 12.
Length; 64 mm.
Head; 10 mm.
Tube; Wound paper.
Colour; Primrose
   yellow.
Print; Light brown.
Base; Brass.
Closure; Rolled
   turn-over.
Wad; White card,
   print vermilion
   red.
Business; Gunmaker.
Case; Eley Bros,
   Ltd.

I. M. CRUDGINGTON, LTD:
7 Green Street, Bath, Avon, England.

Wordings were condensed on the plastic tubes.

"SPA" 6
SPECIALLY LOADED
I. M. CRUDGINGTON LTD.
GUNMAKERS
7 GREEN STREET
BATH
MADE IN GREAT BRITAIN

'A'   'B'

"S P A"
SPECIALLY LOADED
I. M. CRUDGINGTON LTD.
GUNMAKERS
7 GREEN STREET
BATH
MADE IN GREAT BRITAIN

DATA
Gauge; 12.
Length; 70 mm.
Head; 8 mm.
Tubes; Wound pink
   paper. Later
   smooth pink
   plastic.
Print; Black.
Bases; 'A' reinforced
   brass. 'B' steel
   with brass wash.
Closure; Six fold
   crimp.
Business; Gunmakers.
Wetproof; Clear
   lacquered.

I. M. CRUDGINGTON, LTD:
7 Green Street. Later at,
37 Broad Street, Bath, Avon,
England.

THE
CRUDGINGTON
CARTRIDGE
I. M. CRUDGINGTON LTD.
GUNMAKERS
7 GREEN STREET, BATH
TEL: 4928
IMPORTED CASE BRITISH LOADED

I. M. CRUDGINGTON LTD.
GUNMAKERS
37 BROAD STREET, BATH
TEL: 64928

Later had red fine ribbed plastic tubes.
Loading; Hull Cartridge.

7 GREEN STREET, BATH
TEL: 4928
37 BROAD STREET, BATH
TEL: 64928

DATA
Gauge; 12.
Length; 70 mm.
Head; 8 mm.
Tube; Wound white
   paper.
Colour; Light
   crimson red.
Print; Black.
Base; Steel with
   a brass wash.
Closure; Six fold
   crimp.
Business; Gunmakers.
Case; Fiocchi,
   Italy.

PLATE 46

IMPERIAL CHEMICAL INDUSTRIES OF
AUSTRALIA & NEW ZEALAND LIMITED:
Deer Park, Melbourne, Victoria, Australia.

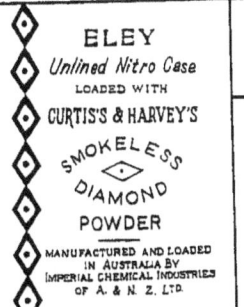  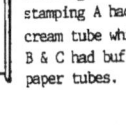

DATA
Gauge; 12.
Length; 64 mm.
Head; 8 mm.
Tube; Wound blue
    paper.
Colour; Middle blue.
Nearest Pantone;
PANTONE® 3025 C.
Print; Black.
Base; Brass, inner
    reinforced.
Closure; Rolled
    turn-over.
Wad; Orange,
    print black.
Circa; 1937.
Business, Cart-
    ridge manufacturers.

ELEY UNLINED NITRO CASE for CURTIS'S
& HARVEY'S SMOKELESS DIAMOND POWDER

IMPERIAL CHEMICAL INDUSTRIES OF AUSTRALIA &
NEW-ZEALAND (I.C.I.A.N.Z.):
Deer Park, Melbourne, Victoria, Australia.

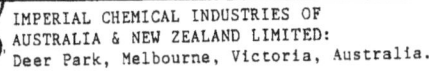 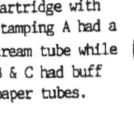 

Cartridge with
stamping A had a
cream tube while
B & C had buff
paper tubes.

Gauge; 20. DATA
Length; 64 mm.
Head; 7 mm.
Tubes; Wound coloured
    papers.
Colours; Cream or
    buff.
PANTONE® 1345 C.
PANTONE® 163 C.
    respectively.
Prints; Black.
Base; Brass.
Closure; Rolled
    turn-over.
Wad; White card,
    print black.
Business; Manu-
    facturers.

ELEY 20 GAUGE CASE

IMPERIAL CHEMICAL INDUSTRIES OF AUSTRALIA &
NEW-ZEALAND (I.C.I.A.N.Z):
Deer Park, Melbourne, Victoria, Australia.

Wad
not
known

EMPRESS
Made & Loaded in Great Britain

EB
L
EMPRESS
Made & Loaded in Great Britain

I saw this cartridge when I visited
Australia during 1985. As it states
that it was made and loaded in
Great Britain, I take it to have
been loaded for the Australian market
and to have been marketed by I.C.I.A.N.Z.
It was not listed in Eley-Kynoch
ammunition catalogues for Great Britain.

DATA
Gauge; 12
Length; 64 mm.
Head; 8 mm.
Tube; Wound grey
    paper.
Colour; Grey.
Print; Black.
Base; Brass.
Closure; Rolled
    turn-over.
Wad; Not known.
Business;
    Ammunition
    manufacturers.

IMPERIAL CHEMICAL INDUSTRIES OF AUSTRALIA &
NEW-ZEALAND, LTD. (I.C.I.A.N.Z.):
Deer Park, Melbourne, Victoria, Australia.

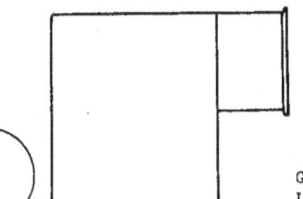 

DATA
Gauge; 12.
Length; 52 mm.
Head; 16 mm.
Tube; Wound Eley's
    brick red paper.
Printing; nil.
Base; reinforced
    brass.
Closure; rolled
    turn-over.
Wad; White card,
    no printing.
Business;
    Ammunition
    manufacturers.
Circa; 1949 - 1956.

NOBEL SCAREBIRD CARTRIDGES

IMPERIAL CHEMICAL INDUSTRIES OF AUSTRALIA
& NEW-ZEALAND (I.C.I.A.N.Z.), LTD:
Deer Park, Melbourne, Victoria, Australia.

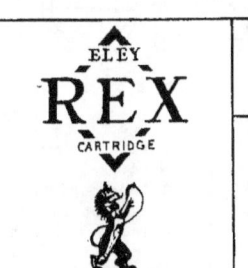  

ELEY
R E X
CARTRIDGE   MANUFACTURED AND LOADED
             IN AUSTRALIA BY
             IMPERIAL CHEMICAL INDUSTRIES
             OF A. & NZ. LTD.

DATA
Gauge; 12.
Lengths; 64 mm.
Heads; 8 mm.
Tubes; Wound coloured
    papers.
Colours; Grey, orange
    or red.
Printings; Black.
Bases; Reinforced
    brass.
Closures; Rolled
    turn-overs.
Wad shown; White
    card, print black.
Business; Ammo
    manufacturers.
Circa; 1939.

IMPERIAL CHEMICAL INDUSTRIES OF AUSTRALIA &
NEW-ZEALAND (I.C.I.A.N.Z.):
Deer Park, Melbourne, Victoria, Australia.

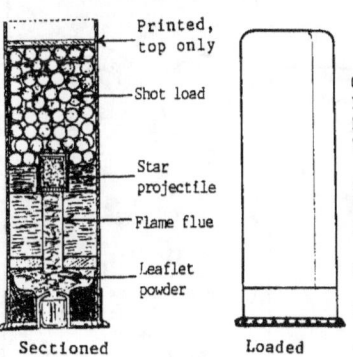

Printed,
top only
Shot load
Star
projectile
Flame flue
Leaflet
powder

Sectioned   Loaded

ELEY ROCKET CARTRIDGE
SHOWS THE FLIGHT OF THE SHOT

DATA
Gauge; 12.
Length; 63 mm.
Head; 8 mm.
Tube; Wound blue
    paper.
Colour; Greyish blue.
Print; Nil.
Base; Reinforced
    brass.
Closure; Rolled
    turn-over.
Wads; White or grey
    cards, print black.
Business;
    Ammunition
    manufacturers.
Circa; Late 1930's.

PLATE 47

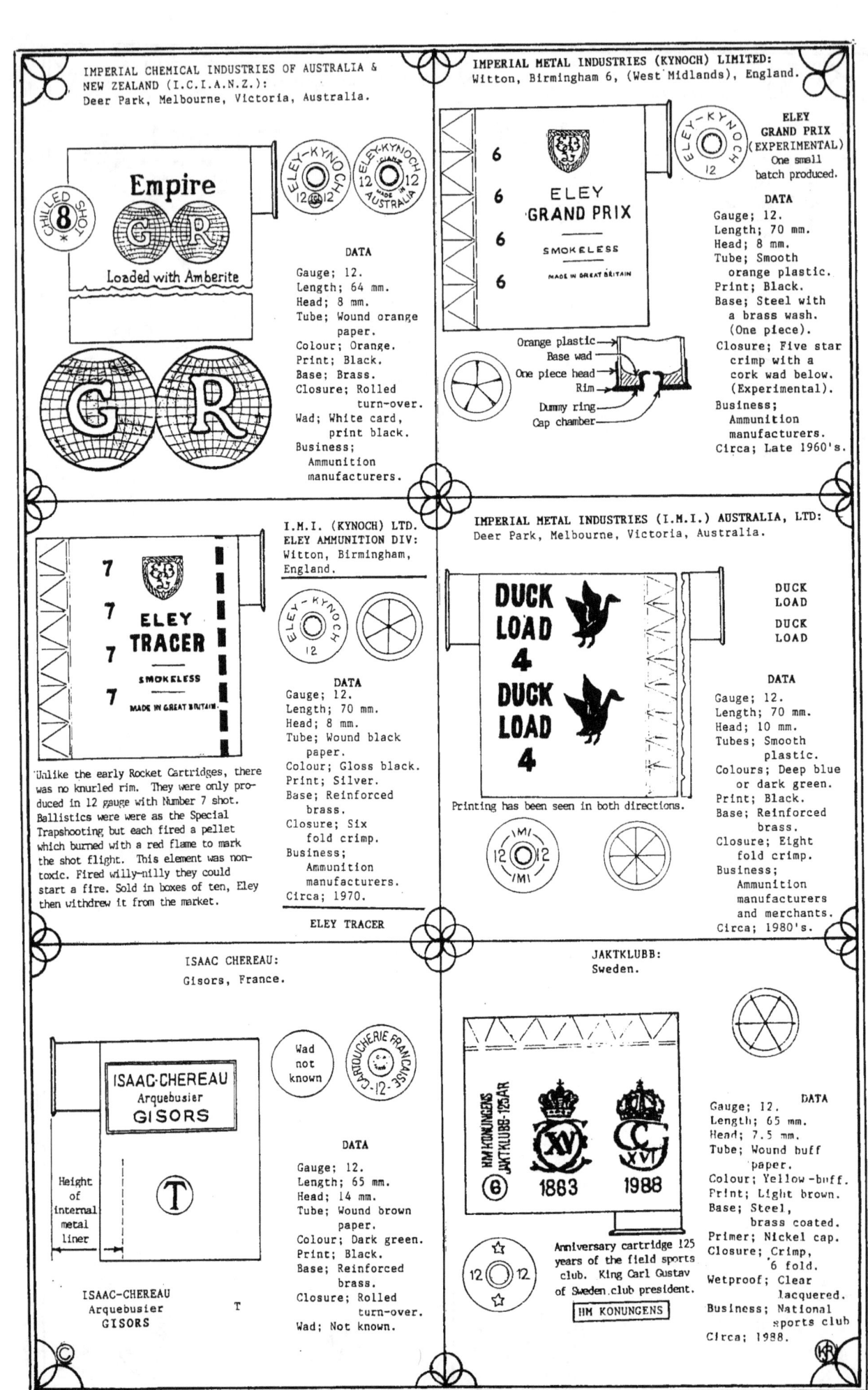

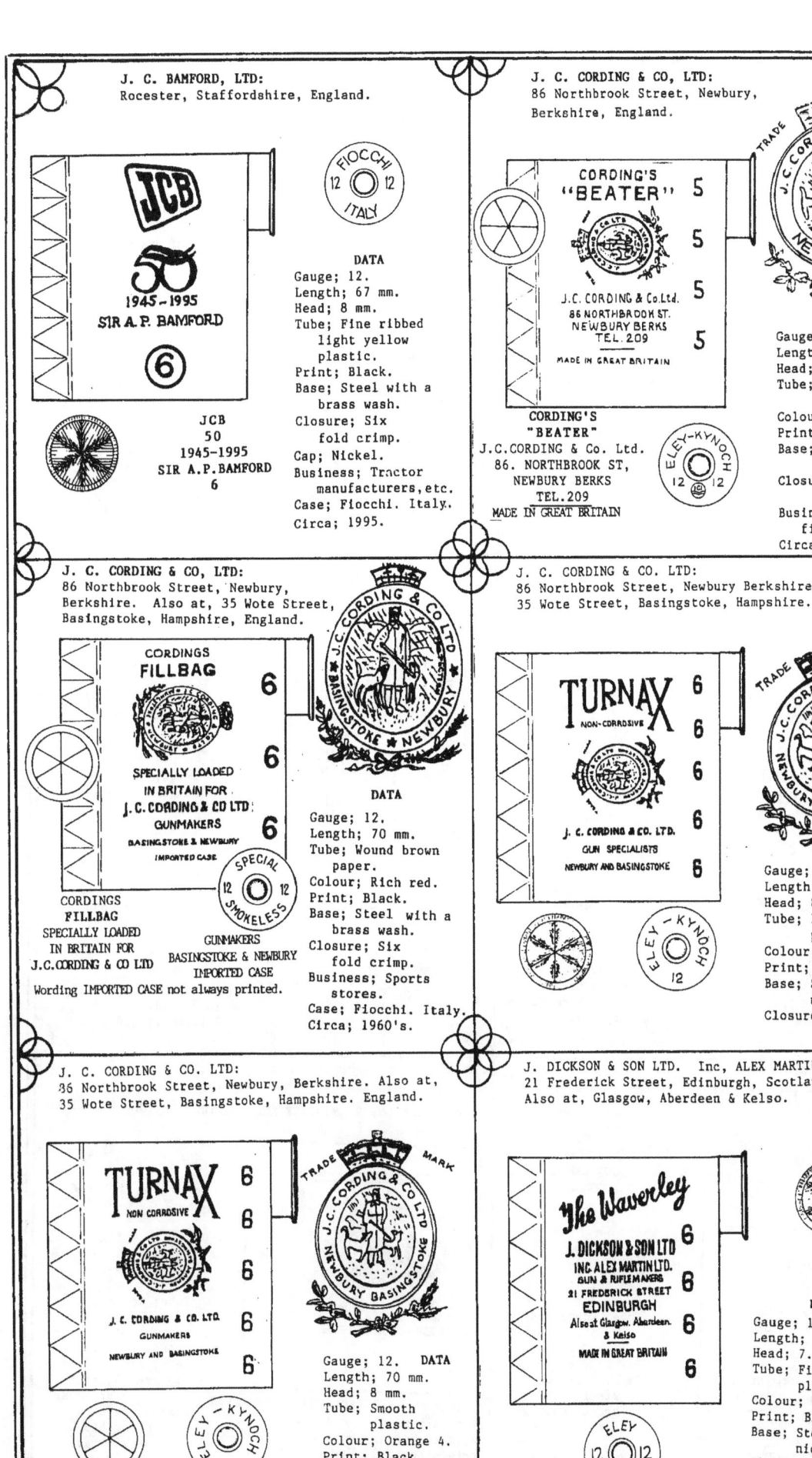

PLATE 49

J. DICKSON & SON LTD. Inc, ALEX MARTIN LTD:
21 Frederick Street, Edinburgh, Scotland.
Also at, Glasgow, Aberdeen & Kelso.

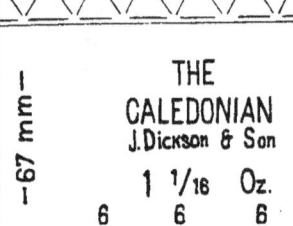

THE CALEDONIAN
J. Dickson & Son
1 1/16 Oz.
6 6 6

-67 mm-

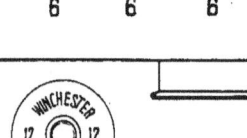

DATA
Gauge; 12.
Length; 67 mm.
Head; 8 mm.
Tube; Vac formed,
    smooth plastic.
Colour; Red 3.5.
Print; Black.
Base; Steel,
    brass coated.
Closure; Crimp,
    6 fold.
Business; Gun and
    rifle
    makers.

J. GILMAN & SON LTD:
Corners of, Stafford Street & Corporation Street,
Birmingham, Midlands, England.

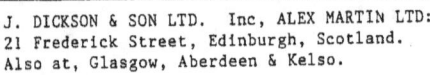

This drawing has been made from a set of photographs.

Registered No 18596
J. GILMAN & SON LTD.
CORNER
STAFFORD STREET
AND
CORPORATION STREET
BIRMINGHAM

DATA
Gauge; 12.
Length; 64 mm.
Head; 8 mm.
Tube; Wound paper.
Colour; Red.
Print; Black.
Base; Brass.
Closure; Rolled
    turn-over.
Wad; White card,
    print black.

KENT CARTRIDGE MANUFACTURING COMPANY LTD:
Branbridges Industrial Estate, East Peckham,
Tonbridge, Kent.

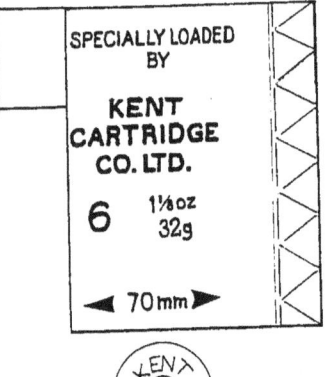

SPECIALLY LOADED BY
KENT CARTRIDGE CO. LTD.
6   1⅛oz
    32g
◄ 70mm ►

DATA
Gauge; 12.
Length; 70 mm.
Head; 16 mm.
Tube; Fine ribbed
    plastic.
Colour; Flame red 2.
Print; Black.
Base; Steel,
    brass coated.
Closure; Crimp,
    6 fold.
Circa; 1994.

KINGSTONE LISLE SHOOT:
Vale of the White Horse, Nr Wantage,
Oxfordshire, England.

KINGSTONE LISLE SHOOT
⑥
67.5mm

KINGSTONE LISLE SHOOT
67.5mm

DATA
Gauge; 12.
Length; 67.5 mm.
Head; 8 mm.
Tube; Fine ribbed
    orange plastic.
Colour; Dull orange.
Print; Black.
Base; Steel with
    a brass wash.
Closure; Six
    fold crimp.
Business; Private
    shoot.
Case, Eley Hawk,
    Ltd.
Circa, 2000.

KIRKEE FACTORY:
Government of India's Factory, Kirkee, Poona, India.

 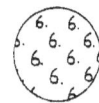

K.F.
"SPECIAL"
LONG RANGE
CARTRIDGE

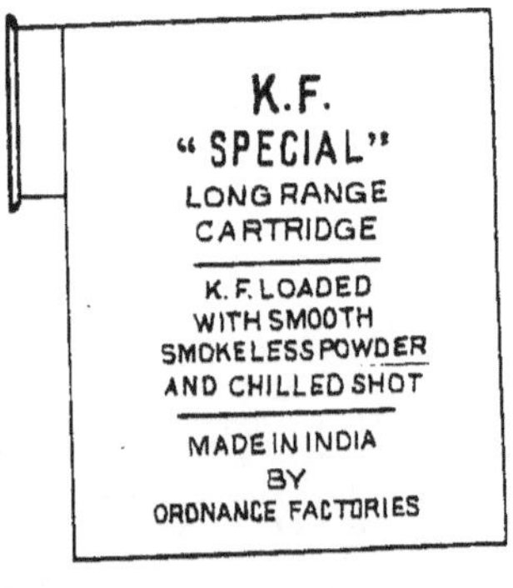

K.F.
"SPECIAL"
LONG RANGE
CARTRIDGE
K.F. LOADED
WITH SMOOTH
SMOKELESS POWDER
AND CHILLED SHOT
MADE IN INDIA
BY
ORDNANCE FACTORIES

DATA
Gauge; 12.
Length; 64 mm.
Head; 8 mm.
Tube; Wound red
    paper.
Colour; Crimson.
Print; Black.
Base; Brass or
    steel with a
    brass coating.
Closure; Rolled
    turn-over.
Wad; White card,
    print black.
Business;
    Ordnance
    factory.

KOLN-ROTTWEILER AG:
Troisdorf, Western Germany.

HEADSTAMPING; VEREINIGTE KOLN-ROTTWEILER PULVEREABRIKEN

Rottweiler
Jagdpatrone
Kriegsjahr 1915
Rauchloses
Jagdpulver

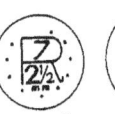 

GERMAN	ENGLISH TRANSLATION
Rottweiler	Rottweiler
Jagdpatrone	Hunting cartridge
Kriegsjahr 1915	War year 1915
Rauchloses	Smokeless
Jagdpulver	Hunting powder

Circa; 1915-1918.

DATA
Gauge; 12.
Length; 64 mm.
Head; 7 mm.
Tube; Wound brown
    paper.
Colour; Dirty grey.
Print; Black.
Base; Iron or steel.
Closure; Squared
    turn-over.
Wad; White card,
    print black.
Cap; Large brass.
Business; Powder
    and ammunition
    manufacturers.

PLATE 50

KRUCKL (KEN RUTTERFORD'S UNITED KINGDOM
COLLECTORS LIST):
White Gates, Wickham, Newbury, Berkshire, England.

LIBERTY CARTRIDGE COMPANY:
Mount Carmel, Connecticut, U.S.A.

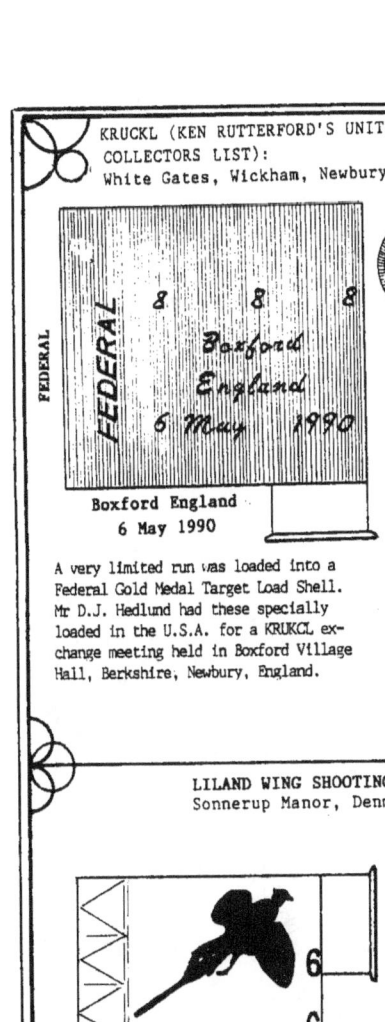

Boxford England
6 May 1990

A very limited run was loaded into a Federal Gold Medal Target Load Shell. Mr D.J. Hedlund had these specially loaded in the U.S.A. for a KRUKCL exchange meeting held in Boxford Village Hall, Berkshire, Newbury, England.

DATA
Gauge; 12.
Length; 68 mm.
Head; 12 mm.
Tube; Burgundy ribbed plastic.
Print; Golden yellow.
Base; Reinforced brass.
Closure; Eight fold pie crimp.
Business; Private cartridge collectors club.
Case; Federal Cartridge Corp, Minnesota, U.S.A.

LIBERTY BULK

DATA
Gauge; 12.
Length; 70.
Head; 28 mm.
Tube; Wound brown paper.
Colour; Venous blood red.
Print; Nil.
Base; Reinforced brass.
Closure; Rolled turn-over.
Wad; White card, print black.
Business; Ammunition manufacturers.

LILAND WING SHOOTING:
Sonnerup Manor, Denmark.

LORD MONTAGU:
Beaulieu Manor Estate, Beaulieu,
South Hampshire, England.

LILAND WINGSHOOTING
SONNERUP MANOR
DENMARK
BRITISH LOADED

DATA
Gauge; 12.
Length; 64 mm.
Head; 12 mm.
Tube; Wound white paper.
Colour; Crimson red.
Print; Black.
Base; Steel with a brass coating.
Closure; Six fold crimp.
Wetproof; Clear lacquered.
Case; Fiocchi, Italy.
Loading; Hull Cartridge.

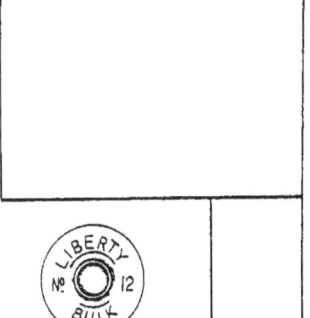

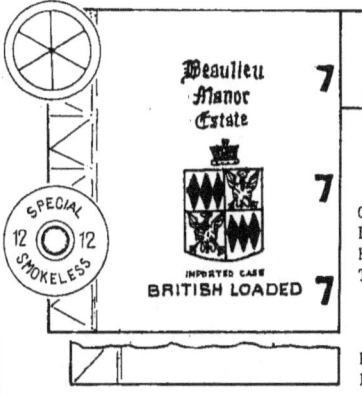

Beaulieu Manor Estate   IMPORTED CASE
BRITISH LOADED

DATA
Gauge; 12.
Lengths; 65 mm, 70 mm.
Heads; 8 mm.
Tubes; Wound white or brown paper. Later, red plastic.
Printings; Black.
Bases; Steel with brass washes.
Closures; Six fold crimps.
Business; Private cartridge.
Case; Fiocchi, Italy. Italy.

LUCKING: (THE NAME OF THE ORIGINAL IS NOT KNOWN).
Manufactured as a novelty, some others then ordered quantity batches of this cartridge.
Origin; England.

LYALVALE LIMITED:
1650 Pershore Road, Birmingham, B30 3BL . England.

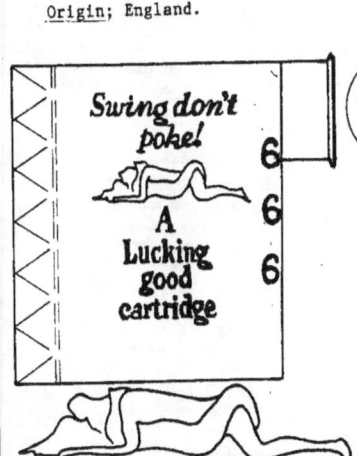

SWING DON'T POKE!

DATA
Gauge; 12.
Length; 70 mm.
Head; 12 mm.
Tube; Wound white paper.
Colour Crimson red.
Print; Black.
Base; Steel, brass coated.
Closure; Crimp, 6 fold.
Case; Fiocchi.
Loader; Hull Cartridge Co, Ltd.
Wetproof; Lacquered.
Circa; 1985-1990.

DATA
Gauge; 12.
Length; 68.5 mm
Head; 26 mm.
Tube; Fine ribbed plastic.
Colour; Maroon 3.
Print; Gold.
Base; Steel, brass coated.
Closure; Crimp, 6 fold.
Circa; 1994.

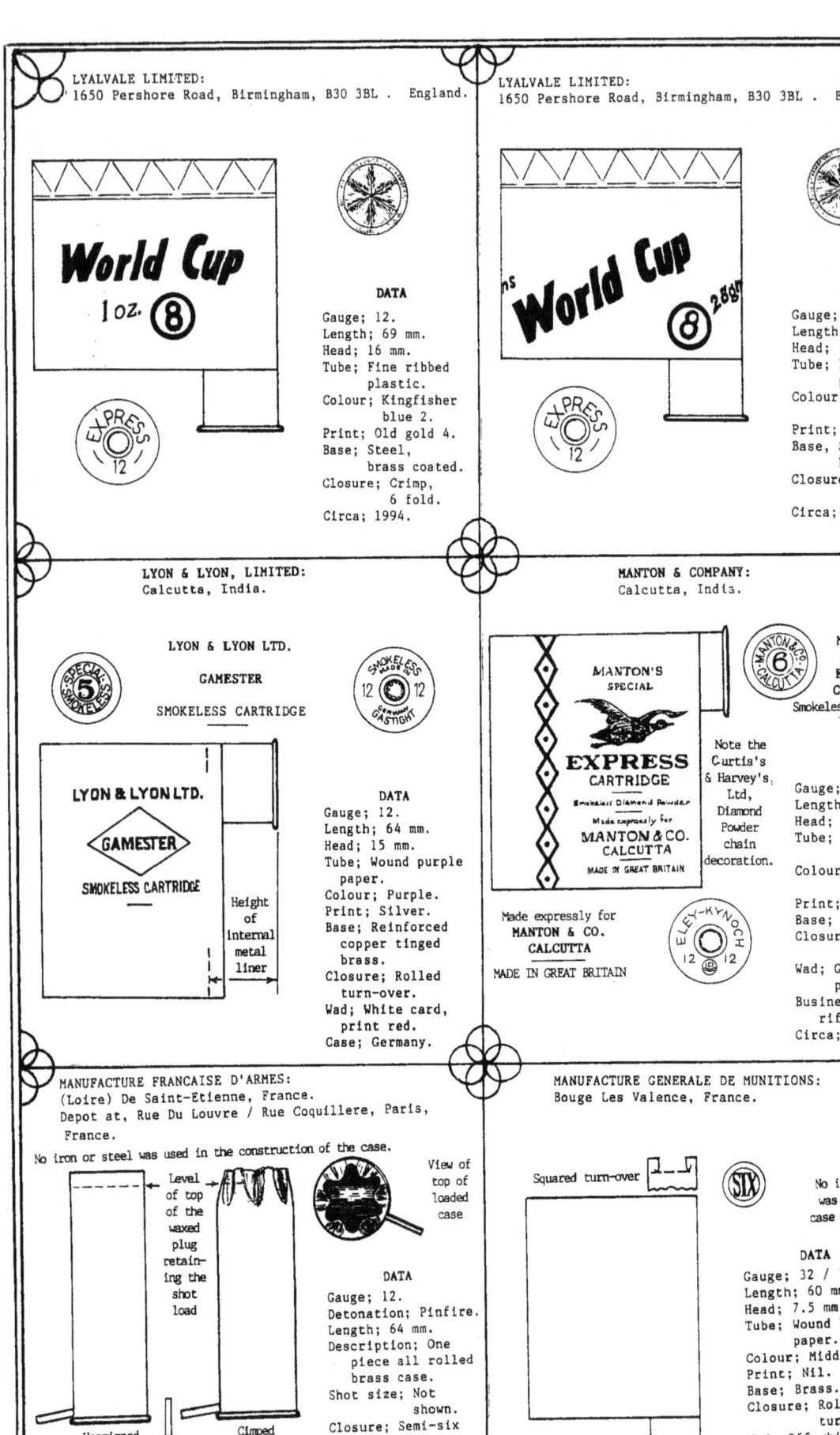

PLATE 52

MANUFACTURE GENERALE DE MUNITIONS:
Bouge Les Valence, France.

MGM   T

DATA
Gauge; 12.
Length; 64 mm.
Head; 11 mm.
Tube; Wound brown paper.
Colour; Middle blue.
Print; Black.
Base; Reinforced aluminium.
Closure; Rolled turn-over.
Wad; Brown cork, print dark red.
Business; Ammunition manufacturers.

MARLBOROUGH GUN SHOP:
5 London Road, Marlborough, Wiltshire, England.

MARLBOROUGH CARTRIDGE
MARLBOROUGH GUN-SHOP
5 LONDON ROAD
MARLBOROUGH
Telephone: 2072

DATA
Gauge; 12.
Length; 70 mm.
Head; 8 mm.
Tube; Wound brown paper.
Colour; Deep red.
Print; Black.
Base; Steel with a brass wash.
Cap; Nickel.
Closure; Six flod crimp.
Business; Gunshop.
Loading; Hull Cartridge Co, Ltd. Hull.
Case; Fiocchi. Italy.

This firm is now long extinct.

MARLBOROUGH GUN SHOP:
5 London Road, Marlborough, Wiltshire, England.

THE MARLBOROUGH
Marlborough Gun Shop
5 London Road
Marlborough, Wilts.
6   1⅛ OZ

THE MARLBOROUGH

DATA
Gauge; 12.
Length; 69 mm.
Head; 7 mm.
Tube; Fine ribbed plastic.
Colour; Olive green 4.
Print; White.
Base; Steel, brass coated.
Closure; Crimp, 6 fold.
Business; Gun shop.

MARLBOROUGH GUN SHOP:
5 London Road, Marlborough, Wiltshire, England.

MOONRAKER
OLYMPIC TRAP LOAD
Marlborough Gun Shop
5 London Road
Marlborough, Wiltshire
7½
made in England

DATA
Gauge; 12.
Length; 69 mm.
Head; 7.5 mm.
Tube; Fine ribbed plastic.
Colour; Orange 3.5 .
Print; Black.
Base; Steel, nickel coated.
Closure; Crimp, 6 fold.
Business; Gun shop.

MARSHALL SONS & COMPANY:
Britannia Ironworks, Gainsborough, Lincolnshire, England.

Both head-stampings were used.

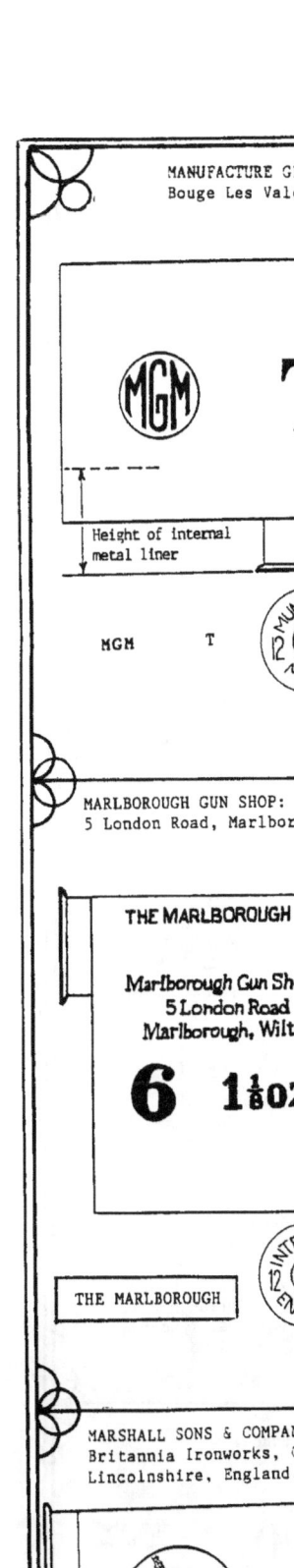

ALLOY END CAP

MARSHALL
OF GAINSBOROUGH
FOR USE ONLY ON MARSHALL DIESEL ENGINES
EQUIPPED FOR POWER STARTING. IT IS DANGER-
OUS TO USE ANY BUT CARTRIDGES SUPPLIED BY
APPROVED DISTRIBUTORS AND BEARING THE
MARSHALL NAME AND REGISTERED TRADE MARK.

DATA
Gauge; 12.
Length; 70 mm.
Head; 3 mm.
Tube; Wound green paper.
Colour; Blue grass (Blueish-green).
Print; Black.
Base; Brass or steel brass coated.
Closure; Six fold crimp.
Business; Steam and diesel manufacturing engineers.
Case; Witton made

MARSHALL SONS & CO:
Gainsborough, Lincolnshire, England.
Cartridge; I.C.I.A.N.Z.: Deer Park, Melbourne, Victoria, Australia.

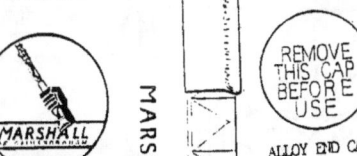

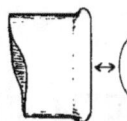 

Australian made by I.C.I.A.N.Z. for Australian owned Marshall tractors.

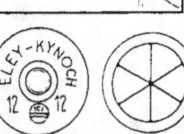
MARSHALL POWER START CARTRIDGE

DATA
Gauge; 12.
Case length; 70 mm.
Alloy cap length; 15 mm - 18 mm.
Head; 7 mm.
Tube; Wound paper.
Colour; Greyish-green.
Print; Black.
Base; Brass.
Filling; Carbon pellets.
Closure; Crimp, 6 fold.

PLATE 53

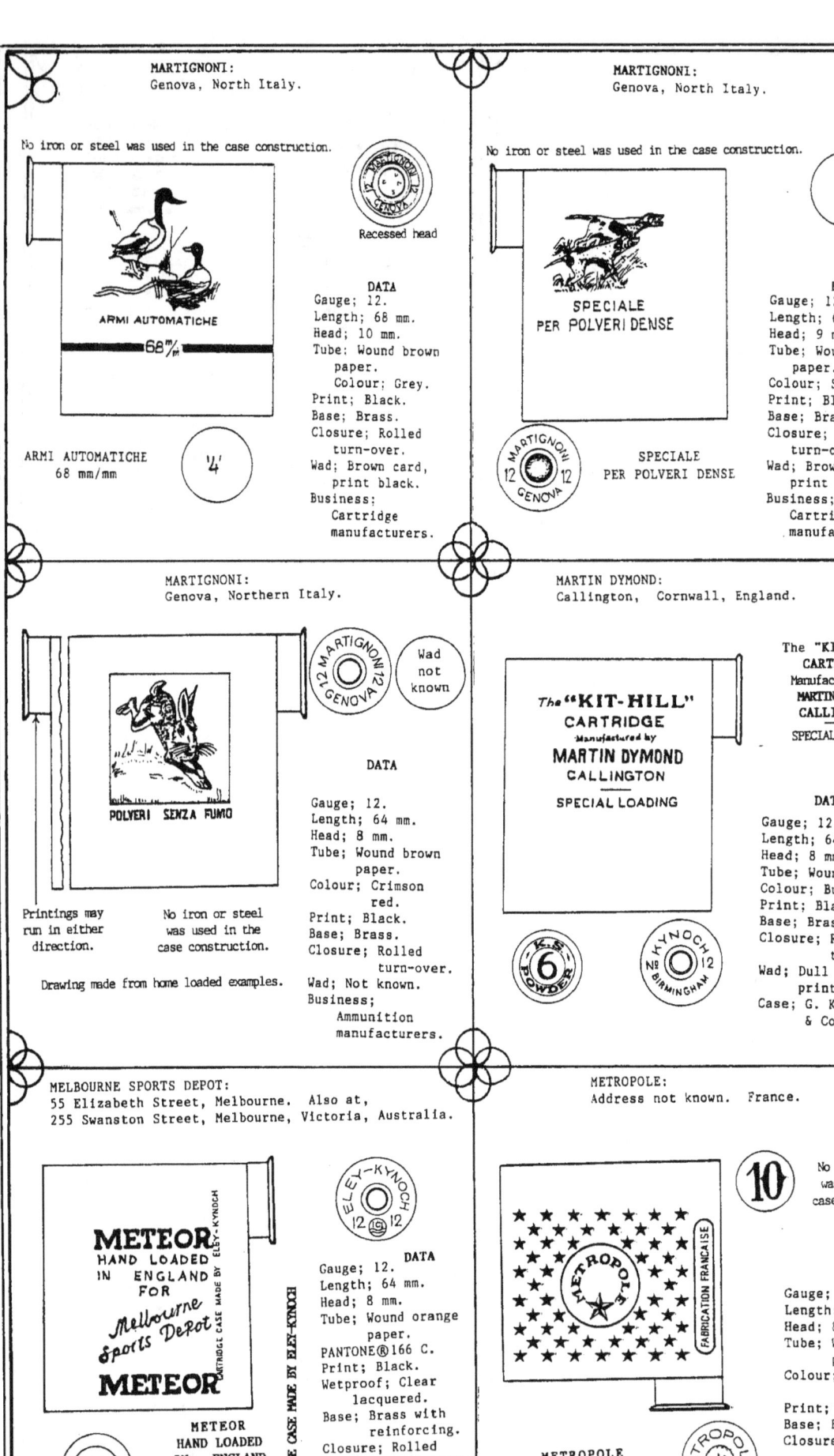

M. GAUPILLAT:
Paris, France.

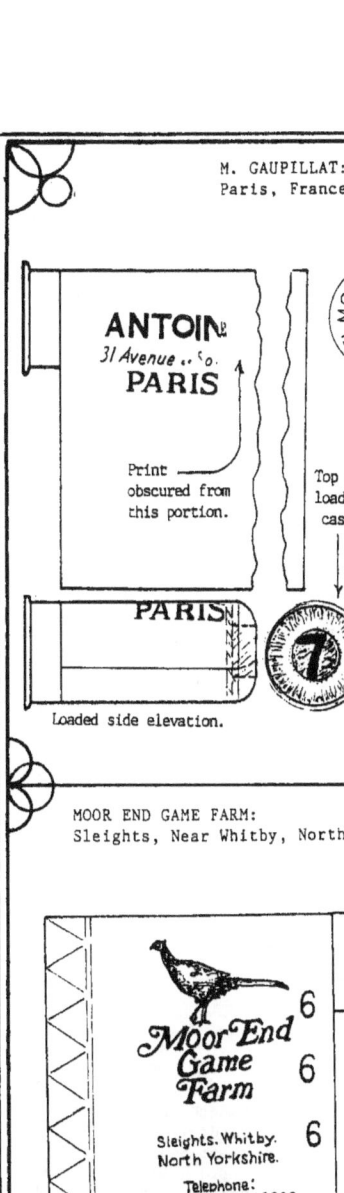
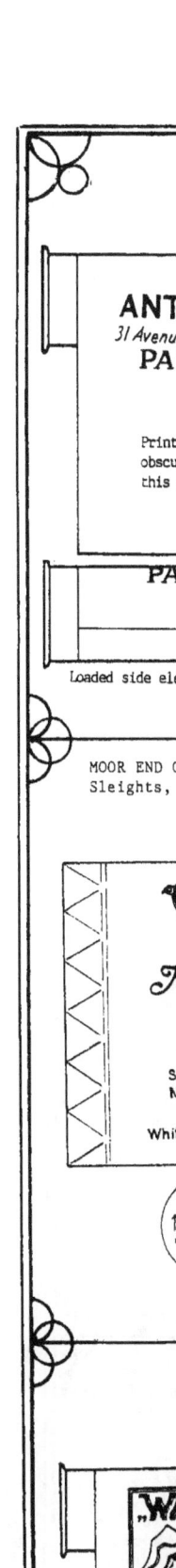

Print obscured from this portion.

Top of loaded case

Loaded side elevation.

No iron or steel was used in the case construction.

DATA
Gauge; 12.
Case length; Not known.
Loaded length; 50 mm.
Head; 8 mm.
Tube; Wound paper.
Colour; Burnt orange.
Print; Black.
Base; Brass.
Closure; Thick roll.
Wad; Brown cork, print black.

MICK SIMMONS, LIMITED:
720 George Street, Sydney, New South Wales, Australia.

THE LIGHTNING
SUPER-CHARGE SMOKELESS
HIGH VELOCITY
EXTRA HEAVY LOAD

DATA
Gauge; 12.
Length; 64 mm.
Head; 8 mm.
Tube; Wound red paper.
Colour; Signal red.
Print; Black.
Base; Reinforced brass.
Closure; Rolled turn-over.
Wad; Orange card, print black.
Business; Sports stores.

MOOR END GAME FARM:
Sleights, Near Whitby, North Yorkshire. England.

DATA
Gauge; 12.
Length; 70 mm.
Head; 8 mm.
Tube; Fine ribbed plastic.
Colour; Red 3.
Print; Black.
Base; Steel, copper coated.
Closure; Crimp, 6 fold.
Business; Game farming.

MULTI-SPORTS:
225 Old Christchurch Road, Bournemouth, Hampshire (Dorset), England.

MULTI-SPORTS
225 OLD CHRISTCHURCH ROAD
BOURNEMOUTH
TEL: 26319

"THE MULTI-SHOT"
BRITISH LOADED
IMPORTED CASE

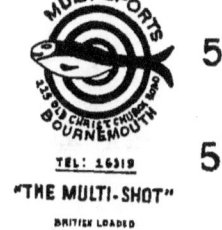

The wordings BRITISH LOADED IMPORTED CASE was not always printed on. Later, these cartridges had red ribbed plastic tubes.

DATA
Gauge; 12.
Length; 69 mm.
Head; 8 mm.
Tube; Wound light brown paper.
Colour; Poppy red.
Print; Black.
Base; Steel with a brass wash.
Closure; Six fold crimp.
Loading; Hull Cartridge Co, Ltd.
Business; Sports store.
Case; Fiocchi, Italy.

MUNITIONSWERKE:
Schoenebeck A/E, Germany.

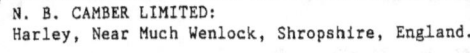

"WALDHEIL"

DATA
Gauge; 16.
Length; 65 mm.
Head; 7.5 mm.
Tube; Wound brown paper.
Colour; Dark brown.
Print; Black.
Base; Reinforced brass.
Closure; Rolled turn-over.
Wad; Shocking-pink card, print black.
Origin; Germany.

N. B. CAMBER LIMITED:
Harley, Near Much Wenlock, Shropshire, England.

THE HARLEY HORNET

N.B. CAMBER LTD.
AGRICULTURAL MERCHANTS
HARLEY, SHREWSBURY, SHROPSHIRE.
(0952 510481)

The small print,
AGRICULTURAL MERCHANTS
HARLEY, SHREWSBURY, SHROPSHIRE.

THE
HARLEY HORNET

DATA
Gauge; 12.
Length; 68 mm.
Head; 7.5 mm.
Tube; Fine ribbed plastic.
Colour; Maroon 3.5.
Print; Black.
Base; Steel, brass coated.
Closure; Crimp, 6 fold.
Business; Agricultural merchants.
Circa; 1993.

PLATE 55

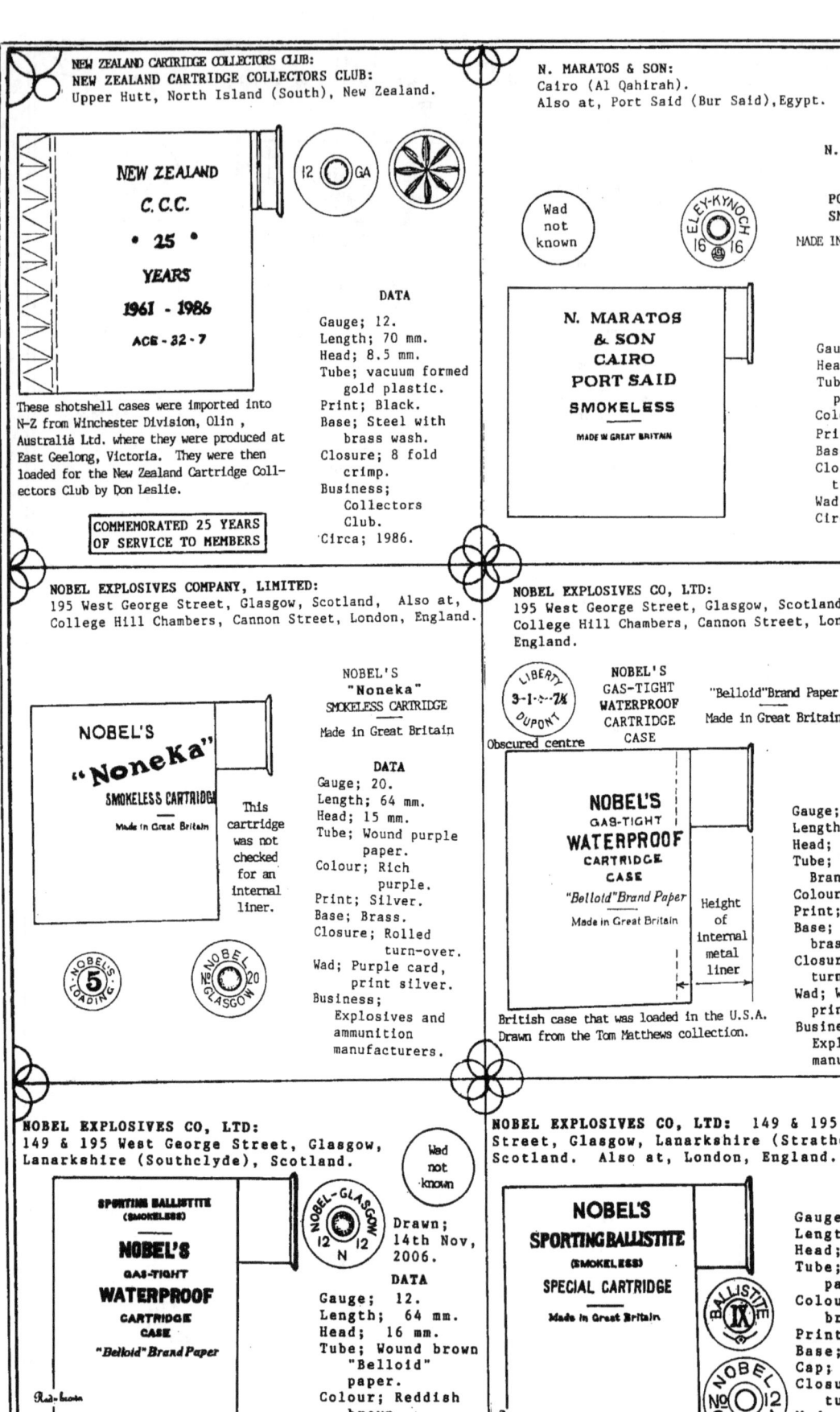

NOBEL INDUSTRIES, LTD:
Witton, Birmingham, Warwickshire (West Midlands), England.

 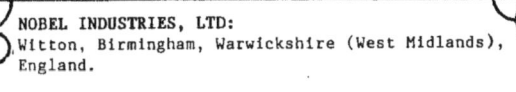 

DATA
Gauge; 20.
Length; 64 mm.
Head; 7 mm.
Tube; Wound cream paper.
Colour; Cream.
Print; Black.
Base; Brass.
Closure; Rolled turn-over.
Wad; Brown card, print black.
Powder; Smokeless Diamond.
Business; Ammo manufacturers.
Circa; 1924.

NOBEL INDUSTRIES, LTD / ELEY BROTHERS, LTD:
Waltham Abbey, Essex, England.

DATA
Gauge; 12.
Head; 16 mm.

Gauge; 12.
Length; 64 mm.
Head; 16 mm.
Tube; Wound cream paper.
Colour; Cream.
Print; Black.
Base; Brass.
Cap; Copper.
Closure; Rolled turn-over.
Wad; Brown card, print black.
Business; Manufacturers.
Circa; 1924.
(drawn from photographs, 28 Nov 06)

NOBEL'S Sporting Ballistite CARTRIDGE WATER RESISTING METAL LINED. A cartridge from the early 1920's, it would have been produced from an Eley Bros Ltd,s London factory. The wad is of Eley Bros.Due to the time of production, I have placed it under Nobel Industries.

NOBEL INDUSTRIES (AUSTRALIA), LTD:
Nobel Factory, West Footscray, Melbourne, Victoria, Australia.

ELEY DUXBAC WATERPROOF LOADED WITH SMOKELESS DIAMOND

DATA
Gauge; 12.
Length; 64 mm.
Head; 8 mm.
Tube; Wound crimson paper.
Colour; Crimson red.
Print; Black.
Base; Reinforced brass.
Closure; Rolled turn-over.
Wad; White card, print dark pink.
Business; Sale of ammunition, etc.
Circa; Early 1920's.

Most likely loaded in Great Britain. Drawn from the Tom Matthews collection.

OAKES & COMPANY, LIMITED:
Madras, India.

DATA
Gauge; 12.
Head; 8 mm.
Tube; Wound paper.
Colour; Mauve.
Print; Black.
Base; Brass.
Closure; Rolled turn-over.
Wad; White card, print red.
Case; Eley Bros, Ltd, London, England.

OAKES' PREMIER Smokeless Cartridge ELEY SPECIAL NITRO CASE

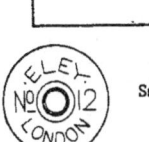

OAKES BROS LTD:
The Station, Hungerford, Berkshire. Also at, Newbury, Berkshire & Wantage, Oxfordshire. England.

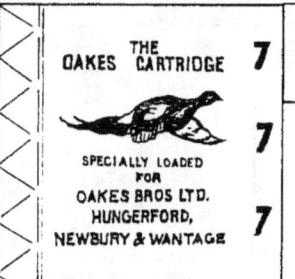

DATA
Gauge; 12.
Length; 69 mm.
Head; 8 mm.
Tube; Fine ribbed plastic.
Colour; Red 3.
Print; Black.
Base; Steel, brass coated.
Closure; Crimp, 6 fold.
Business; Agricultural engineers.

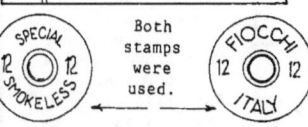

Both stamps were used.

ORBEA:
Vitoria, Spain.

Wad not known

DATA
Gauge; 12.
Length; 64 mm.
Head; 9 mm.
Tube; Wound dark blueish-green paper.
Colour; Dark blueish green.
Print; Black.
Base; Steel with a brass coating.
Closure; Rolled turn-over.
Wad; Not known.
Business; Ammunition manufacturers.

TRUST

This drawing was made from a used case.

ORMSBY GAME SERVICES:
North Ormsby, Louth, Lincolnshire, England.

SPECIALLY LOADED FOR ORMSBY GAME SERVICES NORTH ORMSBY LINCOLNSHIRE 6

DATA
Gauge; 12.
Length; 66 mm.
Head; 9 mm.
Tube; Dark red tough vacuum formed plastic.
Print; Black.
Base; Brass.
Closure; Six fold crimp.
Business; Game farmers.
Case; Winchester Australia.
Circa; 1960's.

P. A. BONETT:
Alexandria, Egypt.

THE MALLARD SMOKELESS CARTRIDGE
P. A. BONETT
ALEXANDRIA
Made in Great Britain

DATA
Gauge; 12.
Length; 64 mm.
Head; 16 mm.
Tube; Wound green paper.
Colour; Dark green.
Print; Black or dark blue.
Base; Brass.
Wetproof; Clear lacquered.
Closure; Rolled turn-over.
Wad; Yellow card, print black.
Circa; 1930's.

PACHMAYR GUN WORKS:
1220 S. Grand Avenue, Los Angles, California 90015, U.S.A.

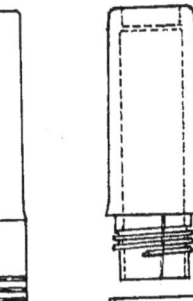

SALT   PEPPER
laurel-green crimson-red

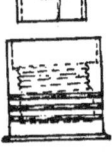

TWO PIECE CRUET SET

DATA
Two part set. Each item has a turned brass base with female threads and an upper plastic container with male threads.
Salt container; Laurel green plastic.
Pepper container; Crimson red plastic.
Height; 63.5 mm.
Head; 21 mm.
Circa; Prior 1986.

P. D. MALLOCH:
34 Scott Street. Also at, 259 Old High Street, Perth, Perthshire (Tayside), Scotland.

 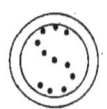

THE RED GROUSE CARTRIDGE
MALLOCH'S OF PERTH
34 SCOTT STREET TEL: 21631

DATA
Gauge; 12.
Length; 69 mm.
Head; 8 mm.
Tube; Wound brown paper.
Colour; Signal red.
Print black.
Base; Steel, brass coated.
Closure; Six fold crimp.
Business; Gunshop.
Case; Fiocchi.
Loading; Hull Cartridge Co, Ltd

PEARSON & COMPANY:
Grimsby, Lincolnshire (Humberside), England.

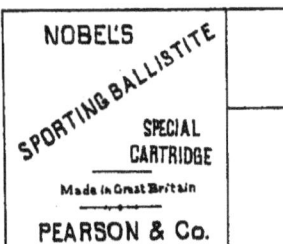 

NOBEL'S SPORTING BALLISTITE SPECIAL CARTRIDGE
Made in Great Britain
PEARSON & Co. GRIMSBY

This drawing was made from a set of photographs.
NOBEL'S SPORTING BALLISTITE SPECIAL CARTRIDGE

DATA
Gauge; 12.
Length; 64 mm.
Head; 16 mm.
Tube; Wound paper.
Colour; Old straw. PANTONE® 134 C.
Print; Black.
Base; Brass.
Closure; Rolled turn-over.
Wad; Red, print black. PANTONE® 186 C.

PETER KNIGHT:
22 Carrington Street, Nottingham, Nottinghamshire, England.

No iron or steel was used in the case construction.

KNIGHTS INVINCIBLE

KNIGHTS' INVINCIBE

DATA
Gauge; 12.
Length; 64 mm.
Head; 8 mm.
Tube; Wound paper.
Colour; Dull red.
Print; Black.
Closure; Rolled turn-over.
Wad; Brown card, print black.
Business; Gunmaker.
Case; Nobel Industries, Ltd.
Circa; 1921.

P. JARRY:
Angouleme, Charente, Mid-west France.

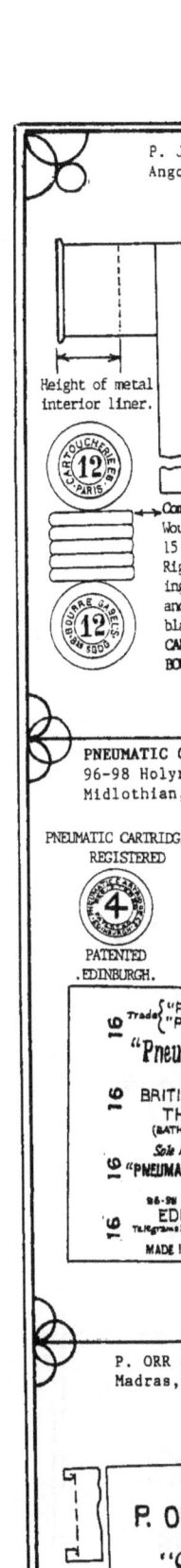

P. JARRY
Armurier
ANGOULEME

Height of metal interior liner.

Compression Wad;
Wound paper sleeve, Length 15 mm, Colour maroon, Waxed, Riged, Cork chippings filling, Rolled turn-over top and bottom, Wads yellow with black print.
CARTOUCHERIE Est. PARRIS.
BOURRE GABEL'S. Bte SGDG.

DATA
Gauge; 12.
Length; 64 mm.
Head; 22 mm.
Tube; Wound brown paper.
Colour; Tan brown.
Print; Black.
Base; Reinforced brass.
Closure; Rolled turn-over.
Wad; Pea green, red print, compressable.
Business; Armourer.

PNEUMATIC CARTRIDGE CO, LTD.
96-98 Holyrood Road, Edinburgh, 8,
Scotland.

"Pneuma"
(Registered Trade Mark)
CARTRIDGE
Specially loaded by
"PNEUMATIC" CARTRIDGE
CO. LTD.
96-98 HOLYROOD ROAD
EDINBURGH. 8
Grams: "Pneuma, Edinburgh"
MADE IN GREAT BRITAIN

Height of reinforcing→
"Pneuma"
(Registered Trade Mark)
CARTRIDGE
Specially loaded by
"PNEUMATIC" CARTRIDGE
CO. LTD.
96-98 HOLYROOD ROAD
EDINBURGH, 8
Grams: "Pneuma, Edinburgh"
MADE IN GREAT BRITAIN

DATA
Gauge; 12.
Length; 64 mm.
Head; 8 mm.
Tube; wound grey paper.
Colour; Greenish grey.
Print; Black.
Base; Reinforced brass.
Cap; Copper.
Closure; Rolled turn-over.
Wad; Dark red, print black.
Business; Cartridge loading and merchants.

PNEUMATIC CARTRIDGE CO, LTD:
96-98 Holyrood Road, Edinburgh 8, Trade{"PNEUMA" "PNEUMATIC"} Marks
Midlothian, Scotland.

PNEUMATIC CARTRIDGE Co
REGISTERED
PATENTED
.EDINBURGH.

"Pneumatic Special"
Loaded with
BRITISH MATERIAL
THROUGHOUT
(BATHGATE'S PATENT)
Sole Manufacturers
"PNEUMATIC" CARTRIDGE Co.
LTD.
96-98 HOLYROOD ROAD
EDINBURGH, 8
TELEGRAMS:"Pneuma."Edinburgh
MADE IN GREAT BRITAIN

DATA
Gauge; 16.
Length; 64 mm.
Head; 7.5 mm.
Tube; Wound eau-de-nil paper.
Print; Black or navy blue.
Base; Reinforced brass.
Closure; Rolled.
Wad; Dark orange, print black.
Business; Cartridge sales.

POLISH STATE AMMUNITION:
Pronit Chemical Factory, Pionki, Poland.

EAGLE
TRAP
LOAD.

DATA
Gauge; 12.
Length; 70 mm.
Head; 9 mm.
Tube; Wound brown paper, outer semi-ribbed.
Colour; Dark red. PANTONE® 1797.
Print; Dark blue, PANTONE® 281 C.
Base; Steel, brass coated.
Closure; Crimp, 6 fold.
Business; Ammunition manufacturers.

P. ORR & SONS:
Madras, India. Also in, Rangoon, Burma.

P. ORR & SONS
"Challenge"
Smokeless Cartridge
MADRAS & RANGOON

The cartridge case was made by Messrs Eley Brothers Ltd, of London, England.

DATA
Gauge; 12.
Length; 64 mm.
Head; 7.5 mm.
Tube; Wound paper.
Colour; Dark red 4.
Print; Black.
Base; Brass.
Closure; Rolled squared turn-over.
Wad; Dark red 4, print black.
Wetproof; Waxed impregnated.

P. ORR & SONS, LTD:
Madras, India. Also, Rangoon, Burma.

ELEY
"GRAND PRIX"
CARTRIDGE
SPECIALLY LOADED WITH
SMOKELESS ◊ DIAMOND
FOR
P. ORR & SONS LTD,
MADRAS & RANGOON
Made in Great Britain

ELEY
"GRAND PRIX"
CARTRIDGE

SPECIALLY LOADED WITH
SMOKELESS DIAMOND
FOR
P.ORR & SONS LTD.
MADRAS & RANGOON
Made in Great Britain

DATA
Gauge; 12.
Length; 64 mm.
Head; 8 mm.
Tube; Wound Middle blue paper.
Colour; Middle blue.
Print; Navy blue.
Base; Reinforced brass.
Closure; Rolled turn-over.
Wad; Brown card, no printing.
Circa; 1930's.

POUDERIES REUINES DE BELGIQUE:
Belgium.

MARQUE
"CLERMONITE"
DEPSEE

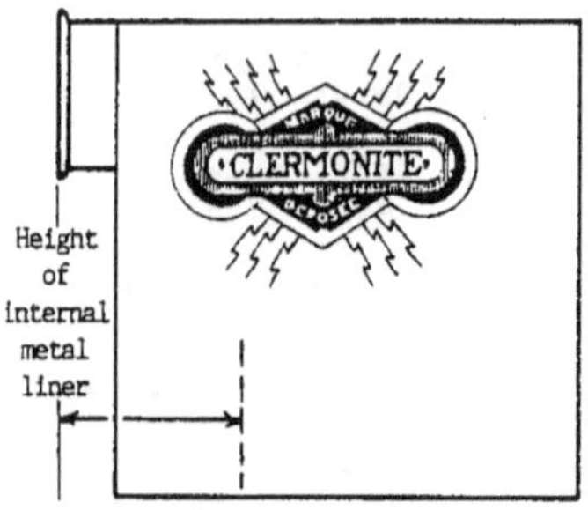

DATA
Gauge; 20.
Length; 64 mm.
Head; 7.5 mm.
Tube; Wound paper.
Colour; Light green.
Print; Black.
Base; Reinforced brass.
Closure; Rolled turn-over.
Wad; Yellow, print black.
Business; Ammunition manufacturers.

This firm was formed after World War One. Several explosives companies amalgamated and they included Muller & Cie.

POUDERIES REUINES DE BELGIQUE:
Belgium.

MARQUE
"CLERMONITE"
DEPSEE

Wad, *PRB*CHARGEMENTORIGINAL 8

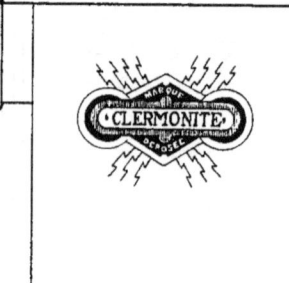

DATA
Gauge; 12.
Length; 65 mm.
Head; 8 mm.
Tube; Wound pale green paper.
Colour ; Apple green.
Print; Black.
Base; Reinforced brass.
Closure; Rolled turn-over.
Wad; White card, print black.
Case; British.
Business; Ammunition manufacturers.

This firm was formed after World War One. Several explosives companies amalgamated and they included Muller & Cie.

PULVERFABRIK (POWDER FACTORY). HASLOCHA/MAIN:
I have no information about what appears to be a German firm.

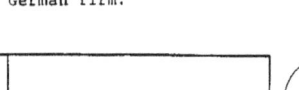

No iron or steel was used in the case construction.

DATA
Gauge; 16.
Length; 64 mm.
Head; 8 mm.
Tube; Wound brown paper.
Colour; Brownish-buff.
Print; Black.
Base; Brass.
Closure; Rolled turn-over.
Wad; White card, print red.
Cap; Copper.
Internal liner; Nil.

Olympia
Haslocher
rauchloses
Blattchenpulver
Olympia
Rostfrei

PULVERFABRIK (POWDER FACTORY). HASLOCHA/MAIN:
I have no information about what appears to be a German firm.

DATA
Gauge; 16.
Length; 64 mm.
Head; 7 mm.
Tube; Wound brown paper.
Colour; Dark crimson red.
Print; Black.
Base; Steel, brass coated.
Closure; Rolled turn-over.
Wad; Yellow, print black..
Cap; Large copper.

Extra beste
JAGDPATRONE
Schutzmarke „Pasan"
RAUCHLOS.
ABSOLUT ROSTFREI
Geschlossenes Schussbild
Ausserordenil Durchschlag
Versagerfrei

ENGLISH TRASLATION.
Extra best hunting cartridge.
Td Mk. "Pheasant.
SMOKELESS.
Absolute rust free.

P. W. BARKE:
103 Hednesford Road, Heath Hayes, Near Cannock, Staffordshire, England.

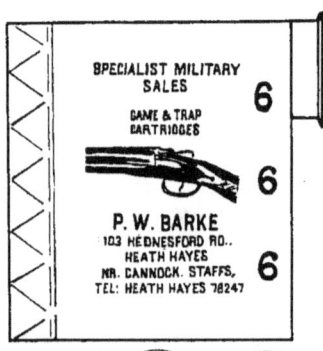

The loadings were in Italian Fiocchi cases by the Hull Cartridge Company Limited.

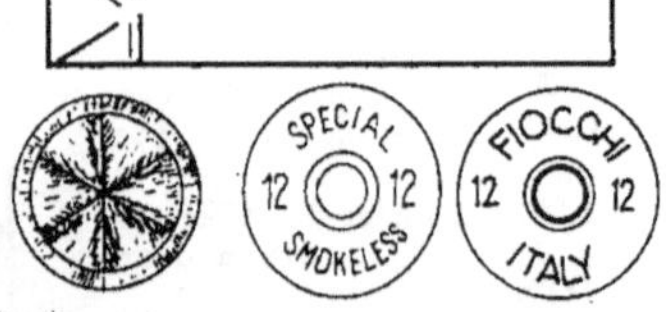

DATA
Gauge; 12.
Length; 69 mm.
Head; 7.5 mm.
Tube; Fine ribbed plastic.
Colour; Red 2.5 .
Print; Black.
Base; Steel, brass coated.
Closure; Crimp, 6 fold.

R.A.F. LAKENHEATH ROD & GUN CLUB:
R.A.F. Lakenheath Air Force Base, Suffolk.

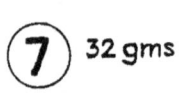 

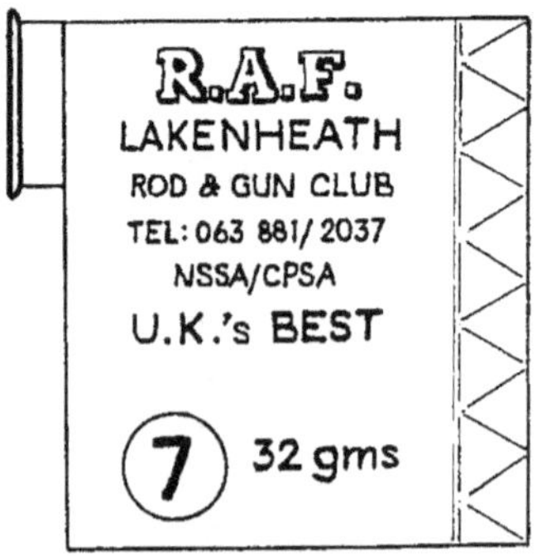

DATA
Gauge; 12.
Length; 67 mm.
Head; 7 mm.
Tube; Medium ribbed plastic.
Colour; Summer Green 3.
Print; Black.
Base; Steel, brass coated.
Closure; Crimp, 6 fold.
Business; Armed Service field sports.

PLATE 60

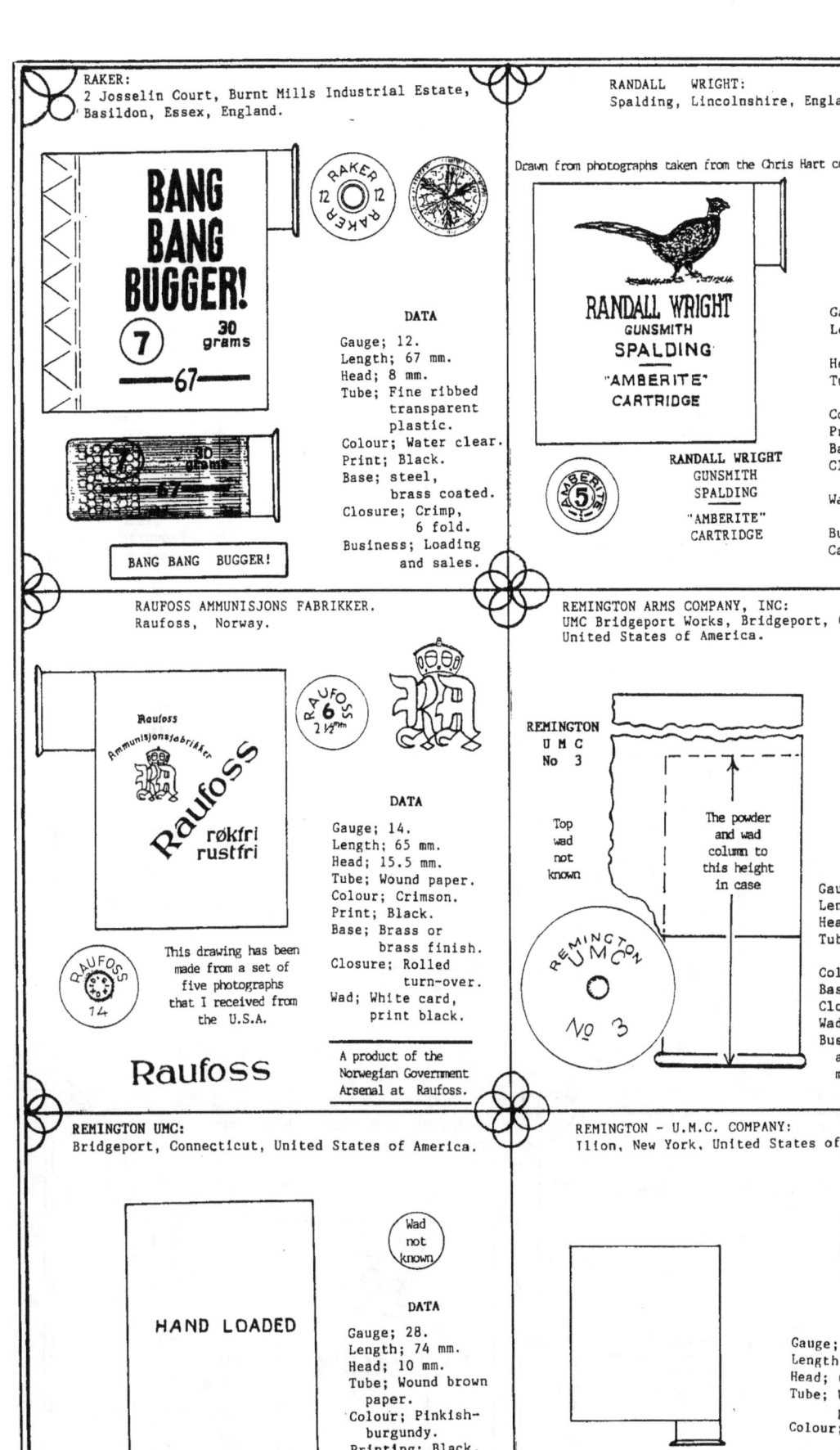

PLATE 61

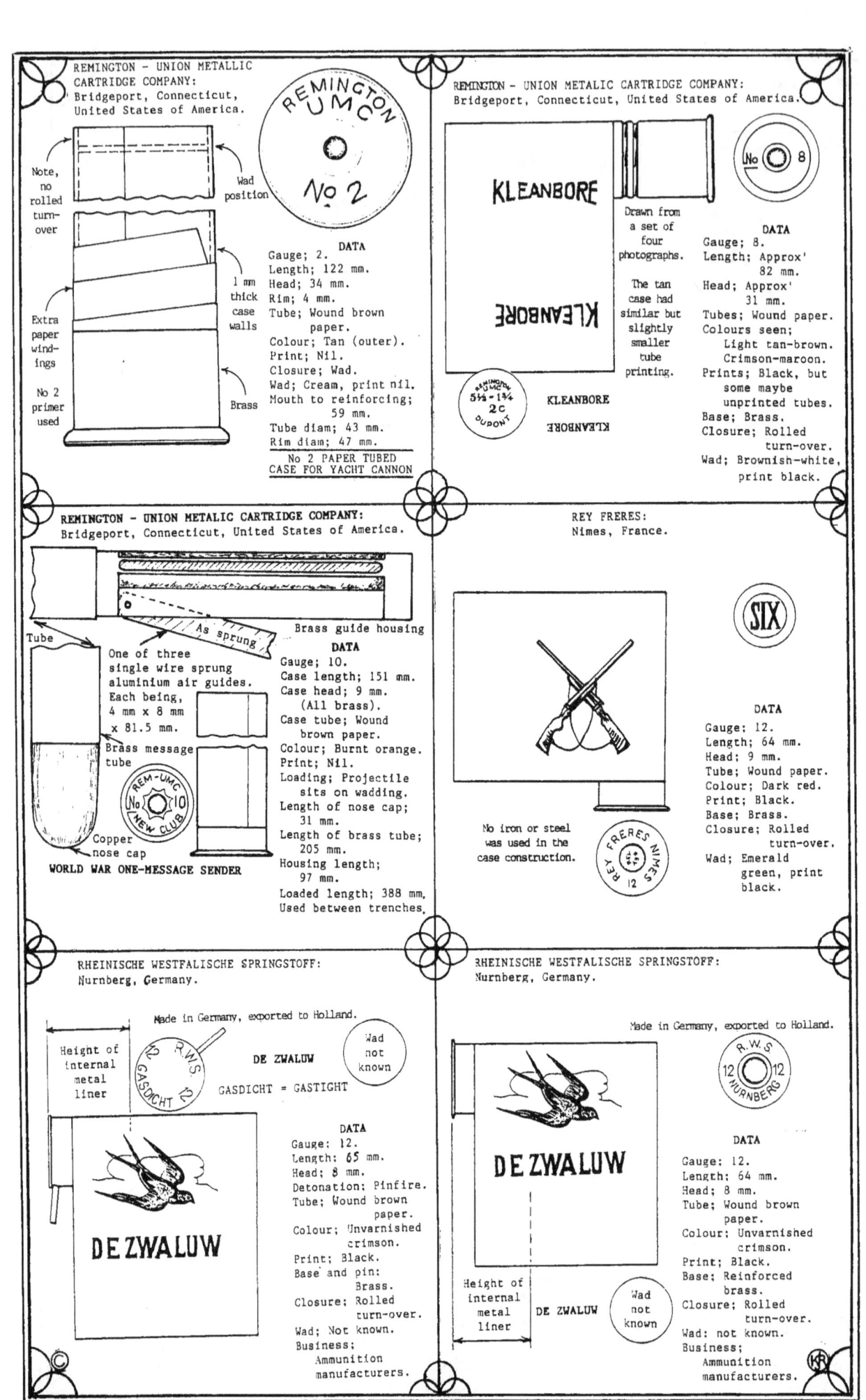

PLATE 62

RHEINISCHE-WESTFALISCHE SPRENGSTOFF, A.G:
Nurnberg, West Germany.

DATA
Gauge; 16.
Length; 65 mm.
Head; 6.5 mm.
Tube; Wound brown paper.
Colour; Salmon red.
Print; Black.
Base; Reinforced brass.
Closure; Rolled turn-over.
Wad; White card, print black.
Case; H. Utendoerffer.
Cap; R.W.S. (brass).
Business; Ammunition manufacturers.

GERMAN	ENGLISH TRANSLATION
MARKE EINHORN	Mark (Td Mk) Unicorn
RAUCHLOS	Smokeless
Rostfrei	Rust free

ROBERT JONES:
Monarch Gun Works, Manchester Street, Liverpool,
Lancashire (Merseyside), England.

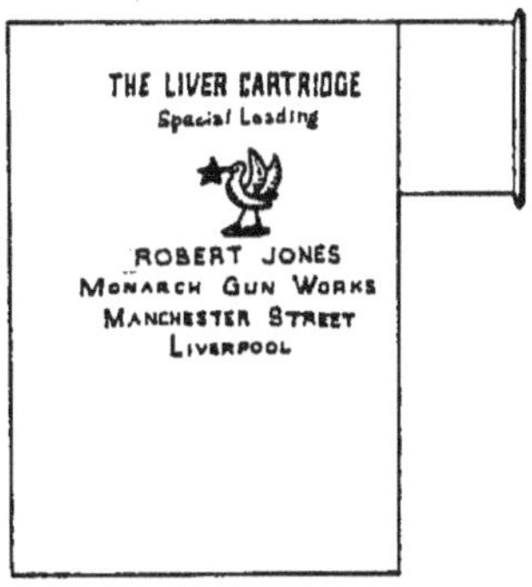

DATA
Gauge; 12.
Length; 64 mm.
Head; 16 mm.
Tube; Wound paper.
Colour; Nut brown.
Print; Black.
Base; Brass.
Closure; Rolled turn-over.
Wad; White card, print black.
Business; Gunmaker.

THE LIVER CARTRIDGE

ROBIN HOOD AMMUNITION COMPANY:
Swanton, Vermont, North-East, United States of America.

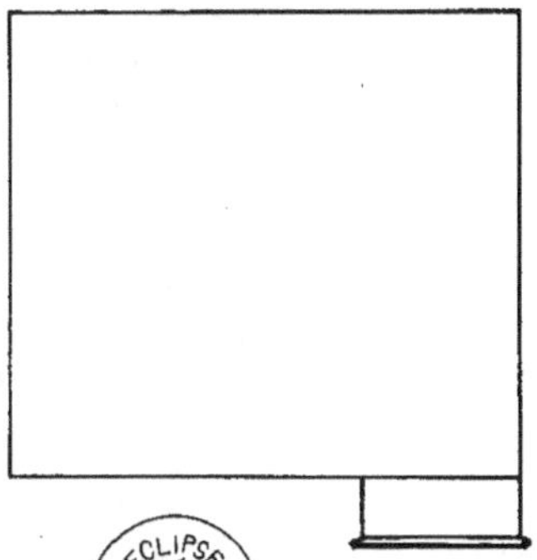

DATA
Gauge; 12.
Length; 66 mm.
Head; 9 mm.
Tube; Wound pink paper.
Colour; Pink.
Print; Nil.
Base; Brass.
Closure; Rolled turn-over.
Wad; White card, print black.
Business; Gunpowder and ammunition manufacturers.

RONNIE CROWE:
63 Maldon Road, Great Baddow, Essex, England.

DATA
Gauge; 12.
Length; 69 mm.
Head; 8 mm.
Tube; Wound brown paper.
Colour; Soot black.
Print; Silver.
Base; Steel with brass coating.
Closure; Six fold crimp.
Business; Gun and field sports shop.
Case; Northern Italy.

| THE CHELMER Specially loaded for RONNIE CROWE | 63, MALDON ROAD GREAT BADDOW ESSEX Tel; Chelmsford 71246 Imported Case |

R. CROWE LTD:
63 Maldon Road, Great Baddow, Near Chelmsford,
Essex, England.

Ronnie Crowe has been well known for his Sporting Bygone Stall at country fairs.

DATA
Gauge; 12.
Length; 70 mm.
Head; 7.5 mm.
Tube; Wound white paper.
Colour; red.
Print; Black.
Base; Steel, brass coated.
Closure; Crimp, 6 fold.
Wetproof; Lacquered.
Case; Fiocchi.
Loading; Hull Cartridge.
Business; Gun and sports store.

SANDRINGHAM RABBIT CLEARANCE SOCIETY, LTD:
Sandringham, North Norfolk, England.

| SANDRINGHAM RABBIT CLEARANCE SOCIETY LTD. NORFOLK | 1¼ oz. Loaded by G.L. WOODS & SONS Ovington, Norfolk |

DATA
Gauge; 12.
Length; 70 mm.
Head; 8 mm.
Tube; Wound orange paper.
Colour; Orange.
Print; Black.
Base; Steel, brass coated.
Closure; Six fold crimp.
Business; Rabbit clearance.
Circa; Late 1960's.

PLATE 63

SAYER'S:
Address and country not known.

SAYER'S
"Bulzi"
HARD HITTING
SMOKELESS
CARTRIDGE.

Loaded in Great Britain

DATA
Gauge; 12.
Length; 65 mm.
Head; 7 mm.
Tube; Wound brown paper.
Colour; Orange.
Print; Black.
Base; Reinforced brass.
Cap, large brass copper coated.
Closure; Rolled turn-over.
Wad shown; Red card, print black (May not be the original).

SCHULTZE COMPANY LIMITED. Also known as **SCHULTZE GUNPOWDER COMPANY LIMITED:**
3 Bucklersbury, London. Also at, 28 Gresham Street, London E.C., England.

The
"CAPTAIN"
The SCHULTZE Co. Ltd.
LONDON

Made in Great Britain

DATA
Gauge; 20.
Length; 64 mm.
Head; 7 mm.
Tube; Wound green paper.
Colour; Pale hay-green.
Print; Black.
Base; Brass.
Closure; Rolled turn-over.
Wad; Rich red, print black.
Business; Gunpowder and cartridge manufacturers.

This brand honoured Captain Schultze.

S. COHEN, SONS & COMPANY:
315 Sturt Street, Ballarat, Victoria. Also at, 380 Lonsdale Street (West), Melbourne, Victoria, Australia.

Advertised as long distant killing.

THE AK-U-RATE
SMOKELESS CARTRIDGE
— or —
SURE & DEADLY

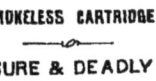

THE AK-U-RATE
SMOKELESS CARTRIDGE
SURE & DEADLY

DATA
Gauge; 12.
Length; 64 mm.
Head; 8.5 mm.
Tube; Wound cream paper.
Print; Red.
Base; Brass.
Closure; Rolled turn-over.
Wad colour; Not recorded.
Business; Hardware merchants.
Case; Kynoch, Ltd. Witton, Birmingham, England.

SELLIER & BELLOT:
Formerly, ZUNDHUTCHEN und PATRONENFABRIK:
Schoenbeck, Magdeburg, Eastern Germany.

Beste gasdichte
Patronenhulse
mitunfehlbarer Zundung.

Aus bestem Material
hergestellt und vorzuglich
gearbeitet.

DATA
Gauge; 12.
Length; 65 mm.
Head; 8 mm.
Tube; Wound orange paper.
Colour; Orange;
Print; Black.
Base; Reinforced brass.
Closure; Rolled turn-over.
Wad; White card, print black.
Cap; Large copper.
Business; Ammunition manufacturers.

SELLIER & BELLOT:
Formerly, ZUNDHUTCHEN und PATRONENFABRIK:
Schoenbeck, Magdeburg, Eastern Germany.

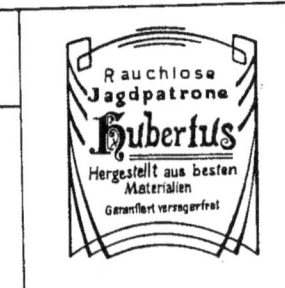

Rauchlose
Jagdpatrone
Hubertus
Hergestellt aus besten
Materialien.
Garantiert versagerfrei.

DATA
Gauge; 12.
Length; 65 mm.
Head; 7 mm.
Tube; Wound light brown paper.
Colour; Waxed yellow.
Print; Black.
Base; Reinforced brass.
Closure; Rolled turn-over.
Wad; White card, print purple.
Business; Ammunition manufacturers.

Note the extra letter E in the headstamp.

SHIMWELL BROTHERD (PTY),LTD:
(Address not known). South Africa.

Drawn from the Tom Matthews collection.

"UNITY"
SUPER
VELOCITY
CARTRIDGE
Specially loaded for
SHIMWELL BROS.
(PTY) LTD.
SOUTH AFRICA
WATER RESISTING
MADE IN GREAT BRITAIN

DATA
Gauge; 12.
Length; 64 mm.
Head; 16 mm.
Tube; Wound dark green paper.
Colour; Dark green.
Base; Reinforced brass.
Wetproof; Clear lacquered.
Closure; Rolled turn-over.
Wad; Yellow, print black.
Case; England.

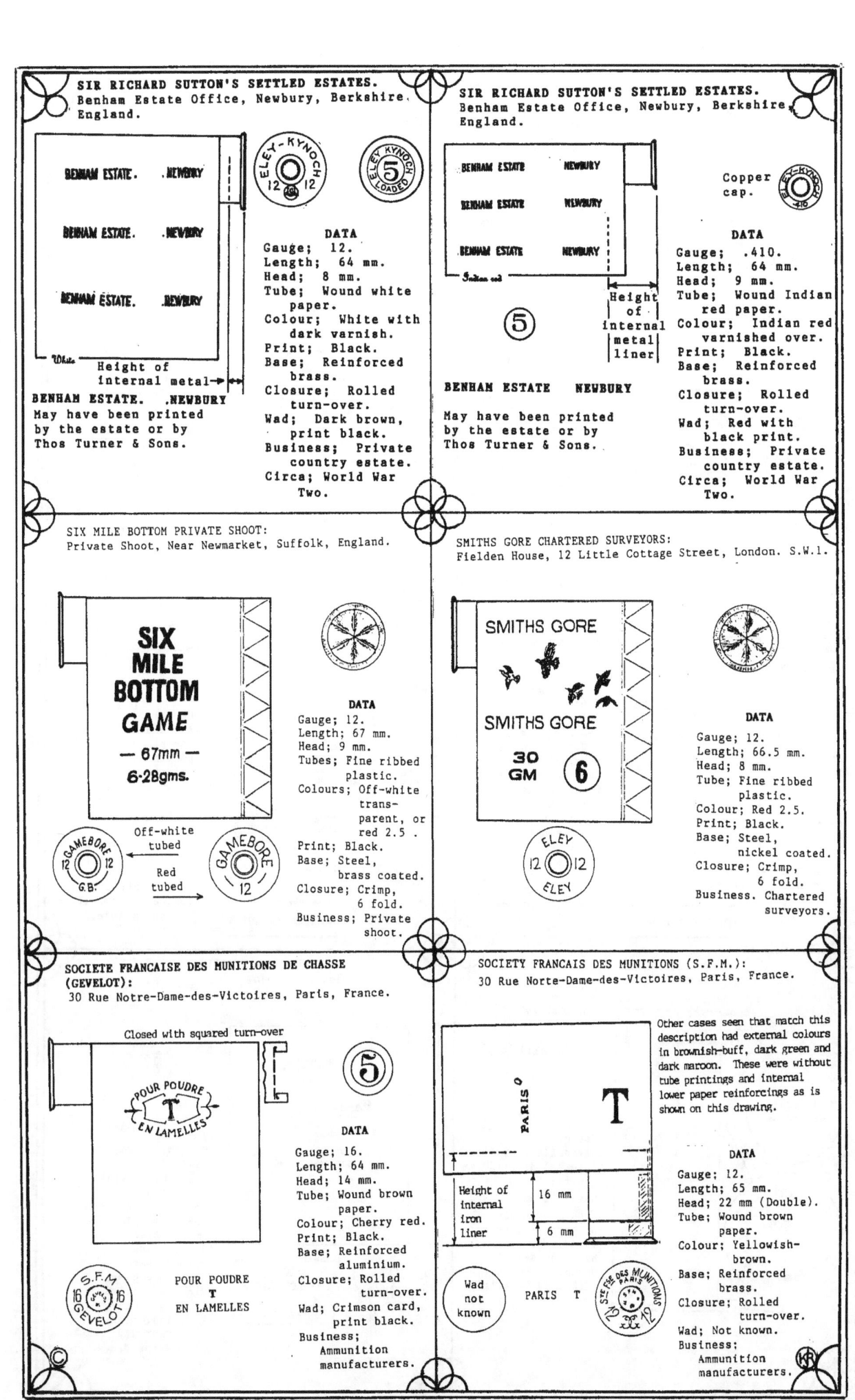

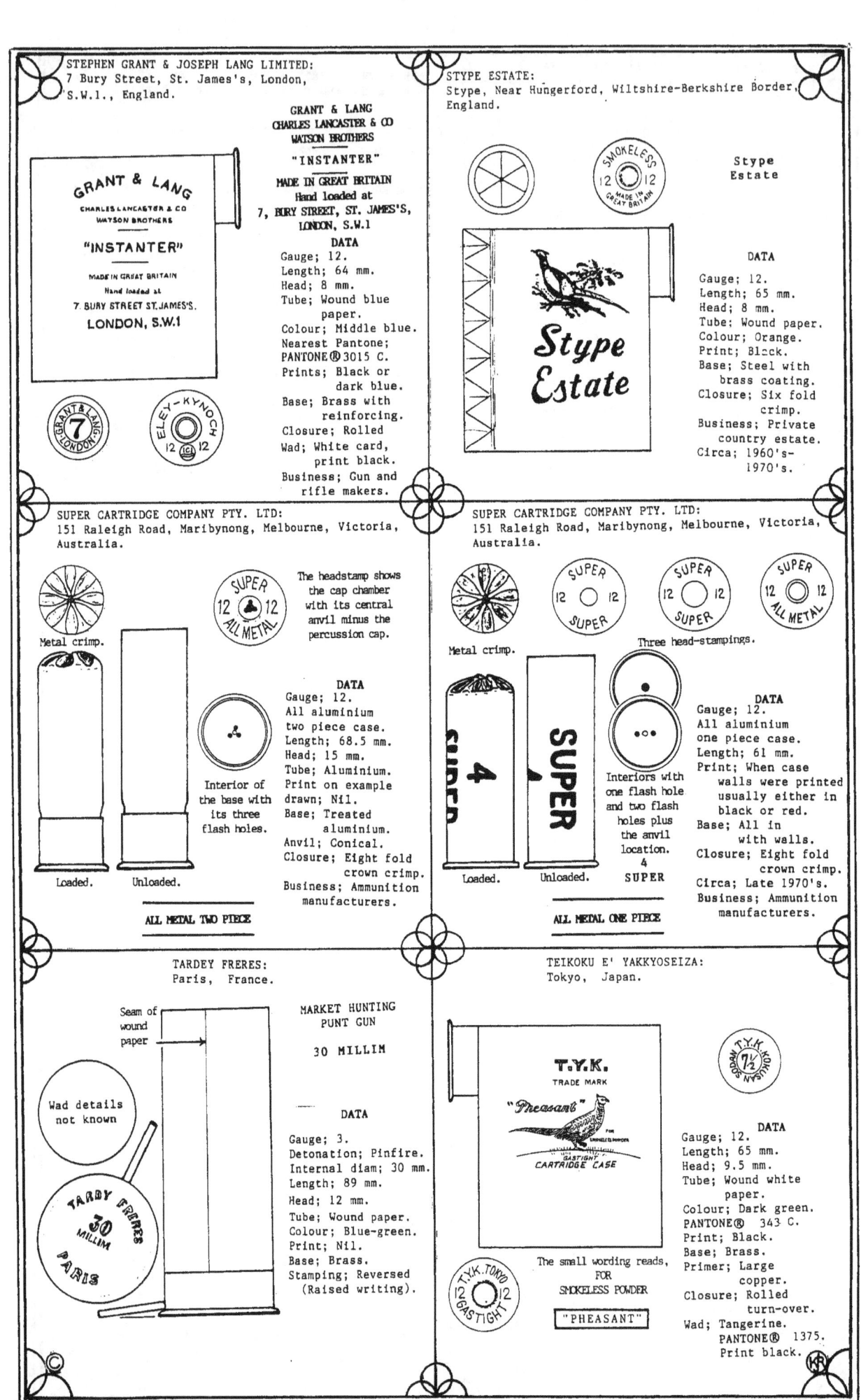

THE CARTRIDGE:
16 Smith Street, Warwick, Warwickshire, England.

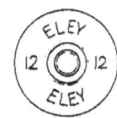

DATA

Gauge; 12.
Length; 67 mm.
Head; 7 mm.
Tube; Fine ribbed
  plastic.
Colour; Crimson
  red 3.
Print; Black.
Base; Steel,
  nickel coated.
Closure; Crimp,
  6 fold.
Business; Field
  sports.

THE CARTRIDGE:
16 Smith Street, Warwick, Warwickshire, England.

DATA

Gauge; 12.
Length; 70 mm.
Head; 8 mm.
Tube; Fine ribbed
  plastic.
Colour; Orange 3.
Print; Black.
Base; Steel,
  nickel coated.
Closure; Crimp,
  6 fold.
Business; Field
  sports.

THE GUN COUNTER:
67 High Street, Wallingford, Oxfordshire. England.

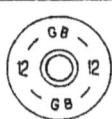

DATA

Gauge; 12.
Length; 69 mm.
Head; 7 mm.
Tube; Medium ribbed
  plastic.
Colour; Flame red 2.5.
Print; Black.
Base; Steel,
  brass coated.
Closure; Crimp,
  6 fold.
Business; Field
  sports
  store.

THE GUN COUNTER;
67 High Street, Wallingford, Oxfordshire. England.

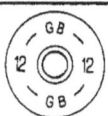

DATA

Gauge; 12.
Length; 69 mm.
Head; 7 mm.
Tube; Medium ribbed
  plastic.
Colour; Blue 3.5.
Print; Black.
Base; Steel,
  brass coated.
Closure; Crimp,
  6 fold.
Business; Field
  sports
  store.

THE HINGSTON-SMITH ARMS COMPANY LIMITED:
Winnipeg, Manitoba, Canada.

DATA

Gauge; 12.
Length; Approx' 64 mm.
Head; Not known.
Tube; Wound paper.
Colour; Vermilion.
Print; Black.
Base; Brass.
Closure; Rolled
  turn-over.
Wad; Yellow card,
  print black.
Business; Canadian
  agents, arms and
  sports dealers.

I have never seen the actual cartridge. Its details were sent to me along with a sketch. The nationality must be Canadian although it was loaded at Hendon, London, England. The case was French and the powder came out of Switzerland. I do not know where the shot and wadding came from. H.R.H. The Prince of Wales used their shells in 1902.

PROVISIONAL DRAWING

THE MEMBURY ESTATE:
Membury, Near Axminster, Devonshire, England.

DATA

Gauge; 12.
Length; 65 mm.
Head; 12 mm.
Tube; Wound brown
  paper.
Colour; Pine green.
Print; Black.
Base; Steel, brass
  coated.
Closure; Six fold
  crimp.
Wetproof; Clear
  lacqured.
Business; Private
  estate.
Circa; 1998.

PLATE 67

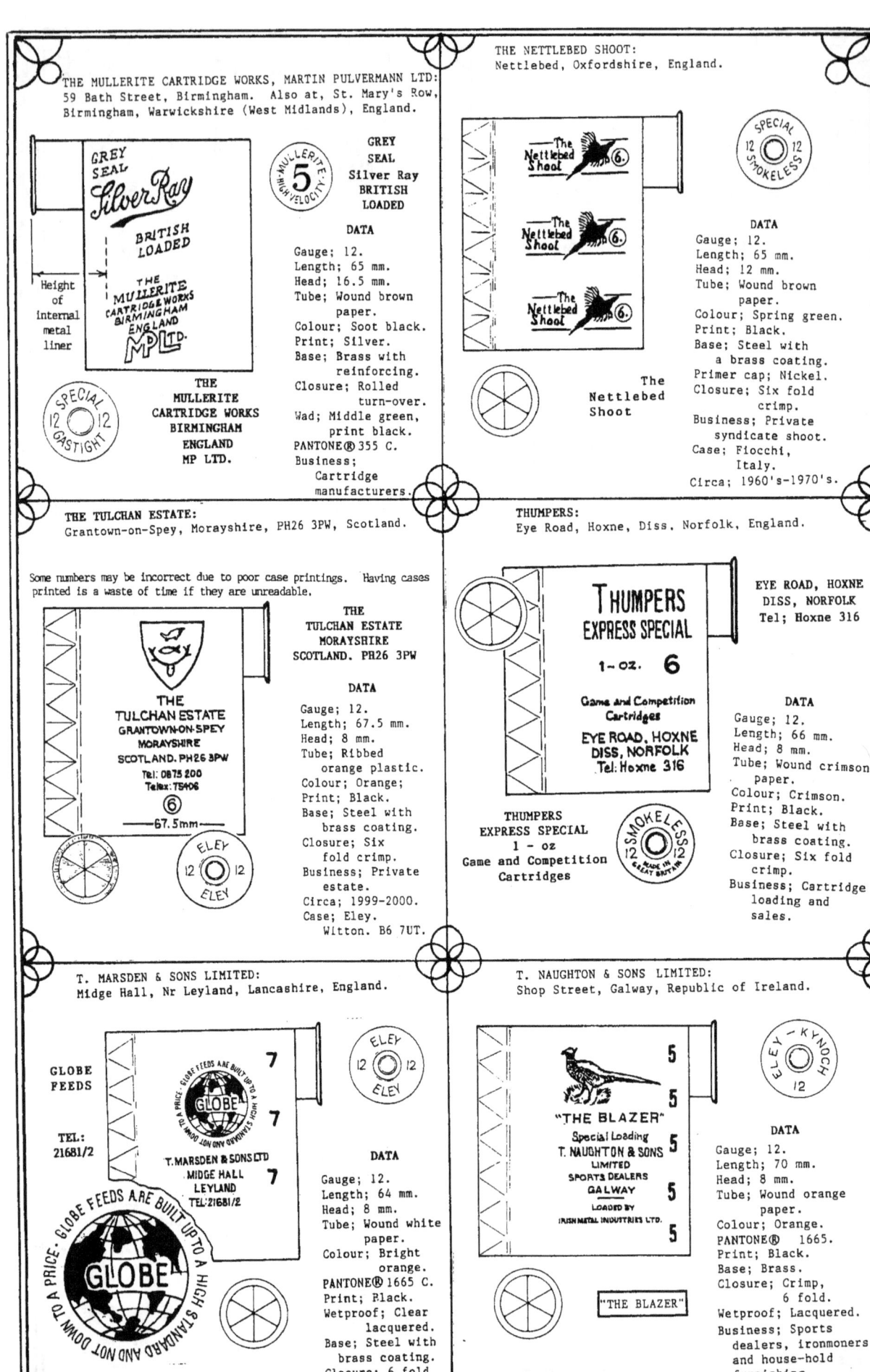

PLATE 68

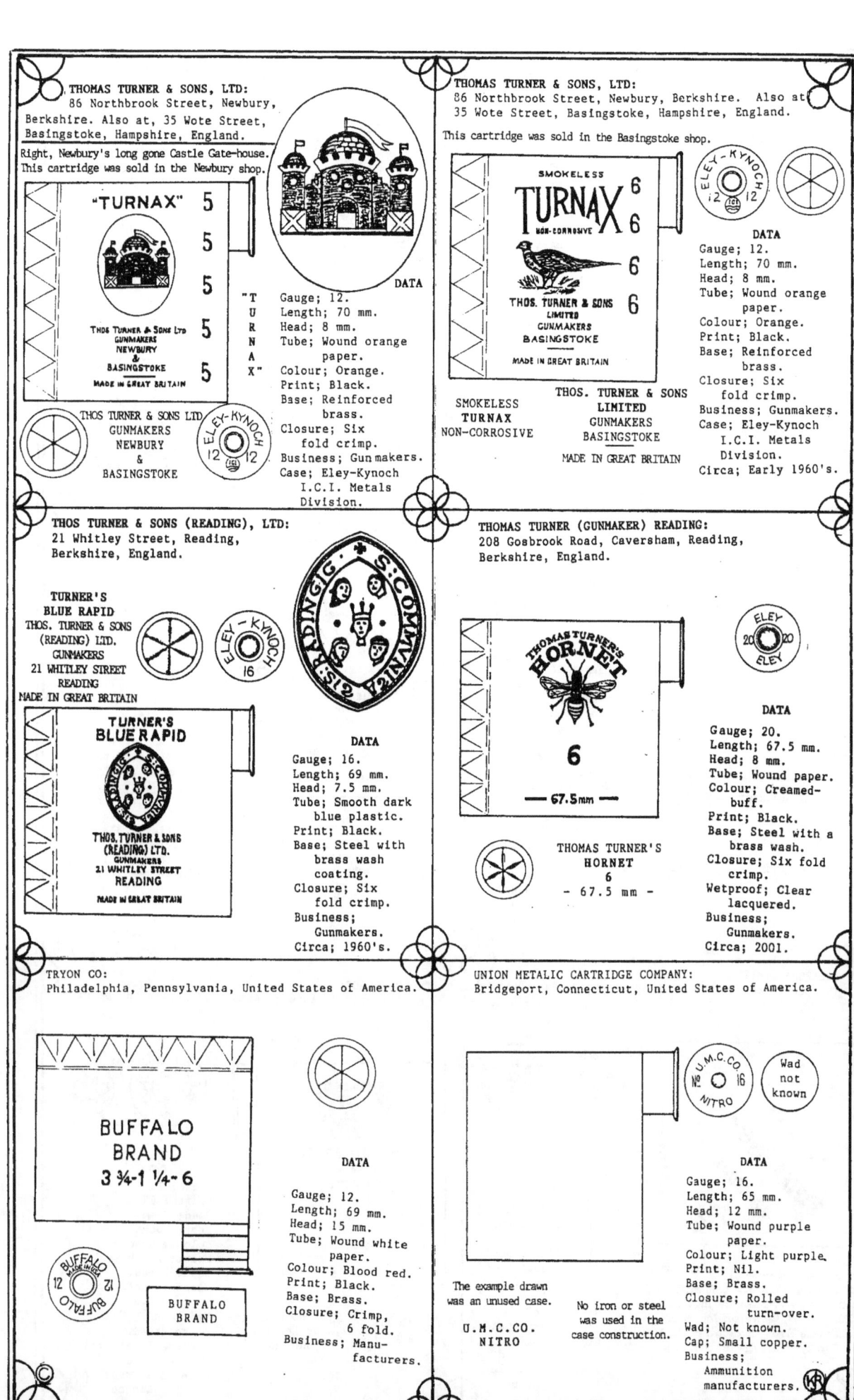

PLATE 69

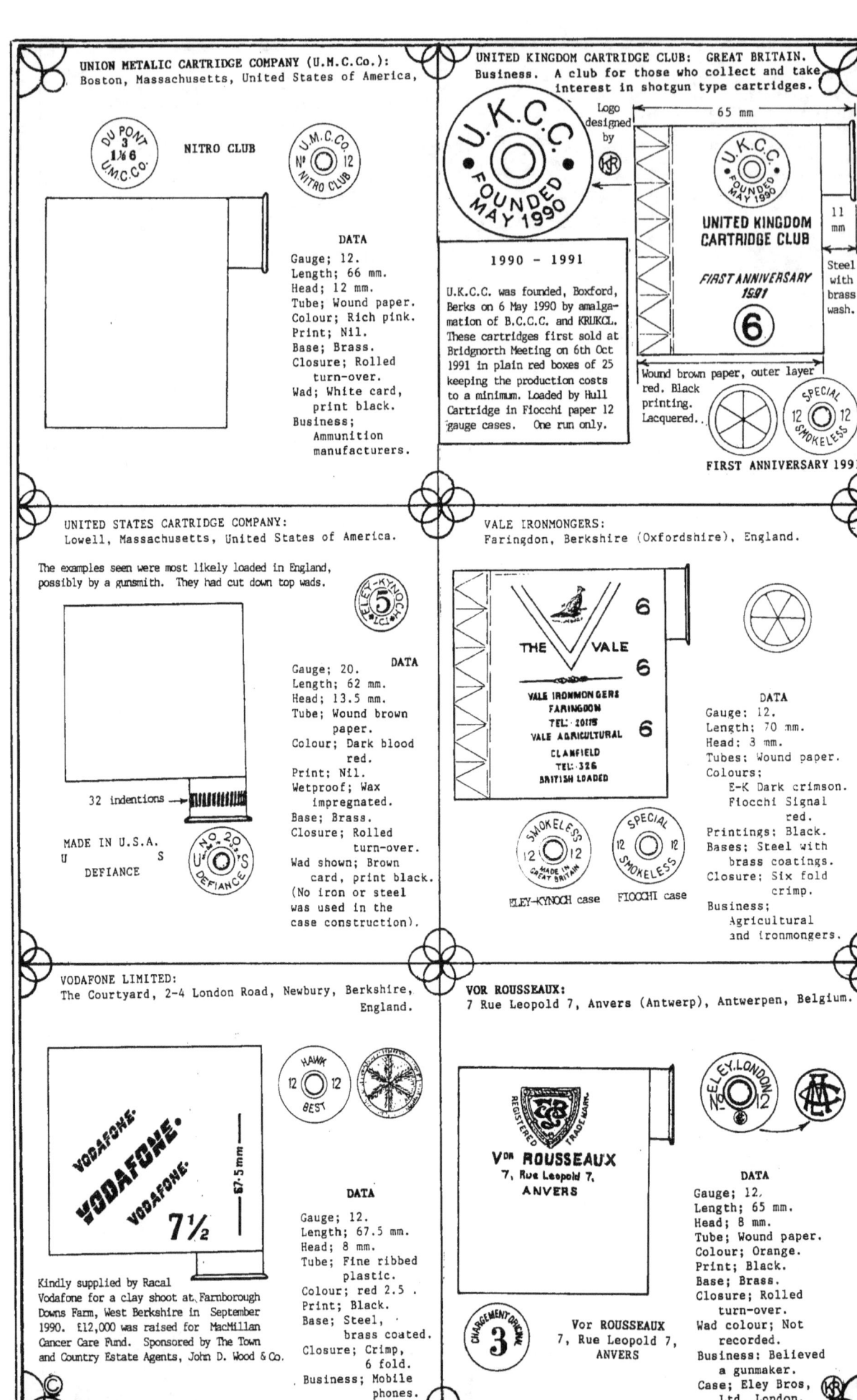

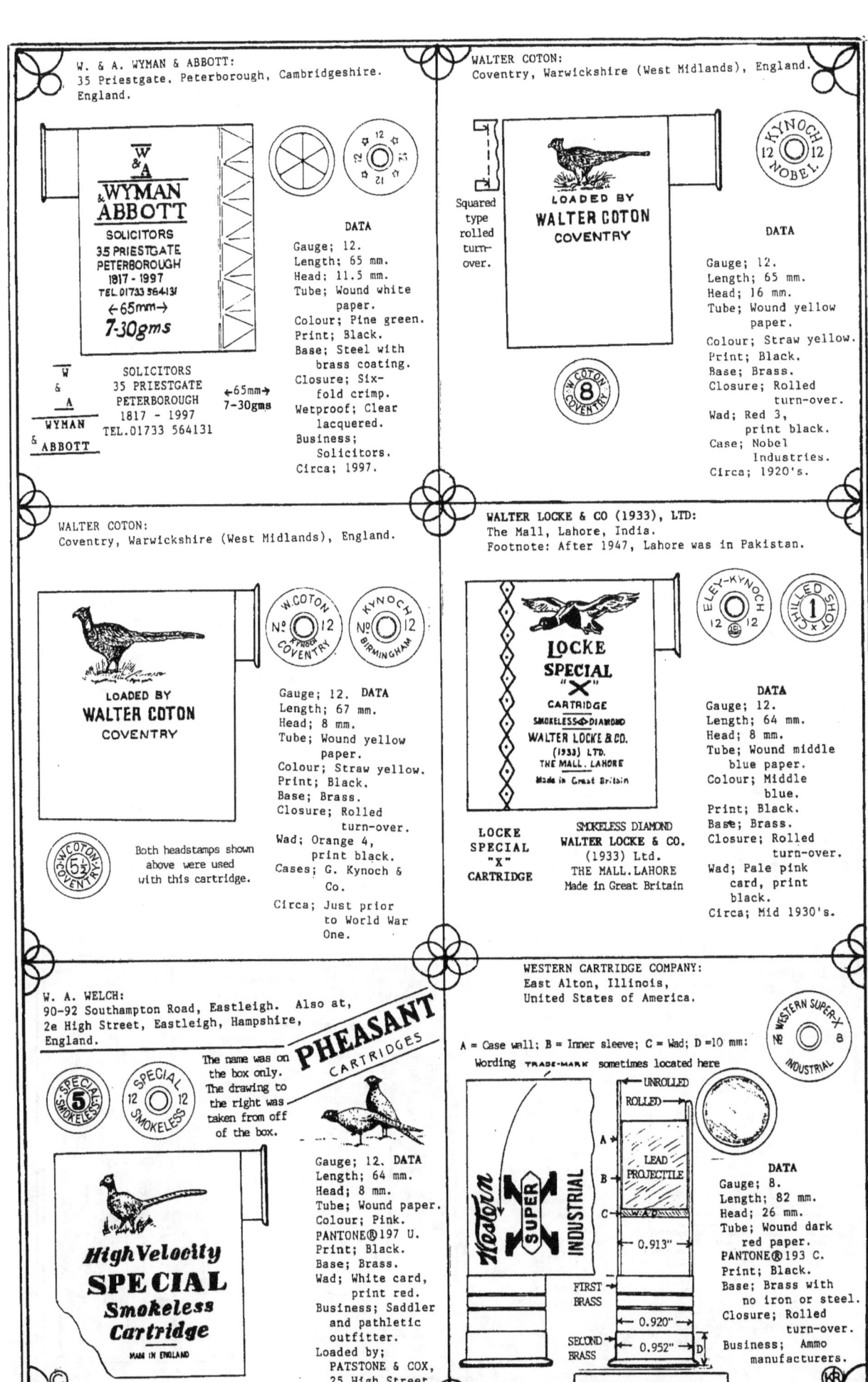

PLATE 71

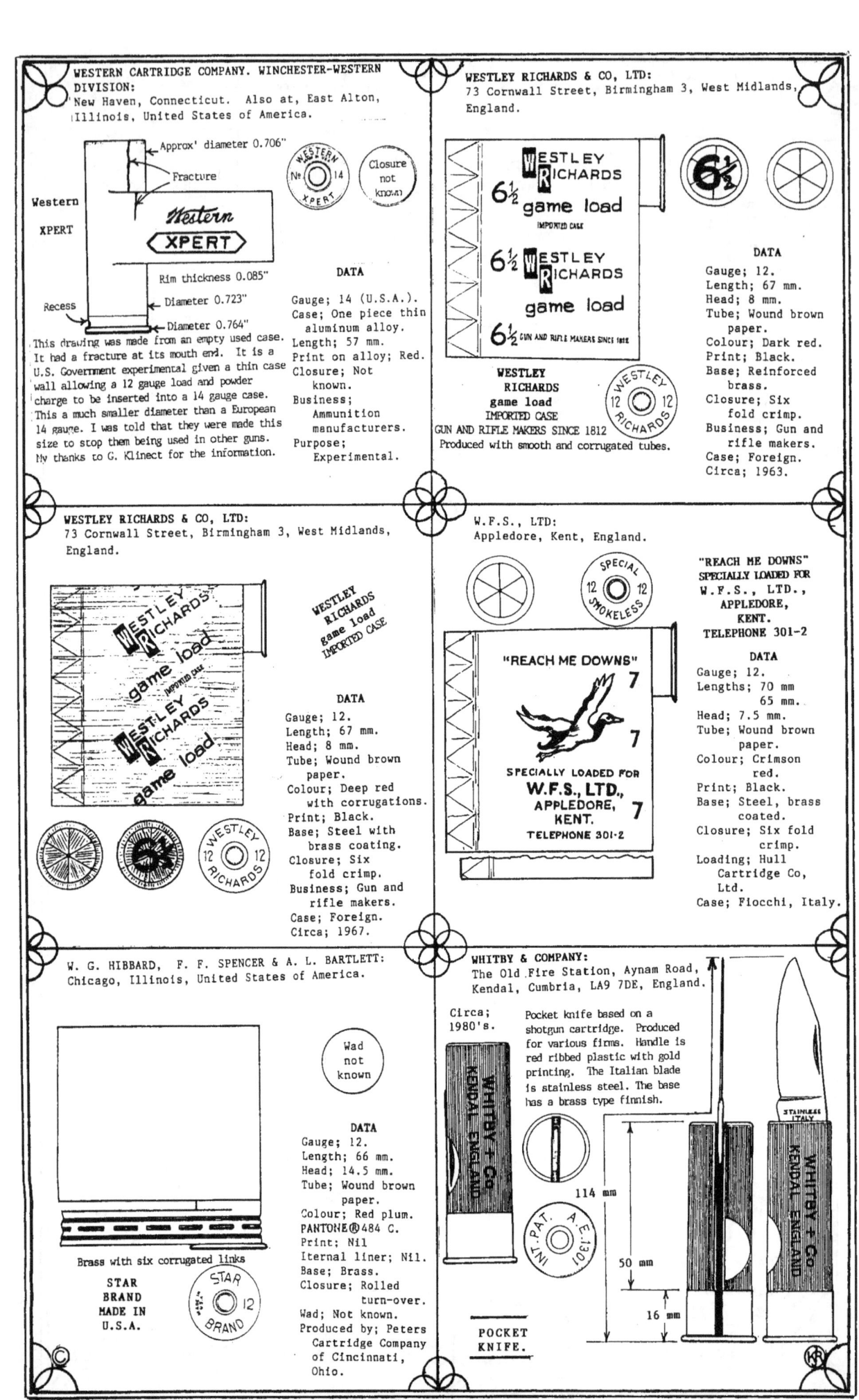

W. H. TISDALL, LTD:
Wellington & Christchurch, New-Zealand.

"Perfection" Cartridge
LOADED ONLY BY
W. H. TISDALL, LTD.
WELLINGTON & CHRISTCHURCH

DATA

Gauge; 12.
Length; 64 mm.
Head; 8 mm.
Tube; Wound red paper.
Colour; Eley Bros red quality.
Print; Black.
Base; Brass.
Closure; Rolled turn-over.
Wad; Pale brown card, print black.
Business; Gun and ammunition dealers.

W. H. TISDALL LIMITED:
Auckland, Hamilton & Wellington, North Island.
Also at, Christchurch, South Island, New Zealand.

"THE RETRIEVER"

DATA

Gauge; 12.
Length; 64 mm.
Head; 7 mm.
Tube; Wound paper.
Colour; Poppy red.
Print; Black.
Base; Brass.
Closure; Rolled turn-over.
Wad; Grey, print black.
Case by; Nobel Explosives Co, Ltd., Scotland.

W. H. TISDALL, LIMITED:
Auckland, Wellington, Christchurch & Hamilton, New Zealand.

W.H.TISDALL,Ltd.
AUCKLAND—WELLINGTON
CHRISTCHURCH—HAMILTON
"THE RETRIEVER"
Made in Great Britain

DATA

Gauge; 12.
Length; 64 mm.
Head; 8 mm.
Tube; Wound orange paper.
Colour; Orange.
Print; Black.
Base; Reinforced brass.
Closure; Rolled turn-over.
Wad; Yellow card, print black.
Business; Gun and ammunition dealer.
Circa; 1930's.

WILHELM COLLATH:
Gewehr-u-Patronen (Gun, rifle & Cartridge Factory),
Frankfurt A/O, East Germany.

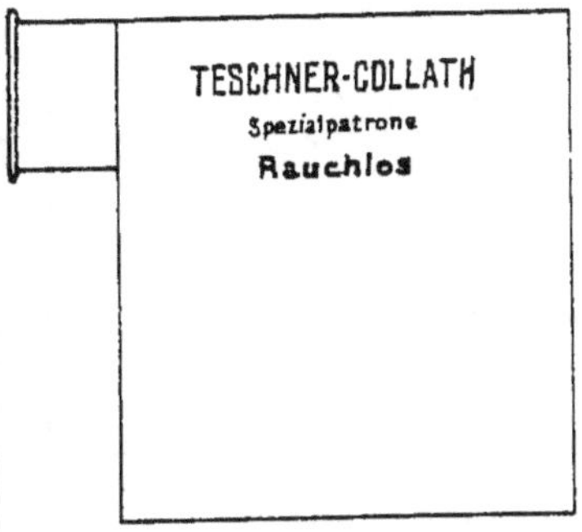

TESCHNER-COLLATH
Spezialpatrone
Rauchlos
(Special cartridge, Smokeless)
Experimental central pinfire.

DATA

Central Pinfire.
Gauge; (3).
Equivalent gauge; 14.
Length; 73.5 mm.
Head; 14 mm.
Tube; Wound paper.
Colour; Brownish cimson.
Print; Black.
Base; Brass.
Closure; Not known.
Business; Gun and cartridge maker.

WILHELM COLLATH & SOHNE:
Gewehr-u-Patronen (Gun, Rifle & Cartridge Factory),
Frankfurt A/O, East Germany.

Drawing made from a set of photographs.
"TESCO"
Experimental central pinfire.

This cartridge had a bottle shaped head with a thin tapered rim. A large copper cap was fitted.

Collath gauge equivalents.
No, 0 = 10 gauge
No, 1 = 12 gauge
No, 2 Not used
No, 3 = 14 gauge
No, 4 = 16 gauge
No, 5 = 18 gauge
No, 6 = 20 gauge
No, 7 = 24 gauge
No, 8 = 28 gauge

DATA

Central Pinfire.
Gauge; (5).
Equivalent gauge; 18.
Length; 74 mm.
Head; 12.5 mm.
Tube; Wound paper.
Colour; Greyish-green.
Print; Black.
Base; Brass.
Closure; Not known.
Business; Gun and cartridge maker.

WILHELM COLLATH & SOHNE:
Gewehr-u-Patronen (Gun, Rifle & Cartridge Factory),
Frankfurt A/O, East Germany.

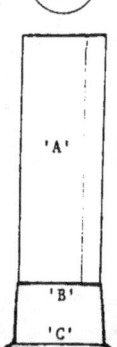

DRAWING DIAMETERS
'A' = 0 666"
'B' = 0 705"
'C' = 0 731"
'D' = 0 803"

DATA

Gauge; (5).
Equivalent gauge; 18.
Length; 65 mm.
Head; 14 mm.
Tube; Wound paper.
Colour; Light redish brown.
Print; Nil.
Base; Brass.
Cap large copper
Wetproof; Waxed.
Closure; Rolled turn-over.
Wad; Light sky blue, print black.
Business; Gun and cartridge maker.

PLATE 73

WILKINSON'S: Penrith, Cumberland (Cumbria).

"THE BEACON"
WILKINSON'S
PENRITH'S
SPORTS DEPOT
PHONE 220
MADE IN GREAT BRITAIN

Red

Internal reinforcing →

"THE BEACON" WILKINSON'S
PENRITH'S SPORTS DEPOT
PHONE 220
MADE IN GREAT BRITAIN

DATA
Gauge; 12.
Length; 64 mm.
Head; 8 mm.
Tube; Wound red paper.
Colour; Crimson.
Print; Black.
Base; Reinforced brass.
Cap; Copper.
Closure; Rolled turn-over.
Wad; Yellow, print black.
Business; Field sports.
Circa; 1930's.

WILLIAM EVANS: (Gunmaker).
63 Pall Mall, London E.C., England.
LIBERTY CARTRIDGE CO: (Cartridge manufacturers).
Mount Carmel. Connecticut. U.S.A.

British case exported to U.S.A where it was loaded.
Drawing of a shell in the Dale Hedlund collection.

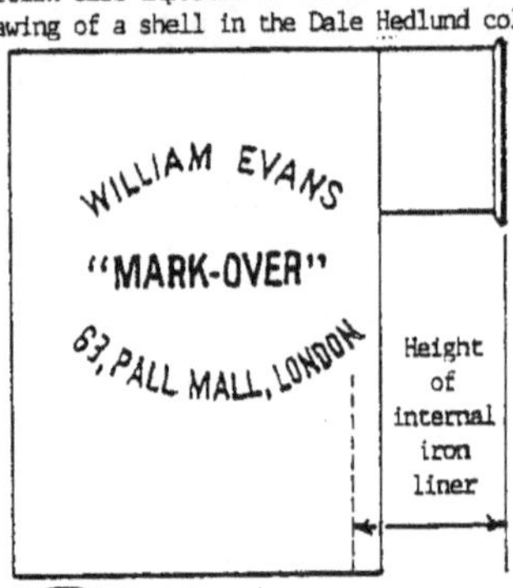

WILLIAM EVANS
"MARK-OVER"
63, PALL MALL, LONDON

Height of internal iron liner

WILLIAM EVANS
"MARK-OVER"
63, PALL MALL, LONDON

DATA
Gauge; 12.
Length; 64 mm.
Head; 16 mm.
Tube; Wound burgundy paper.
Colour; Burgundy.
Print; White.
Base; Reinforced brass.
Closure; Rolled turn-over.
Wad; White card, print pink.
Case; English.
Load; American.

WILLIAM EVANS:
63 Pall Mall, London, E.C., England.

WILLIAM EVANS
"MARK OVER"
63 PALL MALL, LONDON
MADE IN GREAT BRITAIN

Height of the interior steel liner.

Made in Great Britain

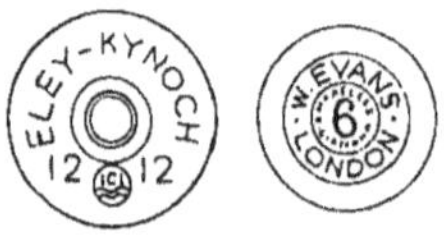

Both versions of 'Made in Great Britain' were used on this cartridge. Those with spring green tubes and black case wall printings were circa, 1938-1939.

"MARK OVER"

DATA
Gauge; 12.
Length; 64 mm.
Head; 16 mm.
Tube; Wound green paper.
Colours; Dark green, print black or dark blue. Spring green, print black.
Base; Brass.
Closure; Rolled turn-over.
Wad; Red, print black.
Circa; 1930's.
Business; Gunmaker.

WILLIAMSON & SON:
34 Bull Ring, Ludlow, Shropshire, England.

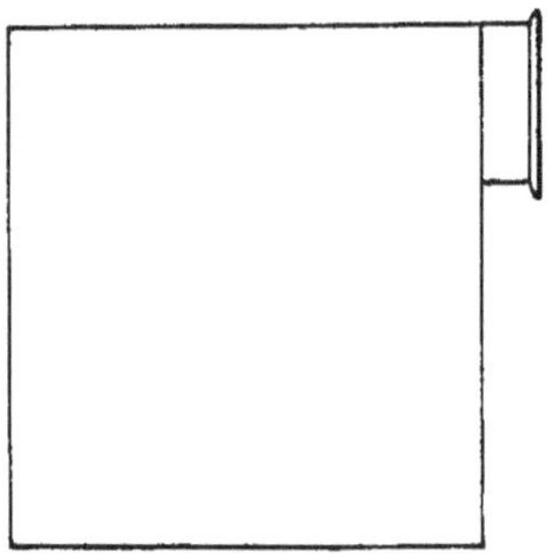

DATA
Gauge; 16.
Length; 64 mm.
Head; 7 mm.
Tube; Wound brown paper.
Colour; Dark brown.
Print; Nil.
Base; Brass.
Closure; Rolled turn-over.
Wad; White card, print red.
Case; G. Kynoch, Ltd. Witton quality.
Business; Gunmakers.

WILKINSON:
Sports Depot, Penrith, Cumberland (Cumbria), England.

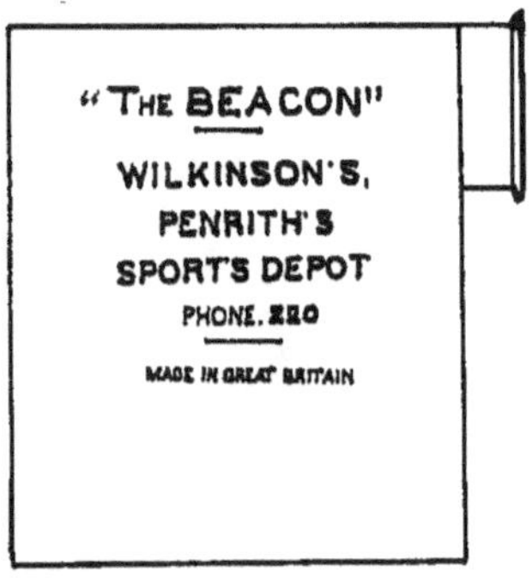

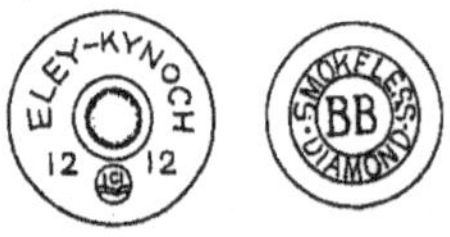

"THE BEACON"
WILKINSON'S,
PENRITH'S
SPORTS DEPOT
PHONE. 220
MADE IN GREAT BRITAIN

"THE BEACON"
WILKINSONS'S,   PHONE. 220
PENRITH'S   MADE IN GREAT BRITAIN
SPORTS DEPOT

DATA
Gauge; 12.
Length; 64 mm.
Head; 8 mm.
Tube; Wound red paper.
Colour; Crimson.
Print; Black.
Base; Reinforced brass.
Wetproof; Lacquered.
Closure; Rolled turn-over.
Wad; Yellow, print black.
Business; Sports shop.
Circa: 1930's.

WILTSHIRE ROD & GUN:
23 High Street, Swindon, Wiltshire. England.

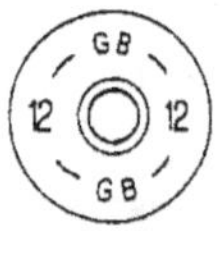

WILTSHIRE ROD & GUN
23 HIGH STREET,
SWINDON,
WILTSHIRE.
TEL: 0793 47455   30gms.
⑥

GB 12 ⊙ 12 GB

DATA
Gauge; 12.
Length; 68.5 mm.
Head; 7 mm.
Tube; Medium ribbed plastic.
Colour; Red 3.5.
Print; Black.
Base; Steel, brass coated.
Closure; Crimp, 6 fold.
Business; Field sports store.

PLATE 74

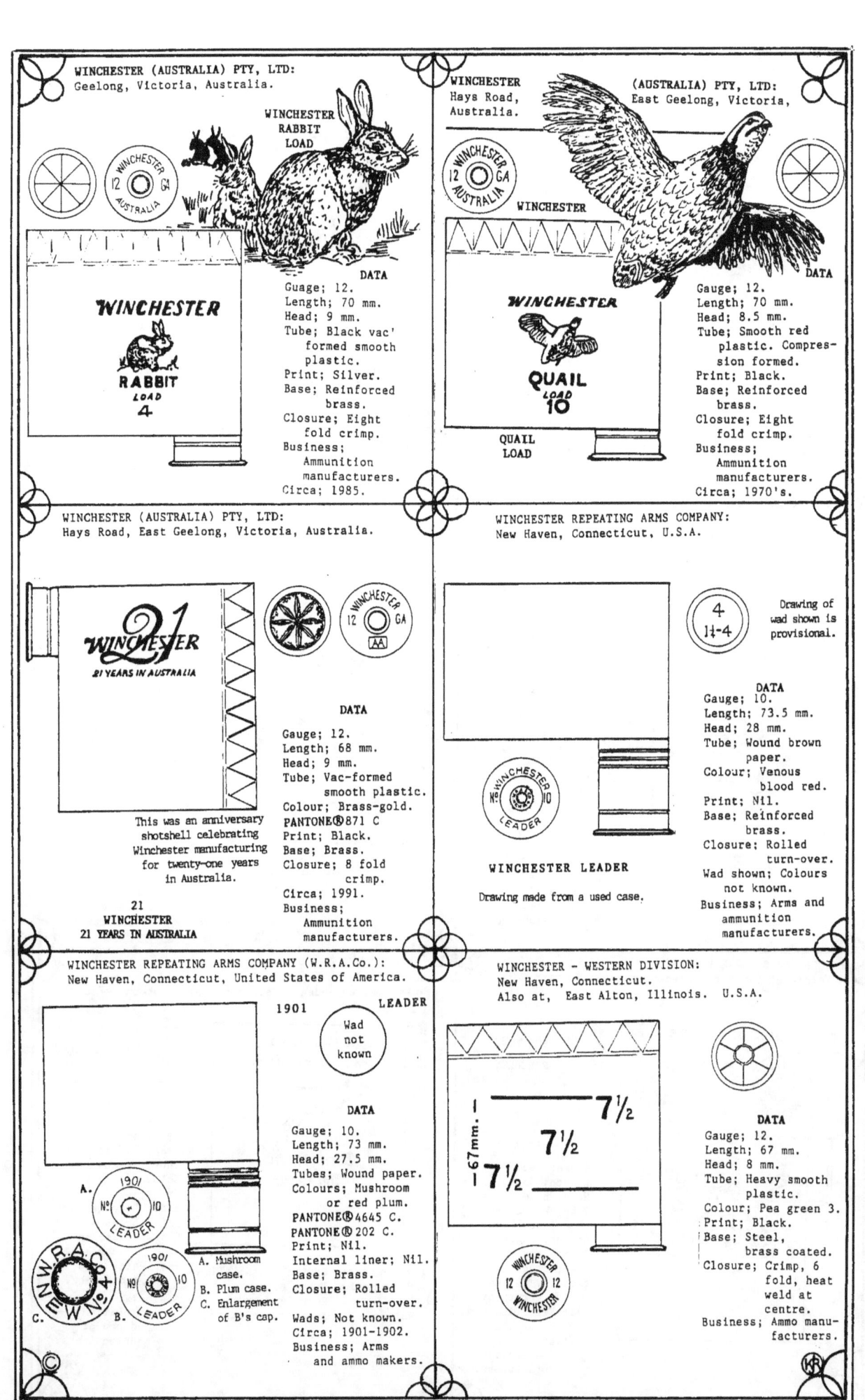

PLATE 75

W. JEFFERY & SON:
12 George Street. Later at, 3 Russell Street, Plymouth, Devonshire, England.

Wording on the scroll is; TURRIS FORTISSIMA EST NOMEN JEHOVA

JEFFERY & SON
GUNMAKERS
PLYMOUTH

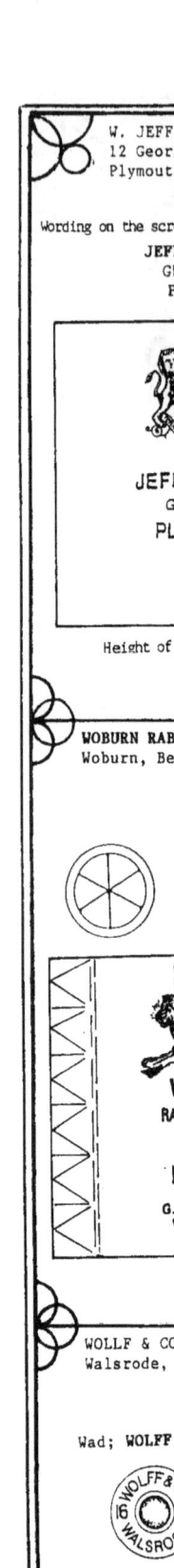

Height of internal metal liner

DATA

Gauge; 12.
Length; 64 mm.
Head; 10 mm.
Tube; Wound paper.
Colour; Orange-buff.
Print; Black.
Base; Brass.
Closure; Rolled turn-over.
Wad; White card, print black.
Business; Gunmakers.
Case; Kynoch & Co.

W. JEFFERY & SON:
3 Russell Street, Plymouth, Devonshire, England.

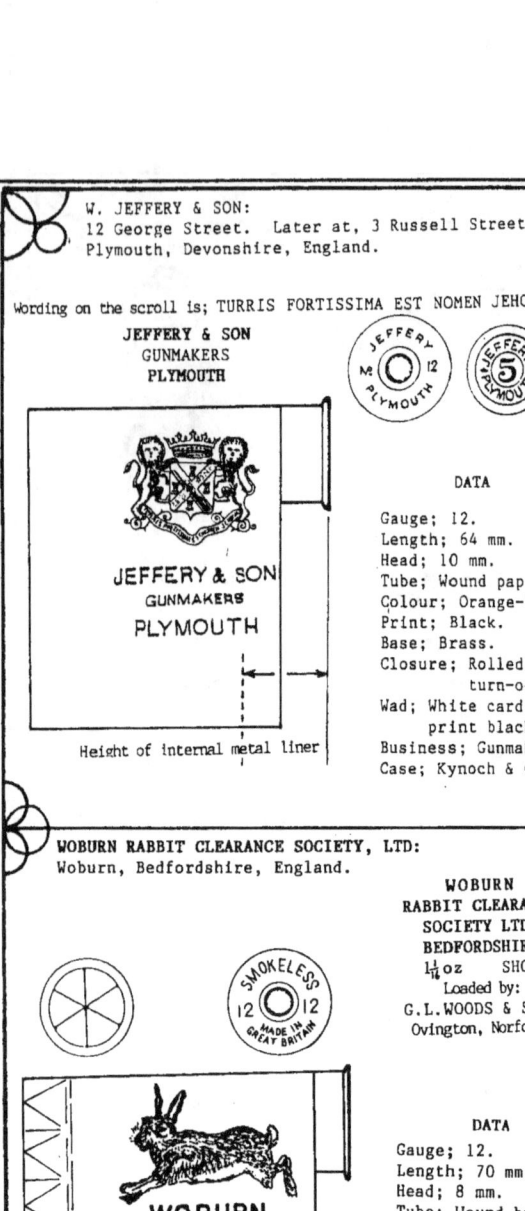

The DATA and drawing is for the 16 gauge

THE
"SKY HIGH"
NON RUSTING
SPECIAL SMOKELESS
BRITISH HAND LOADED
W.JEFFERY & SON
GUNMAKERS
RUSSELL ST.
PHONE 1477 PLYMOUTH
FOREIGN MADE CASE

These black shells were sold in 12 and 16 gauge. No iron or steel was used in their construction. Jefferys' moved from Russell St, in 1928.

DATA

Gauges; 16 & 12.
Lengths; 64.5 mm.
Head; 7 mm.
Tube; Wound brown paper.
Colours; Soot black.
Prints; Silver.
Base; Brass.
Closure; Rolled turn-over.
Wad; White card, print pink.
Case; German.
Circa; Prior to 1929.
Business; Gunmakers.

WOBURN RABBIT CLEARANCE SOCIETY, LTD:
Woburn, Bedfordshire, England.

WOBURN
RABBIT CLEARANCE
SOCIETY LTD.
BEDFORDSHIRE
1¼ oz   SHOT
Loaded by:
G.L.WOODS & SONS
Ovington, Norfolk.

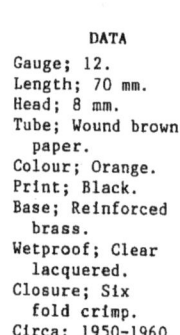

DATA

Gauge; 12.
Length; 70 mm.
Head; 8 mm.
Tube; Wound brown paper.
Colour; Orange.
Print; Black.
Base; Reinforced brass.
Wetproof; Clear lacquered.
Closure; Six fold crimp.
Circa; 1950-1960.

WOLFF & CO (GESELLSCHAFT):
Walsrode, Luneberg (Niedersachsen), Western Germany.

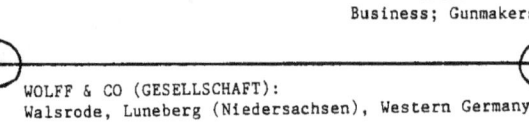

Height of internal metal liner

Extra Gasdicht
"Cymax Standard"
Rauchlos   Rostfrei
geladen mit
rauchlosem Jagd-Blättchen-Pulver
und Jdeal-Hartschrot

DATA

Gauge; 12.
Length; 64.5 mm.
Head; 8 mm.
Tube; Wound paper.
Colour; Light red.
Print; Black.
Base; Reinforced brass.
Closure; Rolled turn-over.
Wad; White card, print black.
Cap; Sinoxid
Business; Ammunition and powder manufacturers.

WOLFF & CO (GESELLSCHAFT):
Walsrode, Luneberg (Niedersachsen), Western Germany.

Wad; WOLFF & Co WALSRODE 3 mm .5

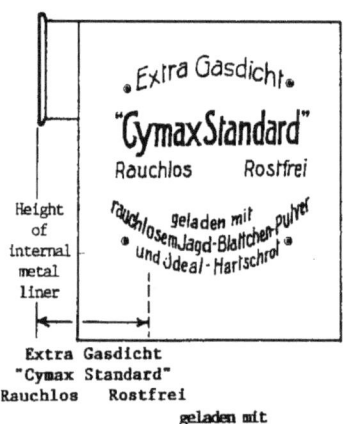

ROSTFREI
RAUCHLOS
Birkhann-Marke

DATA

Gauge; 16.
Length; 65 mm.
Head; 8 mm.
Tube; Wound brown paper.
Colour; Poppy red.
Print; Black.
Base; Steel.
Closure; Rolled turn-over.
Wad; Vermilion red, print black.
Business; Powder and ammunition manufacturers.

WOLFF & CO (GESELLSCHAFT):
Walsrode, Luneburg (Niedersachsen), Western Germany.

Wolf-Marke
rauchlos u rostfrei
Wolff & Co.
Walsrode

ENGLISH TRANSLATION
Trade Mark.
Smokeless and free from rust.

DATA

Gauge; 12.
Length; 64 mm.
Head; 6.5 mm.
Tube; Wound paper.
Colour; Pale yellow.
Print; Black.
Base; Reinforced brass.
Closure; Rolled turn-over.
Wad; White card, print black.
Business; Ammunition and powder manufacturers.

PLATE 76

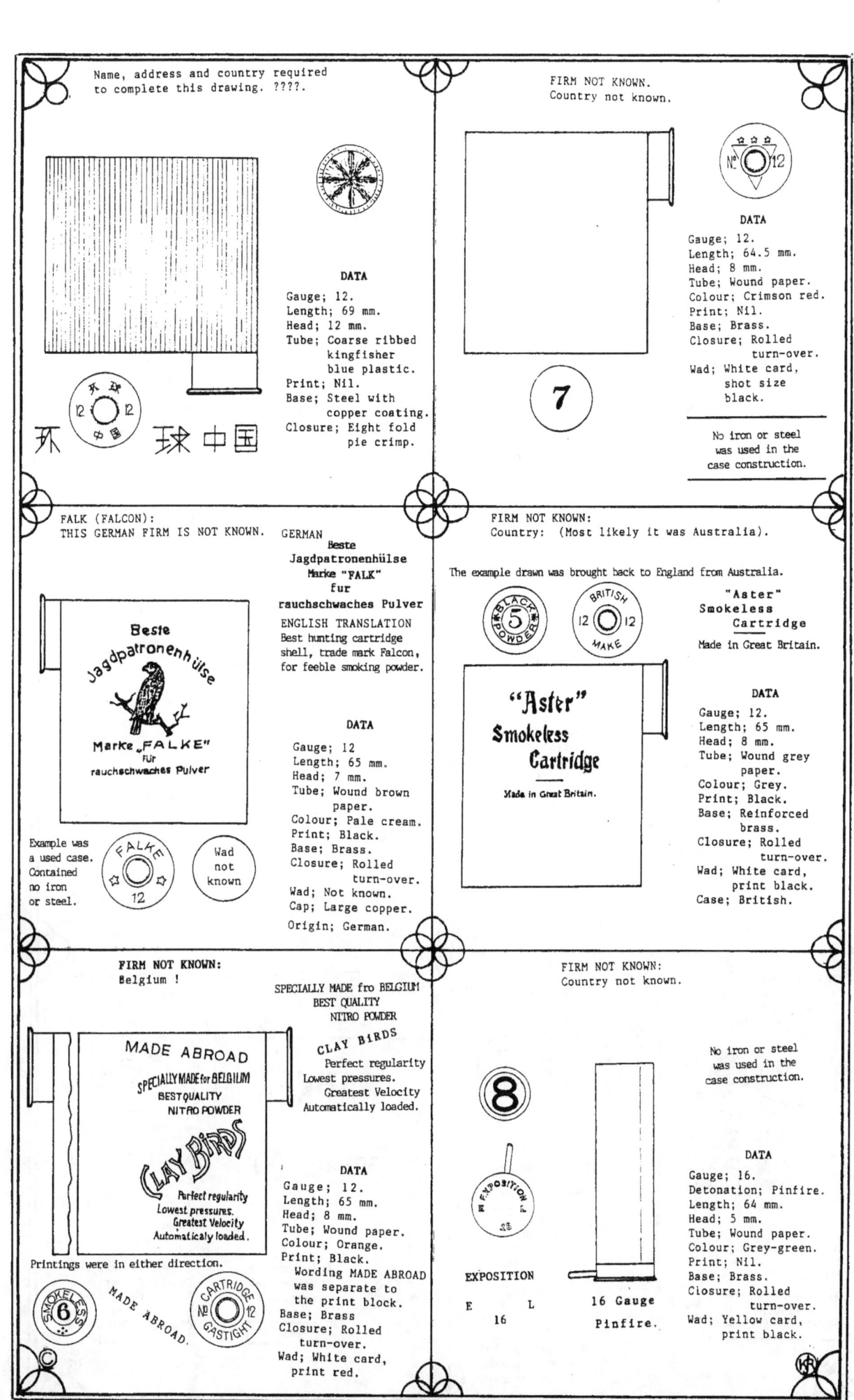

PLATE 77

FIRM NOT KNOWN:
Address not known. France.

 No iron or steel was used in the case construction. T

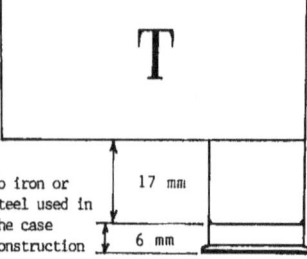

No iron or steel used in the case construction   17 mm
                                                  6 mm

DATA
Gauge; 12.
Length; 54 mm.
Head; Double 23 mm.
Tube; Wound brown paper.
Colour; Crimson.
Print; Black.
Base; Brass.
Closure; Rolled turn-over.
Wad; Light brown card, print black.
Cap; Brass.

FIRMS NAME AND ADDRESS IS NOT KNOWN.

DATA
Gauge; 16.
Length; 64 mm.
Head; 7 mm.
Tube; Wound EDN paper.
Colour; Eau-de-nil.
Print; Black.
Base; Reinforced brass.
Cap; Copper.
Closure; Rolled turn-over.
Wad; White card, print black.
Case by; Eley-Kynoch I.C.I.
Circa; 1930's.

"LODA"
SMOKELESS
CARTRIDGE
MADE AND LOADED
IN ENGLAND

LUX.
The firm, country and address is not known.

The drawing was made from a used case.

DATA
Gauge; 12.
Length; 65 mm.
Head; 5 mm.
Tube; Wound brown paper.
Colour; Brown.
Print; Nil.
Base; Brass.
Closure; Rolled turn-over.
Wad; Not known.

No iron or steel was used in the case construction.

FIRM OR OWNERS NAME NOT KNOWN:
Country possibly England.

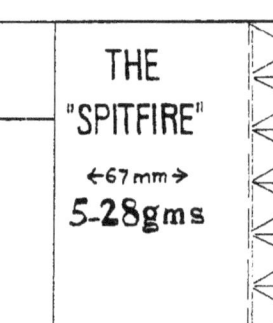

THE
"SPITFIRE"
← 67 mm →
5-28gms

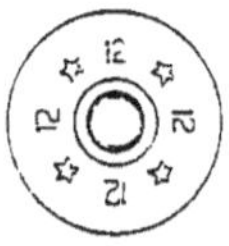

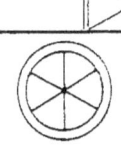

DATA
Gauge; 12.
Length; 67 mm.
Head; 15.5 mm.
Tube; Wound brown paper.
Colour; Light brownish red.
Print; Black.
Base; Steel with brass coating.
Closure; Six fold crimp.
Circa; 1999-2000.

FIRM NOT KNOWN:
Case constructed by; NOBEL'S EXPLOSIVES COMPANY, LIMITED:
Kingsway House, Kingsway, London, England.

  Wad not known

"RINGER"
SMOKELESS CARTRIDGE
IMPROVED SHELL
Made in Great Britain

The origin of this case is still a mystery, but it was definitely manufactured by Nobel's Explosive Co, Ltd. Many unused cases have since come to light.

"RINGER"
SMOKELESS CARTRIDGE

DATA
Gauge; 12.
Length; 65 mm.
Head; 8 mm.
Tube; Wound tan paper.
Colour; Orange-tan.
Print; Black.
Base; Brass.
Closure; Rolled turn-over.
Wad; Not known.
Business; Explosives and cartridge makers.

WANKER: (THE NAME FOR THIS CARTRIDGE IS NOT KNOWN).
Somewhere in England.

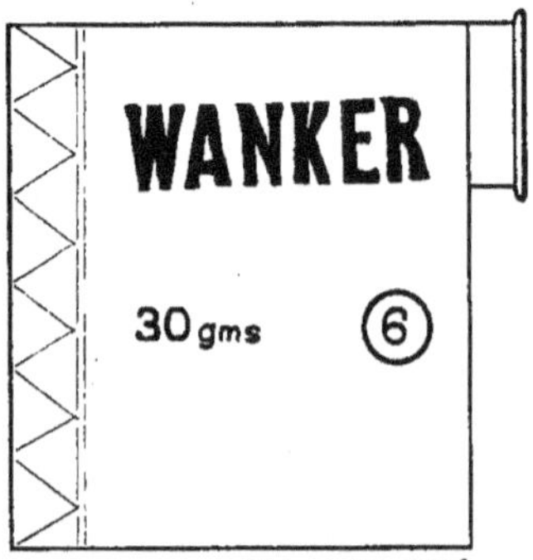

WANKER
30gms 6

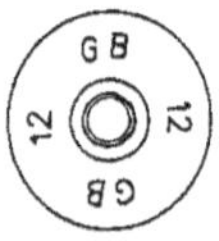

 Without the proof, I will not put a heading name to this cartridge.
WANKER

DATA
Gauge; 12.
Length; 67 mm.
Head; 8 mm.
Tube; Black fine ribbed plastic.
Colour; Black.
PANTONE® Black 6 U 2X.
Print; Silver.
Base; Steel, brass coated.
Closure; Crimp, 6 fold.

PLATE 78

DRAWING HEADSTAMPINGS AND OVER-SHOT CARDS

Drawing headstampings and over-shot cards is not as difficult as it may look. I always draw these at double their size. I then get them reduced by half on a photo copy machine. This being fifty per cent reduction. For drawing these I keep two compasses by me. One fitted with a fine pointed pencil and the other fitted with a thick ball type pen. I often have to shave the outer plastic of the pen down to a smaller diameter to make it fit in the compass. With carpentry you always need to keep your tools sharp. Likewise with drawing, you do need to keep your pencils sharpened. By drawing them at exact double their size then enables you to set your compasses straight against the dimensions to be drawn. Myself, I prefer to work in millimetres. Do remember though that when you reduce your drawings back to normal size that the pen lines then become only half of their thickness. I usually first work out the positioning of all the letters. Once that I am satisfied with them, I then go over them with a drawing pen. If a mistake is made, it can be corrected by sticking a piece of white paper over it and then draw over the top. This paper should not show after it has been photo copied.

To help in positioning the letters or words on the stamping, I then devide my circle up into segments with thin pencil lines. Most times I will devide my circle into four making quarters of it. By placing a rule across the cartridge stamping you can then get a good sighting as to where you should draw in your individual letters. At the same time taking note as at what height say 12 12 or No 12 etc, will be positioned. You will find that they are not always centralized. After the pencil has been inked in, then any other light pencil lines can then be erased with a rubber eraser. You will often find that the two penciled circles made for the outer and inner of the circled wordings will also give you a part positioning for the numbers of the gauge markings.

One thing to remember about drawing. You need to sit down quietly and have patience. I started off by drawing the easy ones. As I got better at it, I then found that I wanted to try and draw those with more detail on them. I had the urge to take up the challenge. The more of it that you do, then the better at it you should become. The headstampings in this book have been drawn over very many years. That is why some are drawn better than others.

  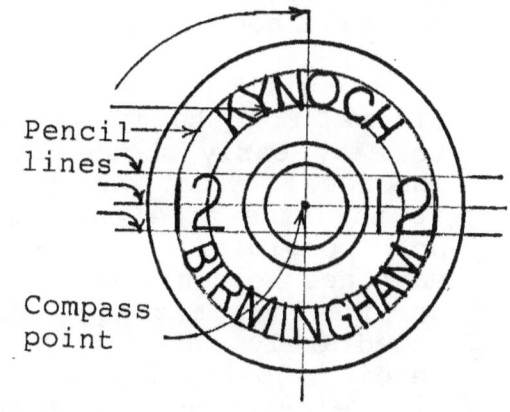

Tops and bottoms drawn at double size.　　　　　With pencil.

UNDERSTANDING THE HEADSTAMP LIST

Altogether there are 2,237 of my headstamp drawings which are all of interest to shotgun cartridge collectors and the many people that enjoy the history of the shotgun cartridge. These drawings have been made over a considerable period in time. Over the last decade or so I have drawn many shotgun cartridges. If a headstamping has been the same on more than one of my drawings, then I have not needed to draw this same stamping twice. This same thing also applied to the over-shot cards. This being so, I have kept a bank of my drawings of the tops and bottoms of many cartridges. These of the reduced drawings which should be at or around their actual size.

If I have not been able to have had an actual cartridge in front of me, or a clear photograph or foil rubbing, then I have not been able to make a drawing. There are hundreds of headstampings that I know of, but as yet, I have not been given the chance to draw them. Many of these are Australian or American. Likewise, old headstamps are literally being dug up every week by people using metal detectors.

You will see that I have shown various similaritys of some of the commoner stampings. Many of the other drawings shown may also have similaritys and also in various gauge sizes. To each of my drawings I have given a reference number. Should this number be followed by the letter R, this then denotes that it was a raised stamping. This practice was used on many very early shotgun cartridges. I have placed my drawings in a semi-alphabetical order. I have made the odd mistake in my alphabetical listing. Having done so there is no way that I could make a correction, but these mistakes are few.

Of all of these stampings, some of them I do know their histories. As there are so many others that I do not know about, I have decided not to place wordings under the drawings. I have left a little space under most of them and this will allow you to write in any notes of your own. Please do not write in telling me that I have missed some of them out. I am aware of this because I could not possibly draw all of them. In any case, I have not been given the chance to do so. Even as I am writing this, somewhere some firm will be busy producing some new ones. Many stampings by various firms have been similar. To give you an instance, the wordings SPECIAL SMOKELESS and SMOKELESS GASTIGHT have been in common use throughout the years and have been used in very many countries.

You will notice that some of the drawings have gone a little bit balloon shaped. Also that some vary in size. This is due to many early photo copy machines that were far from accurate. The ideal situation would have been to have had them all reduced at the same time on a modern machine. Regretfully, this is now not possible. Please remember, without those photo copy machines we could not have had this book. Due to a small number of drawings missing their alphabetical places, I have shown immediately after this listing these missed drawings under the heading 'Belated Additions'. Following on from this is some side elevations of general shotgun cartridges. These are drawn as having paper tubes. If plastic, there would be no seam.

THE
HEADSTAMPINGS

Pin Fire 83

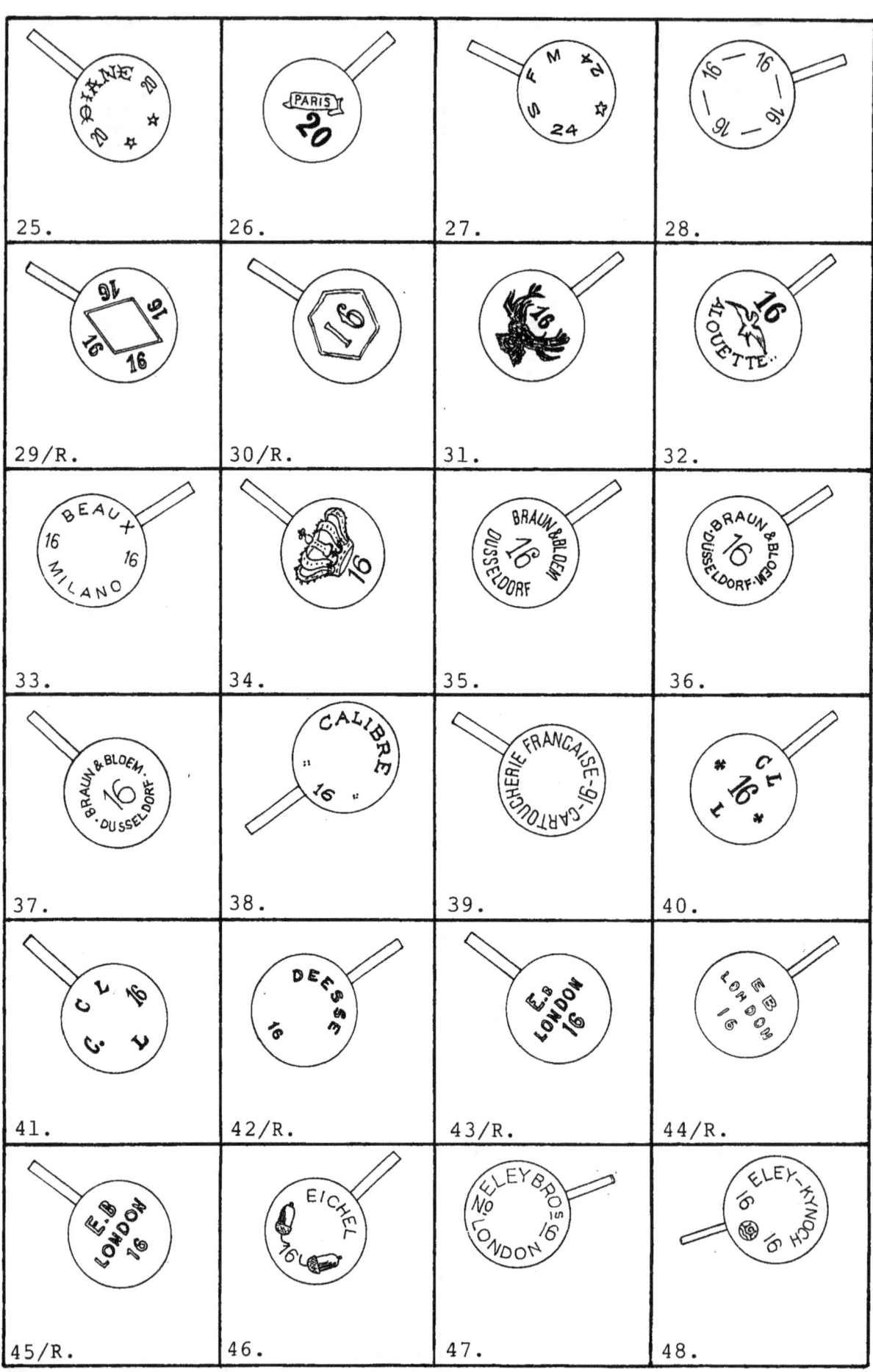

49. ELEY·LONDON Nº GASTIGHT 16	50./R. EXPOSITION 16	51. EXCELSIOR Nº △ 16	52. FF 16 16
53. GEVELOT FABRIQUE PARIS 16	54. FORTUNA 16 ✶ K	55. FORTUNA ✶ K 16	56. GEVELOT 16 PARIS
57. GJ 16 PARIS	58. HIRTENBERG ✶ 16 ✶	59. HIRTENBERG 16 K&C	60. J.HALL.STATION Rd.WIGTON KYNOCH Nº16
61. JOYCE & Cº Nº 16 LONDON	62. MARCEL GAUPILLAT 16 16	63. M·G&Cie 16 G.D.G. PARIS.16	64. NIMROD 16
65. ★ 16 S 16 P 16 R 16	66. PILONI 16 16 LECCO	67. PRIMER 16.	68. R.W.S 16 GASDICHT 16
69. SOCIETE MUNITIONS PARIS 16 16	70. SAMARITAINE 16 IMPORTE D'ITALIE 16	71./R. THOR 16	72. V 16 S K

Pin Fire 85

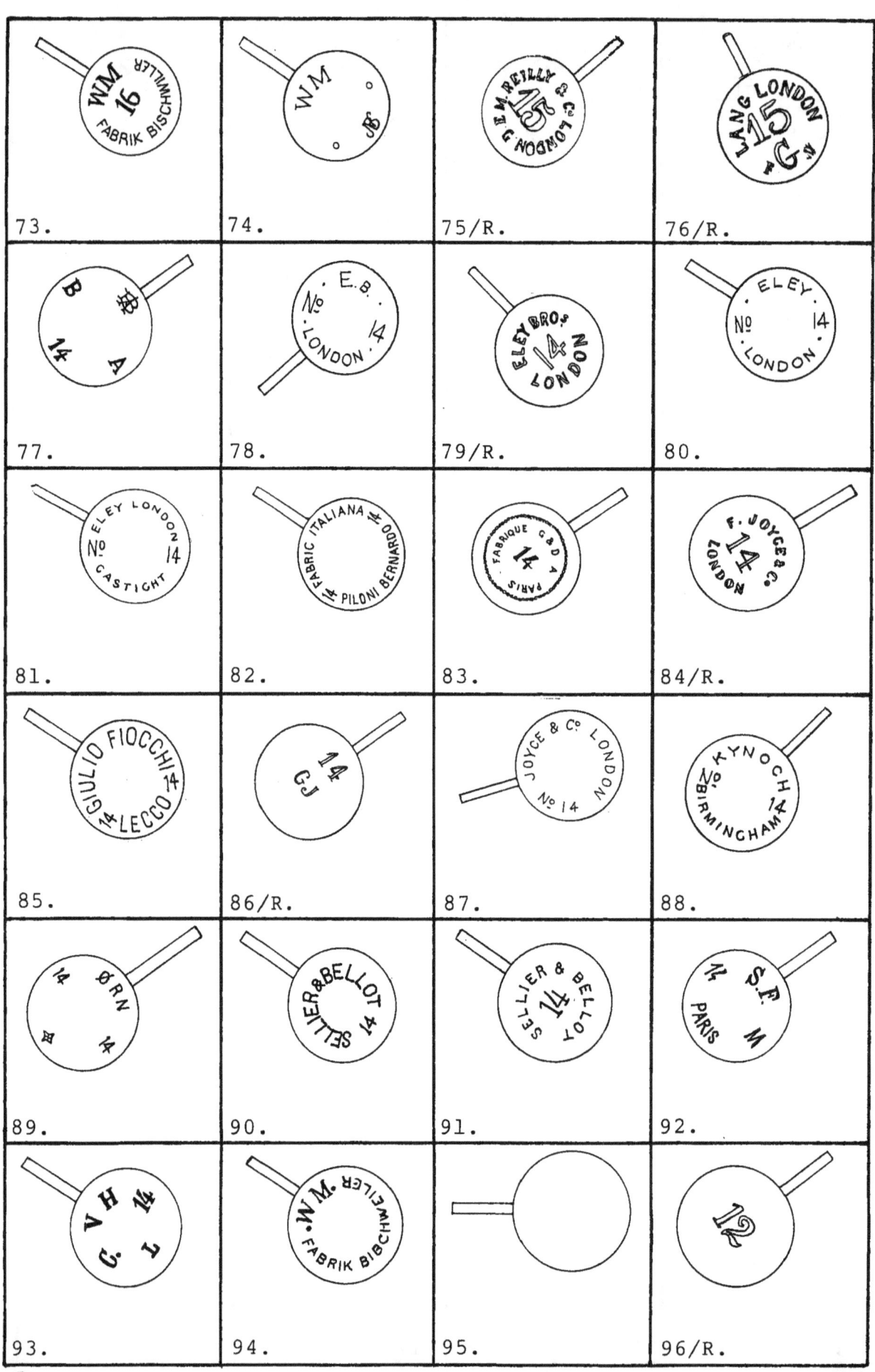

Pin Fire 86

97.	98.	99.	100.
101.	102.	103.	104.
105.	106.	107.	108/R.
109.	110.	111.	112.
113/R.	114.	115/R.	116/R.
117.	118.	119.	120/R.

Pin Fire 87

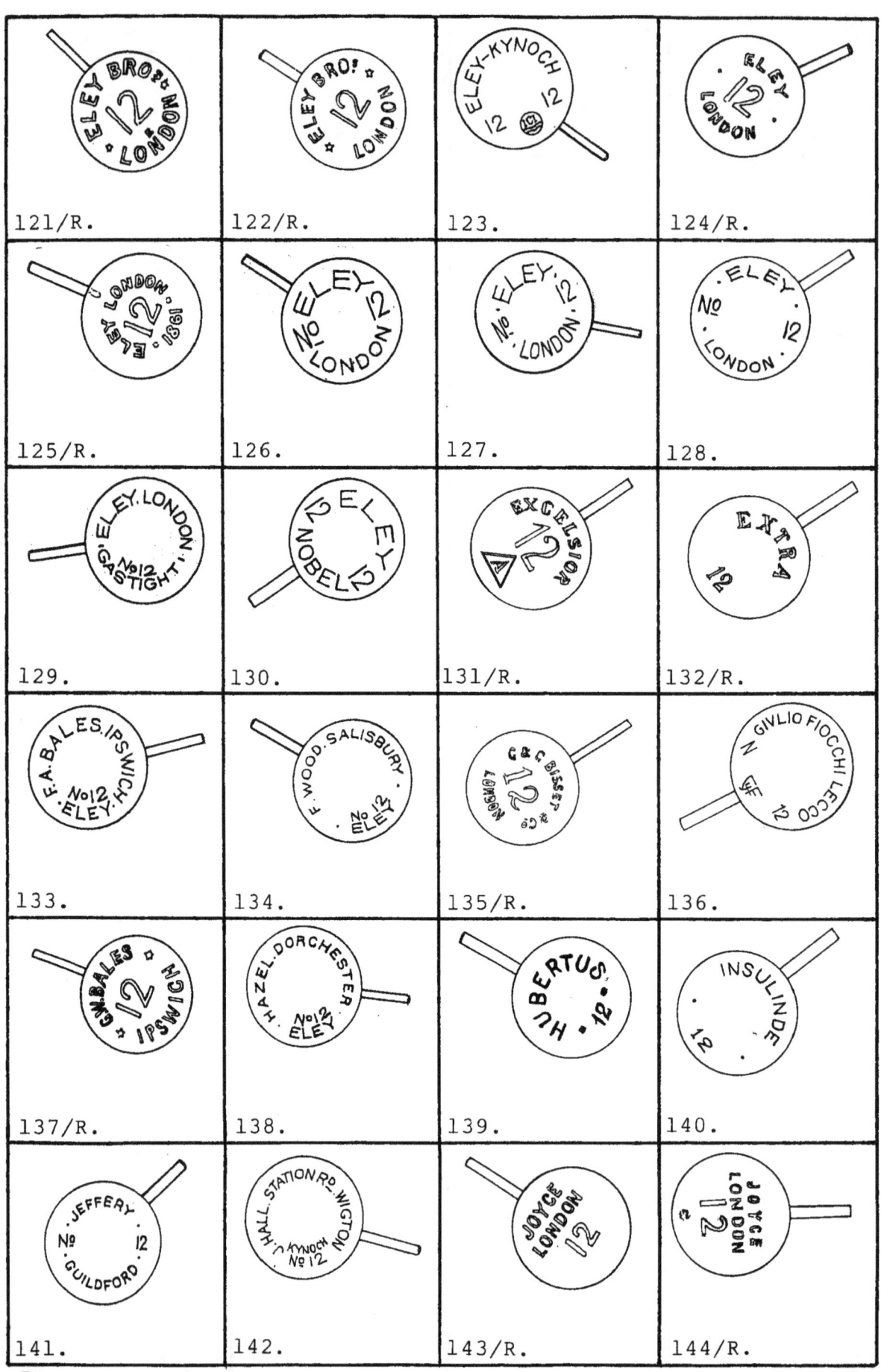

KENT & SON N°12 WANTAGE	KYNOCH N°12 BIRMINGHAM	KYNOCH'S N°12 PATENT	LB 12
145.	146.	147.	148/R.
L. BACHMANN 12 BREVETE	12 LERCAE	L.M & C° 12 WIEN	M. ARENDT 12 LIEGE
149.	150.	151/R.	152.
12 MARKE BLITZ 12	MARQUE DEPOSEE 12 UB PARIS	12 M.F ST ETIENNE 12	12 M.G & CIE PARIS
153.	154/R.	155.	156.
12 MUNITIONS 12 M.G.M	12 MRE FSE DARMES DE ST ETIENNE 12	MARQUE 12 AU LION DE	12 NEMROD 12
157.	158.	159.	160.
OAKES & C° MADRAS N°12 ELEY	12 P A R I S 12	P.J.C & C.IE 12	POND & SON N° BLANDFORD 12
161.	162.	163/R.	164.
POTTER N°12 HIGHWYCOMBE	PREMIATA FABBRICA ITALIANA PILONI BERNARDO 12 LECCO	12 PRIMA 12	PURDEY 12
165.	166.	167.	168/R.

Pin Fire 89

169/R. PURDEY 12	170. RODON 12	171. R.W.S 12	172. R.W.S. 12 GASDICHT
173. SPALE ARM 12	174. F.se DES MUNITIONS PARIS	175. STENNER & Co. TIVERTON. No 12. ELEY	176. 12 ST. ETIENNE 12
177. SVEA 12	178. No TEMPLE & Co BASINGSTOKE 12	179. No TEMPLE & Co BASINGSTOKE 12	180. 12 TRIOMPHE J.I.B 12
181/R. T.TURNER READING 12	182. T.TURNER & SONS READING No 12.	183. T.TURNER & SONS READING No 12. ELEY	184. V H 12 * L * 12
185/R. W.LEECH CHELMSFORD 12	186. WM 12 B	187. W.M. 12 FABRIK BISCHWILLER	188/R. J. LANG LONDON 11 GP
189. 10	190/R. ELEY BRO.s LONDON No 10	191/R. ELEY BRO.s LONDON No 10	192. ELEY. LONDON No 10 GASTIGHT

Pin Fire 90

FABRIQUE GEVELOT 10 PARIS 193.	FABRIQUE GEVELOT 10 G 10 PARIS 194.	GAMMA 10 MGM 195.	G.AUPILLAT PARIS 10 196.
KYNOCH * 10 * 197.	N° KYNOCH 10 BIRMINGHAM 198.	MARQUI AU LION 10 199.	N° B&B 8. D 200.
Fᵃ MONTMᵗʳᵉ 7 CHAUDUN PARIS 8 201/R.	Nº ELEY BROS LONDON 8 202/R.	N° ELEY.LONDON GASTIGHT 203.	R.W.S 8 204.
ELEY BROS 4 LONDON 205/R.	Francse des MUNITIONS PARIS 4 4 206.	FABRIQUE GEVELOT 32 MILLIM PARIS 207/R.	

Pin Fire 91

☆ 208. 9mm	Ⓔ 209.	Ⓔ 210.	Ⓖ 211.
ⒼⒻ 212.	ⓂⒼⓂ 213.		
(D&C.20 SOEMMERDA) 214.			
©			ⓀⓇ

Rim Fire 92

ELEY .360 215.	36 FIOCCHI 36 216.	36 FIOCCHI 36 ITALY 217.	218.
12mm / 12mm 219.	410 / 12m/m 220.	.410 221.	.410 222.
C-Ld IMPERIAL .410 223.	E .410 224.	E-K .410 225.	ELEY .410 226.
ELEY-KYNOCH .410 227.	ELEY-KYNOCH .410 228.	ELEY .410 LONDON 229.	FOREIGN MADE CASE .410 230.
GASTIGHT .410 231.	KYNOCH .410 232.	KYNOCH .410 233.	KYNOCH'S PATENT .410 234.
.410 MADE IN BELGIUM 235.	PETERS $10HV MADE IN USA 236.	REM-UMC .410 MADE IN USA 237.	WESTERN .410 MADE IN USA 238.

Central Fire 93

239. WW 410	240. 14 m/m	241. KYNOCH'S PATENT 14 m/m	242. MGM 14 m/m
243. KYNOCH Nº 32 BIRMINGHAM	244. MADE IN BELGIUM	245. W.W.GREENER Nº 32 LONDON BIRMINGHAM	246. 28 28
247. 28 28	248. 28 28 28 28	249. ELEY 28 28 ELEY	250. ELEY Nº 28 GASTIGHT
251. ELEY-KYNOCH 28 28	252. ELEY-KYNOCH 28 28	253. ELEY Nº 28 LONDON	254. ELEY.LONDON Nº 28 GASTIGHT
255. ELEY 28 28 NOBEL	256. FIOCCHI 28 28 ITALY	257. FIOCCHI 28 28 ITALY	258. GIULIO FIOCCHI LECCO 28
259. KYNOCH.BIRMINGHAM Nº 28	260. KYNOCH GROUSE Nº 28	261. KYNOCH'S PATENT	262. KYNOCH$PATENT Nº 28 GROUSE EJECTOR

Central Fire 94

Central Fire 95

287. CARTOUCHERIE FRANÇAISE -20-	288. CARTOUCHERIE 20 NATIONALE 20	289. C B C 20 20 C B C	290. CHARLES DALY 20
291. CHEDDITE 20	292. CHURCHILL FOREIGN 20 20 MADE CAR LONDON	293. C·L 20 20 CANUCK	294. C·I·L 20 20 IMPERIAL
295. CLEVER VERONA 20	296. CLEVER · VERONA ·20	297. DORHOUT MEES 20	298. ·E·B· No 20 LONDON
299. ELEY · · No 20	300. ELEY No 20 CANADA	301. ELEY 20 20 ELEY	302. ELEY 20 20 ELEY
303. ELEY No 20 GASTIGHT	304. ELEY-KYNOCH 20	305. ELEY-KYNOCH 20 20	306. ELEY-KYNOCH 20 20
307. ELEY-KYNOCH 20 20	308. ELEY-KYNOCH ICI AN 20 20 MADE IN AUSTRALIA	309. ELEY No 20 LONDON	310. ELEY No 20 LONDON

Central Fire 96

311. ELEY No 20 LONDON	312. ELEY No 20 LONDON	313. ELEY No 20 LONDON	314. ELEY No 20 LONDON
315. ELEY No 20 LONDON	316. ELEY No 20 LONDON	317. ELEY LONDON No 20 GASTIGHT	318. ELEY LONDON No 20 GASTIGHT
319. ELEY 20 20 NOBEL	320. ELEY 20 20 NOBEL	321. ELEY 20 20 NOBEL	322. ELEY'S No 20 EJECTOR LONDON
323. 20 EXPRESS	324. EDMOND PARIS ELEY No 20	325. FIOCCHI 20	326. 20 FIOCCHI 20 ITALY
327. 20 FIOCCHI MAX 900 BAR	328. FN 20 20 FN	329. F.T. BAKER LONDON 20	330. 20 GA MADE IN U.S.A.
331. 20 GAUGE BROWNING	332. GEVELOT 20 20 PARIS	333. GEVELOT 20 20 PARIS	334. GEVELOT 20 20 PARIS

GEVELOT 20 20 PARIS 335.	GREEN CHELTENHAM KYNOCH Nº 20 336.	GYTTORP 20 20 GYTTORP 337.	GYTTORP 20 20 MADE IN SWEDEN 338.
Holiday 20 20 GAUGE 339.	HOLLAND & HOLLAND 20 340.	HULL 20 20 CARTRIDGE 341.	JACK RABBIT Nº 20 A.A.CO. 342.
JAS R WATSON & CO 20 20 LONDON 343.	JOYCE Nº 20 LONDON 344.	JOYCE Nº 20 LONDON 345.	KAVANAGH & SON 20 20 DUBLIN 346.
KYNOCH Nº 20 347.	KYNOCH *20* 348.	Nº KYNOCH 20 BIRMINGHAM 349.	Nº KYNOCH 20 BIRMINGHAM 350.
KYNOCH N.L. 20 20 BIRMINGHAM 351.	KYNOCH B.T.L. 20 20 BONAX 352.	KYNOCH Nº 20 GASTIGHT 353.	KYNOCH Nº 20 GROUSE 354.
KYNOCH'S PATENT GROUSE Nº 20 355.	KYNOCH'S GROUSE Nº 20 EJECTOR PATENT 356.	KYNOCH PATENT Nº 20 Nº 2080 CROUSE EJECTOR 357.	Nº KYNOCH 20 SQUIRES, N.Y. 358.

L.B 20 · 359.	LIGNOSE 20 20 RAUCHLOS 360.	MAIONCHI 20 20 ITALY 361.	MAIONCHI 20 20 L.M.I. 362.
MANTON N° 20 CALCUTTA 363.	20 MARTIGNONI 20 GENOVA 364.	1901 N° 20 NEW RIVAL 365.	NITEDAL 20 366.
N° NOBEL 20 GLASGOW 367.	NOBEL-GLASGOW 20 20 N 368.	N° NOBEL'S 20 B BALLISTITE 369.	ORBEA 20 20 VITORIA 370.
PETERS 20 HV 371.	PETERS 20 VICTOR 372.	PRB 20 20 MADE IN BELGIUM 373.	PRINCE of WALES 20 S 374.
PURDEY & SONS N° 20 LONDON 375.	R.B.RODDA&Co N° 20 KYNOCH CALCUTTA 376.	R C 20 20 ITALY 377.	R C 20 20 ITALY 378.
REMINGTON 20 GA PETERS 379.	REM-UMC N° 20 Remington 380.	1901 N° 20 REPEATER 381.	ROSSON DERBY 20 NORWICH 382.

Central Fire 99

383. R.W.S. NURNBERG	384. RWS/GECO ROTTWEIL	385. RUSTLESS 20	386. SAGA LERIDA
387. SBC SPAULO	388. SBP MADE IN CECHOSLOVAKIA	389. SELLIER & BELLOT 20	390. SELLIER & BELLOT 20
391. SMI MADE IN ITALY	392. SMOKELESS 20	393. SMOKELESS GASTIGHT	394. SMOKELESS GASTIGHT
395. SNIABPD ITALY	396. SPECIAL GASTIGHT	397. SPECIAL GASTIGHT	398. SPECIAL SMOKELESS
399. SPECIAL SMOKELESS	400. SPECIAL SMOKELESS	401. SPECIAL SMOKELESS	402. STERLING LONDON
403. S & W USA	404. SWF USA	405. T. BLAND & SONS LONDON	406. TURNER READING & NEWBURY ELEY N°20

Central Fire 100

Central Fire 101

431.	432.	433.	434.
435.	436. HAJI DOSSUL & SONS, KARACHI, No 16, ELEY	437. ALCAN 16 16 MADE IN ITALY INCORPORATED	438. ARTHUR DENNIS No 16 DUNMOW
439. A.SANDERS, MAIDSTONE, No 16, ELEY	440. ATKIN No 16 ELEY'S EJECTOR	441. LOADED IN LONDON BY A.W.GAMAGE LTD. 0. HOLBORN. E.C. CASE MADE IN GERMANY No 16	442. CHAMBERLAIN No 16 ANDOVER
443. CHEDDITE 16 16 UNIVERSEL	444. CHURCHILL FOREIGN 16 16 MADE CASE LONDON	445. CHURCHILL MADE IN No 16 S.F.M. FRANCE LONDON	446. COOPPAL 16 16 WETTEREN
447. COX & SON No 16 SOUTHAMPTON	448. DANARMS 16	449/R. No DAWS 16 PATENT	450. DORHOUT MEES 16
451. E.B. No 16 LONDON	452. E.B. No 16 ELEY LONDON	453. E.CHAMBERLAIN, ANDOVER No 16 ELEY	454. ELEY 16 16 ELEY

Central Fire 102

455. ELEY No 16 GASTIGHT	456. ELEY-KYNOCH 16	457. ELEY-KYNOCH 16 ICI 16	458. ELEY-KYNOCH 16 ICI 16
459. ELEY-KYNOCH 16 ICI 16	460. ELEY No 16 LONDON	461. ELEY No 16 LONDON	462. ELEY No 16 LONDON
463. ELEY No 16 LONDON	464. ELEY No 16 LONDON	465. ELEY No 16 LONDON	466. ELEY.LONDON No 16 DAMP-PROOF
467. ELEY.LONDON No 16 GASTIGHT	468. ELEY LONDON No 16 GASTIGHT	469. ELEY LONDON 16 16 GASTIGHT	470. ELEY N.T. No 16 LONDON
471. ELEY'S EJECTOR No 16 LONDON	472. ELEY 16 16 NOBEL	473. ELEY 16 16 NOBEL	474/R. E.M.REILLY & Co No 16 LONDON
475. E*R No 16 ELEY.LONDON	476. FARMER No 16 LEIGHTON	477. FEDERAL No 16 HI-POWER	478. FEDERAL 16 GA MONARK

Central Fire 103

FIOCCHI 16 16 ITALY 479.	FIOCCHI 16 16 ITALY 480.	F.JOYCE&Co No 16 LONDON 481.	FLOBERT PARIS 16 482.
FLOBERT PARIS 16 483.	FLOBERT 16 16 PARIS 484.	FLOBERT 16 C.F. 16 PARIS 485.	FN 16 16 FN 486.
FN 16 16 MADE IN BELGIUM 487.	16 16 FREDERIKSVÆRK 488.	16 16 FREDERIKSVÆRK 489.	16 GA MADE IN U.S.A. 490.
GENSCHOW 16 16 NORMAL 491.	GEVELOT 16 16 LONDON 492.	GEVELOT 16 16 PARIS 493.	HAREN 16 16 LONDON 494.
H.ATKIN PATENT No 16 No 2090 2 JERMYN STREET 495.	HASLOCH 16 16 NORMAL 496.	H.B. No 16 FISHER 497.	H.CLARKE & SONS. LEICESTER. No 16 498.
H.CLARKE No 16 LEICESTER 499.	A.HENRY.EDINBURGH. No 16 500.	HIRTENBERGER ☆ 16 ☆ 501.	HUSSEY, 81 NEW BOND ST. No 16 H.ELEY. 502.

Central Fire 104

HOLLAND & HOLLAND 16	HOLLAND & HOLLAND No 16 ELEY	HULL CARTRIDGE 16 16	H. UTENDOERFFER NURNBERG 16 RWS N 16
503.	504.	505.	506.
IMPERIA NDXYD 16 M.G.M 16	JACK RABBIT No 16 A.A.Co	J. BURROW No 16 PRESTON	JOHNSON & WRIGHT NORTHAMPTON No 16
507.	508.	509.	510.
JOYCE No 16 LONDON	JOYCE No 16 LONDON	JOYCE & Co No 16 LONDON CHECK BAILEY'S PATENT GAS	J. SWINFEN. MAIDSTONE No 16 ELEY
511.	512.	513.	514.
KAPSELO 16 16 KAUKLAHTI	KRIEGSPATRONE 16	KYNOCH 16	KYNOCH * * 16
515.	516.	517.	518.
No KYNOCH 16 BIRMINGHAM	No KYNOCH 16 BIRMINGHAM	KYNOCH N.T. 16 16 BIRMINGHAM	KYNOCH 16 16 NOBEL
519.	520.	521.	522.
No KYNOCH'S 16 PATENT	KYNOCH'S PATENT No 16 EXPERT SHELL SQUIRES. N.Y.	KYNOCH'S B.TTER. No B. 16 W.COEL.N.Y. PATENT	KYNOCH No 16 "PERFECT"
523.	524.	525.	526.

Central Fire 105

MACPHERSON Nº 16 KYNOCH INVERNESS	16 16 MADE IN HOLLAND	Made in Hungary ⋆ 16 ⋆	MAIONCHI – L.M. – 16 –
527.	528.	529.	530.
MAIONCHI L.M.I. 16	MAIONCHI 16 16 L.M.I.	MALLARD 16 16 C.C.Cº	16 MARTIGNONI 16 GENOVA
531.	532.	533.	534.
METROPOLE 16	MILBURN & SON Nº 16 BRAMPTON	MUNITIONSWERKE 16 16 SCHOENEBECK a/E	1901 Nº 16 NEW RIVAL
535.	536.	537.	538.
NOBEL Nº 16 GLASGOW	NOBEL-GLASGOW 16 16 N	NORMAL KYNOCH'S PATENT Nº 16 CROUSE EJECTOR POWDER Cº	PAWAM 16 16 PIONKI
539.	540.	541.	542.
PETERS Nº 16 LEAGUE	PETERS Nº 16 LEAGUE	PETERLONGO 16 16 INNSBRUCK	POINTER 16 16 C.C.Cº
543.	544.	545.	546.
PULVERFABRIK 16 16 HASLOCH a/MAIN	PURDEY & SONS Nº 16 ZELEY'S EJECTOR	R.C.C. 16 16 LEAGUE	REMINGTON 16 GA PETERS
547.	548.	549.	550.

Central Fire 106

REM-UMC CASE MADE No 16 IN USA Remington 551.	1901 No 16 REPEATER 552.	R HOWSE FRENCH 16 16 MADE CASE SOUTH HILL FAIRFORD 553.	ROTTWEIL 16 16 NORMAL 554.
RUSTLESS 16 555.	RWS/GECO 16 16 ROTTWEIL 556.	RWS/GECO 16 16 ROTTWEIL 557.	S B P 16 16 MADE IN CZECHOSLOVAKIA 558.
SBP 16 16 MADE IN CZECHOSLOVAKIA 559.	SEARS 16 GA TED WILLIAMS 560.	SELLIER & BELLOT 16 561.	S.F.M 16 16 GEVELOT 562.
SMOKELESS 16 16 GASTIGHT 563.	SMOKELESS 16 16 GASTIGHT 564.	SMOKELESS 16 16 GASTIGHT 565.	SMOKELESS 16 16 GASTIGHT 566.
SMOKELESS FOREIGN 16 16 MADE CASE GASTIGHT 567.	SMOKELESS 16 16 MADE IN ENGLAND 568.	SMOKELESS R.W. CASE 16 16 NUREMBERG GASTIGHT 569.	SNIA 16 16 ITALY 570.
SNIABPD 16 16 ITALY 571.	SPARTAN ☆ ☆ 16 572.	SPARTAN 16 16 FRANCE 573.	SPARTAN 16 16 FRANCE 574.

Central Fire 107

SPECIAL 16 16 SMOKELESS 575.	SPECIAL 16 16 SMOKELESS 576.	SPECIAL 16 16 SMOKELESS 577.	SPECIAL 16 16 SMOKELESS 578.
SPECIAL CASE MADE IN 16 16 GERMANY SMOKELESS 579.	SPECIAL FOREIGN MADE CASE 16 16 SMOKELESS 580.	STANDARD 16 16 TYPE CHAMPIONNAT 581.	T.BLAND&SONS 16 16 LONDON 582.
TEC 16 16 TEC 583.	"T-RASET" 16 584.	TRENT FOREIGN MADE 16 16 LOADED IN ENGLAND BY TRENT-GRIMSBY 585.	TURNER, READING & NEWBURY No 16 ELEY 586.
U.M.C.CO. No 16 HIGH-BASE 587.	U.M.C.CO. No 16 MAGIC 588.	U.M.C.CO. No 16 NEW CLUB 589.	U.M.C.CO. No 16 NITRO 590.
U.M.C.CO. No 16 UNION 591.	WALSRODE 16 SINOX 16 NORMAL 592.	W.DARLOW No 16 BEDFORD 593.	WESTERN No 16 FIELD 594.
WESTERN MADE IN U.S.A. No 16 SUPER-X 595.	BRIGHTON & HAILSHAM KYNOCH M. No 16 M. 596.	WESTON, BRIGHTON & HAILSHAM KYNOCH 9 No 16 M. WESTON 597.	WINCHESTER 16 GA WESTERN 598.

Central Fire 108

599. WINCHESTER MADE IN ITALY No 16 SUPER-SPEED	600. WINCHESTER 16 16 WINCHESTER	601. W.J. JEFFERY & Co LTD 16 16 FOREIGN MADE CASE LONDON	602. Wm RICHARDS No 16 PRESTON
603. WOLFF & Co 16 16 WALSRODE	604. W.R. PAPE No 16 NEWCASTLE	605. W-W 16 GAUGE	606. W.W. GREENER No 16
607. W.W. GREENER No 16 LONDON BIRMINGHAM	608. XTRA-RANGE No 16 J.C. HIGGINS	609. J.W. COLLATH FRANKFURT	610. COGSWELL & HARRISON 14 LONDON
611. C. LANCASTER LONDON No 14	612/R. ELEY BROs No 14 LONDON	613. ELEY No 14 LONDON	614. ELEY 14 14 NOBEL
615. GEO.G.BUSSEY & Co No 14 LONDON	616. G.K No 14 LONDON	617. GRENFELL & ACCLES 14 BIRMINGHAM	618. KYNOCH No 14 BIRMINGHAM
619. KYNOCH'S "GROUSE" No 14 PATENT No 2090	620. KYNOCH'S No 14 PATENT	621. KYNOCH'S No 14 PATENT	622. LEON BEAUX 14 MILANO 14

Central Fire 109

623. NARQUE 14 AU LION	624. NOBEL-GLASGOW 14 14 N	625. RAUFOSS 14	626. TURNER CASE MADE 14 14 IN FRANCE READING
627. WESTERN Nº 14 XPERT — Smaller diam than British 14.	628. U.M.C.Cº BRIDGEPORT CONN.	629.	630. 12 12 12g
631. 12 12	632. 12 GA	633. 12 GA	634. 12 12 12 12
635. 12 12 12 12	636. 12 12	637.	638. 12 12g
639. 12	640. Nº 12	641. Nº 12	642. Nº 12
643. Nº 12	644/R. 12 12	645/R. 12 12	646. 12 12

Central Fire 110

Central Fire 111

Central Fire 112

695. A.A.HODGSON KYNOCH LOUTH No 12
696. A.ALLAN GLASGOW No 12
697. A.BARNES ULVERSTON No 12
698. ABARTO ESPANA 12 12
699. AB-LEIBNITZ 12
700. A.B.WYLIE WARWICK No 12
701. ACCLES,LIMITED BIRMINGHAM No 12
702. A.CHAMBERLAIN.SALISBURY.ELEY No12
703. A.CHAMBERLAIN KYNOCH'S PATENT GROUSE EJECTOR SALISBURY No 12
704. A.CONYERS BLANDFORD ELEY No 12
705. ACTIV 12
706. ACTIV 12
707. ADAMS & CO. FINSBURY. LONDON. No12
708. ADGEY & MURPHY FRENCH MADE CASE BELFAST No 12
709. ADLER-MARKE 12
710. A.E.1301 INT.PAT.
711. A.E.RINGWOOD BANBURY 12 12
712. A.E.RINGWOOD MADE IN BANBURY 12 12
713. A.E.WARREN KYNOCH WINDSOR No 12
714. A.F.PUNTER BASINGSTOKE No 12
715. A.F.PUNTER BASINGSTOKE No 12
716. A.F.SMITH HAILSHAM No 12
717. AGNEW & SON EXETER No12
718. AGNEW & SON ELEY EXETER No 12

Central Fire 113

12 12 AGUILA	A.HILL No 12 HORNCASTLE	A.J.DUKES.RUGBY No 12 ELEY	A.J.JEWSON No 12 KYNOCH HALIFAX
719.	720.	721.	722.
A.J.RUSSELL & SONS No 12 KYNOCH MAIDSTONE	ALCAN 12 12 INCORPORATED	ALCAN MADE IN USA 12 12 ALCAN	ALCAN MADE IN USA 12 12 INCORPORATED
723.	724.	725.	726.
ALCOCK & PIERCE No 12 KYNOCH MELBOURNE	ALCOCK & PIERCE ELEY No 12 LONDON MELBOURNE	ALTHAM & SON.PENRITH No.12 ELEY	AMER.ROCK 12 EXPRESS
727.	728.	729.	730.
A.&N.C.S.L No 12 BOMBAY	A.&N.C.S.L No 12 BOMBAY	A.&N.C.S.L No 12 LONDON	A.&N.C.S.LD ELEY No 12 LONDON
731.	732.	733.	734.
A.&N.C.S.LTD No 12 KYNOCH	ANGLIA CARTRIDGE Co 12	ANGLIA CARTRIDGE Co 12	FRANCE·ARMES 12
735.	736.	737.	738.
ARMSTRONG & Co. NEWCASTLE No 12	ARMSTRONG & Co 12 12 NEWCASTLE-UPON-TYNE	ARMSTRONG ELEY NEWCASTLE-ON-TYNE	ARMSTRONG'S PRESSURE REDUCING CASE. KYNOCH No 12
739.	740.	741.	742.

Central Fire 114

ARMSTRONG & CO RECOIL 12 REDUCING NEWCASTLE-UPON-TYNE	ARMUNIT·S 12	ARMURIERS PROFESSIONNELS 12	12 ARMURIERS 12 PROFESSIONNELS
743.	744.	745.	746.
ARMUSA 12 12 ARMUSA	ARMUSA 12 12 ARMUSA	ARMUSA 12 12 SPAIN	ARMY & NAVY C.S.L No12 ELEY
747.	748.	749.	750.
ARMY & NAVY C.S.L No12 LONDON	ARROW 12 GA EXPRESS	ARTHUR ALLAN No 12 GLASGOW	ASAHI 12 12 SKB
751.	752.	753.	754.
ASAHI 12 12 SKB	A.T.FITCHEW No 12 RAMSGATE	ATKIN.2.JERMYN ST.S.W. No12 ELEY	ATKIN.41.JERMYN ST.S.W. No12 ELEY
755.	756.	757.	758.
ATKIN.41.JERMYN ST.S.W. No12 ELEY	ATKINSON No 12 LANCASTER & KENDAL	ATKINSON No 12 ELEY LANCASTER	ATKINSON No 12 LANCASTER & KENDAL
759.	760.	761.	762.
ATKINSON No 12 ELEY LANCASTER & KENDAL	AUBREY LEWIS 12 12 LUTON	AUBREY LEWIS CASE MADE IN 12 BELGIUM 12 LUTON	A.U.DUKES.RUGBY No12 ELEY
763.	764.	765.	766.

Central Fire 115

12 GA AUSTRALIA 767.	AUTOCRAT 12 12 R.H.A.CO 768.	AVERILL & SON No 12 EVESHAM 769.	AVORENKAMP 12 12 GRONINGEN 770.
LOADED IN LONDON FOR A.W.GAMAGE CASE MADE IN GERMANY No 12 HOLBORN E.C. 771.	✯✯✯ 12 63 AZOT 772.	AZOT 12 12 MADE IN USSR 773.	AZOT 12 12 MADE IN USSR 774.
AZOT 12 66 MADE IN USSR 775.	BACHMANN 12 12 BRUXELLES 776.	BAIKAL 12 12 65 777.	BAIKAL 12 12 MADE IN USSR 778.
BAIKAL 12 12 MADE IN USSR 779.	BAILEY No 12 GAS-LEAK-PROOF 780.	BAKER No 12 DARLINGTON 781.	BAKER KYNOCH'S PATENT No 12 GROUSE No 2090 LONDON 782.
BALLS BROS No 12 NEWTON ABBOT 783.	BALMFORTH.ORMSKIRK No 12 ELEY 784.	BARNARD & LEVET No 12 C.H.M.C. LICHFIELD 785.	BARNES No 12 CALNE 786.
8 pellagri-12-baschieri 787.	LA GA-12-BASCHIERI 788.	12 BB 789.	BEAUX 12 12 MILANO 790.

Central Fire 116

791. Leon Beaux & Co (Milano)	792. Beesley London Kynoch's Patent Grouse No 2090	793. Bisley / Bisley	794. Bisley / Bisley
795. B. & J.V. Coultas, Grantham	796. B. & J.V. Coultas, Grantham	797. Blanch & Son, London	798. Blitz / Blitz
799. Bond & Son, Thetford	800. Bond & Son, Eley, Thetford	801. Bond & Son, Eley, Thetford	802. Boreham, Colchester
803. Bornachi, Italy	804. Bornaghi, Italy	805. Boss, London	806. Boss & Co, London
807. Boss & Co, London	808. Boss & Co London, Eley	809. Boss & Co, Kynoch, London	810. Believe to be canceled.
811. Boss & Co, Kynoch's Patent Grouse No 2090, London	812. BPD, Italy	813. B.P.D., Roma	814. B.P.D., Roma

Central Fire 117

815. BRADDELL & SON. BELFAST. No 12	816. BRITAM 12 / BRITAM 12	817. BRITISH MADE LONDON 12	818. BRITISH MADE LONDON 12
819. BRITISH 12 12 MAKE	820. BROWN No 12 MORPETH	821. BROWN No 12 MORPETH	822. BROWNING 12
823. BROWNING 12 12 BROWNING	824. 12 GAUGE BROWNING	825. BSA 12	826. BUFFALO MADE IN USA 12 12 BUFFALO
827. BULLS-EYE No 12 ELEY	828. BURROW. PRESTON No 12 ELEY	829. B.WARREN No 12 KYNOCH WINDSOR	830. CAC 12 12 CAC
831. C.A.C 12 12 N.Z	832. C.A.C 12 12 N.Z	833. C.A.C 12 12 N.Z	834. No 12 CAC RABBIT SHOT BOARD
835. No 12 C.A.C. RABBIT BOARD SHOT	836. CAL 12 12 GA	837. CARLSBAD No 12 AMMO CO	838. CARTOUCHERIE FRANÇAISE. 12.

Central Fire 118

839. C.A.V.I.M. CAL. 12	840. CBC 12 12 CBC	841. C.BOSWELL No 12 KYNOCH 126.STRAND	842. C.BOSWELL KYNOCH'S PATENT GROVE No 12 No 2090 126 STRAND
843. C 12 12 C	844. 12 C C 12	845. C.D.WILLIAMS No 12 KYNOCH BELFAST	846. C.FLETCHER No 12 LEEDS
847. C.G.A.GASTIGHT No 12 KYNOCH	848. C.G.A.WATERPROOF No 12 KYNOCH	849. CHAMBERLAIN ANDOVER No 12	850. CHAMBERLAIN No 12 SALISBURY
851. CHAMBERS No 12 KYNOCH BRISTOL&CARDIFF	852. CHAMBERS No 12 DUNSTABLE	853. CHARLES DALY 12	854. CHARLES HELLIS & SONS No 12
855. CHARLES HELLIS & SONS No 12	856. CHARLES ROSSON 12 12 DERBY	857. CHARLES ROSSON 12 ELEY 12 DERBY	858. CHAS. LANCASTER No 12 KYNOCH LONDON
859. CHAS.E.LANE No 12 PETERCHURCH	860. CHEDDITE 12	861. CHEDDITE 12	862. CHEDDITE 12 ITALIA 12

Central Fire 119

CHEDDITE 12 UNIVERSEL 12	C.H.SPORCO 12 12 LIEGE	S.CHURCHILL.OND ELEY No 12 AGAR ST. STRAND	CHURCHILL MADE IN No 12 8 AGAR ST STRAND
863.	864.	865.	866.
CHURCHILL FOREIGN 12 12 MADE CASE LONDON	CHURCHILL FRENCH 12 SFM 12 MADE CASE LONDON	CHURCHILL MADE IN No 12 FRANCE LONDON	CHURCHILL MADE IN No 12 FRANCE LONDON
867.	868.	869.	870.
C.H.WESTON.BRIGHTON C.&H. No12 ELEY	C-I-L 12 12 CANUCK	C-I-L 12 12 IMPERIAL	C.LANCASTER.LONDON No12 ELEY
871.	872.	873.	874.
C.LANCASTER No 12 ELEY'S R EJECTOR	C. CLARKE No 12 SALISBURY	CLARKE & DYKE No 12 SALISBURY	CLARKE & DYKE No 12 SOUTHAMPTON
875.	876.	877.	878.
CLIMAX SHELL MADE IN U.S.A. 12 12 LOADED IN AUSTRALIA	C.L.LANE 12 12 BRIDGWATER	C.L 12 12 MADE IN BELGIUM	CLEVER 12 12 MIRAGE
879.	880.	881.	882.
CLEVER · VERONA · 12 ·	CLEVER · VERONA 12	CLEVER · VERONA ·12·	CLEVER · VERONA ·12·
883.	884.	885.	886.

Central Fire 120

CLEVER 12 12 VERONA	C.NAYLOR No 12 SHEFFIFLD	C.NAYLOR No 12 SHEFFIFLD	C.NAYLOR No 12 KYNOCH SHEFFIELD
887.	888.	889.	890.
C.O.Co No 12	COGSCHULTZE 12 12 LONDON	COGSCHULTZE 12 12 LONDON	COGSWELL & HARRISON ·12·
891.	892.	893.	894.
COGSWELL & HARRISON LTD No 12	COGSWELL & HARRISON LTD 12	COGSWELL & HARRISON LTD No 12 ELEY	COGSWELL & HARRISON 12 LONDON 12
895.	896.	897.	898.
COGSWELL & HARRISON 12 LONDON 12	COGSWELL & HARRISON 12 LONDON 12	COGSWELL KYNOCH'S No 12 PATENT GROUSE & HARRISON	COGSWELL & HARRISON KYNOCH PATENT GROUSE EJECTOR LTD No 12
899.	900.	901.	902.
COGSWELL & HARRISON KYNOCH'S PATENT LTD GROUSE EJECTOR No 12	COGSWELL & HARRISON LTD 12 PARIS 12	COGSWELL ET HARRISON *12*	COLE & SON No 12
903.	904.	905.	906.
COLE & SON No 12 DEVIZES	COLE & SON No 12 KYNOCH DEVIZES	COLONIAL AMMUNITION No 12 COMPANY, LIMITED	COLTMAN FOREIGN 12 12 MADE CASE BURTON
907.	908.	909.	910.

Central Fire 121

911. COLTMAN FOREIGN 12 12 MADE CASE BURTON	912. COLTMAN FOREIGN 12 12 MADE CASE BURTON	913. COLTMAN & Co FRENCH No 12 CASE BURTON	914. CONYERS DRIFFIELD BLANDFORD & POCKLINGTON ELEY No 12
915. COOPPAL 12 12 MADE IN BELGIUM	916. COOPPAL 12 12 WETTEREN	917. COX & CLARKE No 12 SOUTHAMPTON	918. COX & CLARKE No 12 KYNOCH SOUTHAMPTON
919. COX & SON No 12 KYNOCH SOUTHAMPTON	920. C. PARSONS No 12 NUNEATON	921. C. PINDER No 12 BASINGSTOKE	922. C. PINDER & Co No 12 BASINGSTOKE
923. C. PLAYFAIR & Co No 12 ABERDEEN	924. C. PLAYFAIR & Co No 12 ELEY ABERDEEN	925. C. SMITH & SONS No 12 NEWARK	926. C. SMITH & SONS NEWARK KYNOCH'S PATENT GROUSE No 2090 No 12
927. CURTIS'S & HARVEY Ltd No 12 LONDON	928. CURTIS'S & HARVEY Ltd No 12 LONDON	929. CURTIS'S & HARVEY Ld No 12 LONDON EB L	930. CURTIS'S & HARVEY Ld ELEY No 12 LONDON
931. CURTIS'S & HARVEY ELEY No 12 LONDON	932. CURTIS'S & HARVEY No 12 G.K & Co LONDON	933. *CW-GB* 12 *CW-GB*	934. DAINTITH KYNOCH PATENT No 12 GROUSE EJECTOR WARRINGTON

Central Fire 122

935. DANARMS 12	936. DANARMS 12 DANARMS 12	937. DAP 12 12 ITALY GF	938. DARLOW No 12 BEDFORD
939. DAVIDSON No 12 WELLS	940. DAVIDSON No 12 KYNOCH WELLS	941. DECATHLON ☆ 12 ☆	942. DECATHLON ☆ 12 ☆
943. D.GRAY & Co Y. INVERNESS No 12 ELEY	944. DICKSON 12 12 EDINBURGH	945. DIGBY No 12 SHAFTSBURY	946. DIRCKS-BEATH No 12 AMMO CO
947. DIXIE 12 12 S.C.CO	948. DIXON & Co No 12 KYNOCH ASTON	949. DIXON & Co No 12 KYNOCH BIRMINGHAM	950. DOBSON & ROSSON DERBY No 12
951. DOMINION MADE IN No 12 CANADA IMPERIAL	952. DORHOUT MEES 12	953. DOUILLERE 12 12 FRANCAISE	954. DOUILLERIE 12 12 FRANCAISE
955. DP 12	956. D.WALES.YARMOUTH No 12 ELEY	957. No D.WILLIAMSON 12 LONDON	958. DYER & ROBSON.H.R.B.L?. LON No 12

Central Fire 123

959. Nº 12 / E (crown)	960. Eatonia Shell 12 12	961. EB Nº 12 ELEY LONDON	962. EB Nº 12 ELEY LONDON
963/R. EB Nº 12 LONDON	964. E.B. Nº 12 LONDON	965. E.CHAMBERLAIN Nº 12 ANDOVER	966. CHAMBERLAIN ANDOVER Nº 12 ELEY
967. E.CHAMBERLAIN Nº 12 KYNOCH ANDOVER	968. 12 12 ECLAIR	969. ECLIPSE 12 GA	970. ECLIPSE 12 12 R.H.A.CO.
971. ECO 12 12	972. E.C. 12 12 POWDER	973. E.C.POWDER Nº 12 ELEY EJECTOR	974. EDMONDS & WELLDON Nº 12 RUGBY
975. EDWARDS & SON Nº 12 BELGIAN MADE SHELL PLYMOUTH	976. EDWINSON GREEN -12-	977. EDWINSON GREEN KYNOCH -12-	978. EDWINSON GREEN KYNOCH 12
979. E F HART CLARE Nº 12 ELEY	980/R. E.&G.HIGHAM Nº 12 LIVERPOOL	981. EICHEL 12	982. E.J.BROWN & Cº Nº 12 ROTHERHAM

Central Fire 124

983. E.J. CHURCHILL / KYNOCH'S PATENT GROUSE / No. 2090 / 8 AGAR ST STRAND / 12	984/R. ELEY BROS / No 12 / LONDON	985/R. ELEY BROS / No 12 / LONDON	986. ELEY / 12 12 / ELEY
987. ELEY / 12 12 / ELEY	988. ELEY / 12 12 / ELEY	989. ELEY / No EJECTOR / 12	990. ELEY / No 12 / GASTIGHT
991. ELEY / No 12 / GASTIGHT	992. ELEY "GRAND PRIX" / 12	993. ELEY-KYNOCH / 12	994. ELEY / 12 12 / KYNOCH
995. ELEY-KYNOCH / 12 ICI 12	996. ELEY-KYNOCH / 12 ICI 12	997. ELEY-KYNOCH / 12 ICI 12	998. ELEY-KYNOCH / 12 ICI 12
999. ELEY-KYNOCH / 12 ICI 12	1,000. ELEY-KYNOCH / 12 ICI 12	1,001. ELEY-KYNOCH / 12 ICI 12	1,002. ELEY-KYNOCH / 12 ICI 12
1,003. ELEY-KYNOCH / 12 12	1,004. ELEY-KYNOCH / 12 12 / ICIANZ	1,005. ELEY-KYNOCH / 12 12 / ICIANZ	1,006. ELEY-KYNOCH / I.C.I.A.N.Z. / 12 12 / MADE IN AUSTRALIA

Central Fire 125

1,007.	1,008.	1,009.	1,010.
1,011.	1,012.	1,013.	1,014.
1,015.	1,016.	1,017.	1,018.
1,019.	1,020.	1,021.	1,022.
1,023.	1,024.	1,025.	1.026.
1,027.	1,028.	1,029.	1,030.

Central Fire 126

ELEY LONDON No 12 GASTIGHT 1,031.	ELEY LONDON No 12 NITRO BALL 1,032.	ELEY 12 12 NOBEL 1,033.	ELEY 12 12 NOBEL 1,034.
ELEY 12 12 NOBEL 1,035.	ELEY 12 12 NOBEL 1,036.	ELEY 12 12 NOBEL 1,037.	ELEY 12 12 NOBEL 1,038.
ELEY 12 12 NOBEL 1,039.	No ELEY 12 "WATERPROOF" PEGAMOID 1,040.	No ELEY 12 "WATERPROOF" PEGAMOID 1,041.	ELEY 12 12 P.R.B 1,042.
ELEY 12 12 P.R.B 1,043.	ELEY-ROCKET 12 1,044.	No ELEY'S 12 EJECTOR 1,045.	ELEY'S No 12 EJECTOR LONDON 1,046.
12 12 +ELITE+ 1,047.	ELLICOTT CONED BASE CASE No 12 PATENT No 1814 CARDIFF 1,048.	ELLICOTT No 12 LAUNCESTON 1,049.	E... No 12 LONDON 1,050/R.
E No 12 LONDON 1,051/R.	E No 12 LONDON 1,052/R.	E.M.REILLY & Co ELEY No 12 1,053.	E.P.CARR No 12 KYNOCH NOTTINGHAM 1,054.

Central Fire 127

ERMITAGE 12 12	ERRE 12 12 ITALY	E.R.T. 12 12 ESPAÑA	E.R.T. 12 12 ESPAÑA
1,055.	1,056.	1,057.	1,058.
E.R.T. 12 12 ESPAÑA	ESTATE 12 GA CARTRIDGE	E-SUMMONTE 12 12 ERCOLAND	EUROCOMM 12 12 ITALY
1,059.	1,060.	1,061.	1,062.
EUROPA 12 12 EUROPA	EVANS Nº KYNOCHS PATENT GROUSE ELECTOR 12 LONDON	E.WEST.RETFORD KYNOCH Nº12	E.WILSON.NORWICH Nº12 ELEY
1,063.	1,064.	1,065.	1,066.
Nº E.WOODS 12 LONDON	EXCHEM 12 12 MARK	EXCOPEA 12 12 SPAIN	12 EXPRESS
1,067.	1,068.	1,069.	1,070.
EXPRESS 12	EXPRESS 12	EXTRA DEEP 12 12 GASTIGHT	EXTRA 12 12 MG
1,071.	1,072.	1,073.	1,074.
FABRICATION FRANÇAISE 12 12	FALKE ☆ ☆ 12	FARMER Nº 12 LEIGHTON	FEDERAL 12 GA CARTRIDGE
1,075.	1,076.	1,077.	1,078.

Central Fire 128

FEDERAL 12 GA GOLD MEDAL	FEDERAL Nº 12 HI-POWER	FEDERAL 12 GA HI-POWER	FEDERAL Nº 12 MONARK
1,079.	1,080.	1,081.	1,082.
FEDERAL 12 GA STEEL	N.F.E.WALKER Nº 12 NEWBURY	N.F.H.TIMS Nº 12 TRURO	FIOCCHI 12
1,083.	1,084.	1,085.	1,086.
FIOCCHI 12 12 HELLAS	FIOCCH 12 12 HELLAS	FIOCCHI 12 12 INT.L	FIOCCHI 12 12 INNOCENTI
1,087.	1,088.	1,089.	1,090.
FIOCCHI 12 12 INT.L	FIOCCHI 12 12 ITALY	FIOCCHI 12 12 ITALY	FIOCCHI 12 12 ITALY
1,091.	1,092.	1,093.	1,094.
FIOCCHI 12 12 ITALY	FIOCCHI 12 12 ITALY	FIOCCHI 12 12 U.S.A.	FITCHEW Nº 12 RAMSGATE
1,095.	1,096.	1,097.	1,098.
F.lli SUMMONTE 12 12 RESINA	FLOBERT 12 12 PARIS	12 FN CF 12	FN 12 12 FN
1,099.	1,100.	1,101.	1,102.

1,103. F N / 12 — 12 / MADE IN BELGIUM	1,104. F N / 12 — 12 / MADE IN BELGIUM	1,105. F N / 12 — 12 / MADE IN BELGIUM	1,106. F.N. / 12 — 12 / MADE IN BELGIUM
1,107. ◇ / 12 — 12 / FRANCE	1,108. ◇ / 12 — 12 / FRANCE	1,109. FRANCIS / No — 12 / PETERBOROUGH	1,110. FRANCIS. PETERBORO / No 12 / ELEY
1,111. FRAP / 12 — 12 / ITALY	1,112. ♛ / 12 — 12 / FREDERIKSVÆRK	1,113. F.T. BAKER. LONDON / No 12	1,114. F.T. BAKER LONDON / No 12
1,115. F.T. BAKER. LONDON / No 12 / ELEY	1,116. F.T. BAKER. LONDON / No 12	1,117. F.T. BAKER / KYNOCHS PATENT / No 12 / GROUSE EJECTOR / LONDON	1,118. 12 GA — CAL 12
1,119. 12 GA — CAL 12	1,120. GAFAB / 12 — 12 / GAFAB	1,121. 12 — GA. / GOLD MEDAL	1,122. GALLYON / MADE IN BELGIUM / 12 — 12 / CAMBRIDGE
1,123. 12 GA / MADE IN U.S.A.	1,124. 12 — GA / MADE IN U.S.A.	1,125. GAMEBORE / 12	1,126. GAMEBORE / 12 — 12 / G.B.

Central Fire 130

GARDNER No 12 CHIPPENHAM	12 GAUGE	12 ◇ 12 GAUGE	GAUGE 12 12 GAUGE
1,127.	1,128.	1,129.	1,130.
G BB 12 12 ITALY	GB 12 12 GB	GB 12 12 GB	GB 12 12 GB
1,131.	1,132.	1,133.	1,134.
GB 12 12 SPAIN	G.B. 12 12 SPAIN	C.COONEY No 12 KELLS	G.E.BOND KYNOCH'S PATENT GROUSE No 2090-35 No 12 THETFORD
1,135.	1,136.	1,137.	1,138.
GEO.G.BUSSEY&Co No 12 LONDON	GEORGE BARNITT&Co No KYNOCH 12 YORK	GEORGE GIBBS.LTD. BRISTOL & LONDON. No 12.	GEORGE GIBBS LTD. BRISTOL & LONDON No 12
1,139.	1,140.	1,141.	1,142.
GEV CHEDD 12 12 UNIVERSEL	GEVELOT 12	GEVELOT 12 12 CANADA	GEVELOT 12 12 PARIS
1,143.	1,144.	1,145.	1,146.
GEVELOT 12 12 PARIS	GEVELOT 12 12 PARIS	GEVELOT 12 12 PARIS	GEVELOT 12 12 PARIS
1,147.	1,148.	1,149.	1,150.

GEVELOT 12 12 PARIS 1,151.	G. FIOCCHI No 12 LECCO 1,152.	G.H.DAW'S No 12 PATENT 1,153.	PAT. PEND 12 GA G&H OMAHA 12 CA 1,154.
GIBBS No 12 BRISTOL & LONDON 1,155.	GIBBS No 12 KYNOCH BRISTOL & LONDON 1,156.	12 GIESSE 12 LAMEZIA-T 1,157.	GIULIO FIOCCHI LECCO 12 12 GF 1,158.
GIVLIO FIOCCHI LECCO N 12 GF 1,159.	GIVLIO·FIOCCHI·LECCO No GF 12 1,160.	GIVLIO FIOCCHI 12 12 (MADE IN ITALY) 1,161.	G&L 12 12 CALIBERS 1,162.
G&L 12 12 CYPRUS 1,163.	☆12☆ GLOBAL SHOT.COM 1,164.	GLORIA ☆ ☆ 12 12 ☆ G ☆ 1,165.	G.L.WOODS 12 12 NORFOLK 1,166.
G.L.WOODS 12 12 NORFOLK 1,167.	G.L.WOODS & SONS 12 12 IMPORTED CASE 1,168.	G.L.WOODS & SONS G.12 NORFOLK 12 1,169.	G M G 12 12 CYPRUS 1,170.
G.NEWNHAM No 12 KYNOCH LANDPORT 1,171.	G. NEWNHAM KYNOCH'S PATENT GROUP·T No K.No 2090 12 LANDPORT 1,172.	12 GORDON 12 SYSTEM 1,173.	GRAHAM COCKERMOUTH No 12 1,174.

GREENER No.12 KYNOCH PATENT GROUSE EJECTOR LONDON & BIRMINGHAM	GREENERS No.12 PAT. APD. FOR	GREENFIELD.STORRINGTON No.12 ELEY	GUNMARK 12
1,175.	1,176.	1,177.	1,178.
GUSTAV GENSCHOW & Co AKTIENGESELLSCHAFT 12 12 DURLACH	GUSTAV GENSCHOW & Co AKTIENGESELLSCHAFT 12 12 KARLSRUHE-DURLACH	G.W.BALES No.12 IPSWICH	G.WREN.HUNGERFORD No.12 ELEY
1,179.	1,180.	1,181.	1,182.
GYTTORP 12	GYTTORP 12	GYTTORP * 12 *	GYTTORP 12 12 AMF AB
1,183.	1,184.	1,185.	1,186.
GYTTORP 12 12 GYTTORP	GYTTORP 12 GYTTORP 12 MADE IN SWEDEN	GYTTORP 12 12 MADE IN SWEDEN	HAFIZ GHOUSE & Co No.12 KYNOCH MEERUT
1,187.	1,188.	1,189.	1,190.
H.A.FLINT.HEMEL HEMPSTEAD No.12	HAMMOND BROS ☆ ☆ 12	HAMMOND BROS.WINCHESTER HAMMOND BROS No.12 ELEY	HAMMOND BROS FOREIGN 12 12 MADE CASE WINCHESTER
1,191.	1,192.	1,193.	1,194.
HAMMOND BROS KYNOCH'S PATENT No.12 GROUSE EJECTOR WINCHESTER	HARDY BROS KYNOCH'S PATENT No.12 GROUSE EJECTOR ALNWICK	HARDY BROS LTD No.12 KYNOCH ALNWICK	HARRY WILLIAMS No.12 NEWPORT.I.O.W.
1,195.	1,196.	1,197.	1,198.

Central Fire 133

H.ATKIN PATENT No 2090 2.JERMYN ST.S.W. No 12	H.ATKIN 18 OXENDON STREET.W. No 12	HAWK 12 12 BEST	HAWK 12 12 BEST
1,199.	1,200.	1,201.	1,202.
BEST 12 HAWK 12	H.BARHAM.HITCHIN No12 ELEY	H.C.ELLIOTT 12 12 DARTFORD	H.C.ELLIOTT CASE MADE 12 12 IN BELGIUM DARTFORD
1,203.	1,204.	1,205.	1,206.
H.CLARKE & SONS EXPRESS No 12 CARTRIDGE LEICESTER	H.CLARKE & SONS EXPRESS No 12 CARTRIDGE LEICESTER	HELLIS 12 12 LONDON ENGLAND	HELLIS & SONS KYNOCH PATENT No 12 GROUSE EJECTOR LONDON
1,207.	1,208.	1,209.	1,210.
HELLIS & SONS-LONDON MADE IN BELGIUM 12	HELLIS & SONS-LONDON MADE IN BELGIUM 12	HELLIS & SONS-LONDON MADE IN BELGIUM 12	HELSON No 12 KYNOCH EXETER
1,211.	1,212.	1,213.	1,214.
HENDERSON No 12 DUNDEE	HENRITE EXPLOSIVES 12 12 LONDON	HENRITE EXPLOSIVES 12 12 LONDON	HENRY ATKIN 2.JERMYN STREET KYNOCH'S PATENT GROUSE No 2090 No 12
1,215.	1,216.	1,217.	1,218.
HENRY ATKIN Ld No 12 LONDON	HENRY ATKIN Ld No 12 LONDON	HENRY ATKIN Ld No 12 LONDON K	HENRY ATKIN Ld No 12 LONDON N
1,219.	1,220.	1,221.	1,222.

Central Fire 134

HENRY ATKIN LTD KYNOCH LONDON No 12	HENRY ATKIN LTD KYNOCH PATENT GROUSE EJECTOR LONDON No 12	HERTER'S PAT 12 12	H.HODGSON CASE MADE IN FRANCE IPSWICH & BURY ST EDMUNDS 12 12 SFM
1,223.	1,224.	1,225.	1,226.
HIAWATHA 12 GA ACE	HIAWATHA 12 GA AIRWAY	HIGHAM.OSWESTRY No 12 ELEY	HILL & SON HORNCASTLE No 12
1,227.	1,228.	1,229.	1,230.
HIRTENBERG ✶ 12 ✶	HIRTENBERG ✶ 12 ✶	HIRTENBERG ✶ 12 ✶	HIRTENBERGER ✩ 12 ✩
1,231.	1,232.	1,233.	1,234.
HIRTENBERGER ✩ 12 ✩	H.JONES.WREXHAM No 12 ELEY	HK 12 FREDERIKSVÆRK 12	HK 12 FREDERIKSVÆRK 12
1,235.	1,236.	1,237.	1,238.
H.LUTHY 12 12 NEUCHATEL	H.M.JULIAN No 12 BASINGSTOKE	HOBSON No 12 KYNOCH LEAMINGTON	HOBSON KYNOCH'S PATENT GROUSE No 12 LEAMINGTON
1,239.	1,240.	1,241.	1,242.
HODGSON.RIPON No 12 ELEY	H.HODGSON CASE MADE IN FRANCE IPSWICH & BURY ST EDMUNDS 12 12 SFM	Holiday 12 12 GAUGE	HOLLAND No 12 CIRENCESTER
1,243.	1,244.	1,245.	1,246.

Central Fire 135

HOLLAND & HOLLAND 12	HOLLAND & HOLLAND 12	HOLLAND & HOLLAND No 12	HOLLAND No 12 LONDON
1,247.	1,248.	1,249.	1,250/R.
HOLLAND & HOLLAND No 12 H. ELEY	HOLLAND & HOLLAND KYNOCH H. No 12	HOLLAND & HOLLAND B.E.Y No 12 NITRO PARADOX	HON. G. KEPPEL KYNOCH'S PATENT GROUSE EJECTOR No 12
1,251.	1,252.	1,253.	1,254.
HOOTON & JONES No 12 LIVERPOOL	HOOTON & JONES No 12 LIVERPOOL	HOOTON & JONES No 12 ELEY LIVERPOOL	HOOTON & JONES No 12 KYNOCH LIVERPOOL
1,255.	1,256.	1,257.	1,258.
HORNE No 12 READING	HORSLEY 12 12 YORK	HORTON No 12 MOSSY H. GLASGOW	HORTON. GLASGOW No 12 ELEY
1,259/R.	1,260.	1,261.	1,262.
HUDSON'S BAY No 12 COMPANY	HULL 12 12 CARTRIDGE	HULL CARTRIDGE Co. 12	HUNTER 12
1,263.	1,264.	1,265.	1,266.
HURLSTONE No 12 WARMINSTER	HUSSEY LTD. 81 NEW BOND ST. W. No 12 JOYCE	HUSSA ☆ ☆ 12	H.W. ROBERTS & Co No 12 KYNOCH RHYL
1,267.	1,268.	1,269.	1,270.

Central Fire 136

HYGIENIC ALL-METAL DAMPER	I.C.I. 42 Mk III Z	ICI 12 12 ICI	IMI 12 12 IMI
1,271.	1,272.	1,273.	1,274.
I.M.I. 12 12 VIGENANO	IMPERIAL 12 12 CANADA	IMPERIAL 12 12 CANADA	IVI 12 12 IMPERIAL
1,275.	1,276.	1,277.	1,278.
IMPERIAL 12 12 USA	INMAN MORROW & Co No 12 KYNOCH LEEDS	INTERNATIONAL No 12 REPEATOR	INTERSTATE 12 12 ENGLAND
1,279.	1,280.	1,281.	1,282.
IN. PA. 12 12 ITALY	INT. PAT. A.E.1301	I.P.M. 12 12 I.P.M.	JACK RABBIT No 12 A.A.Co.
1,283.	1,284.	1,285.	1,286.
JAMES B. WARRILOW TRADE MARK No 12 ACCURATE CHIPPENHAM · ENGLAND	JAMES KIRK No 12 K AYR	JARRY 12 12 ANGOULEME	JAS R WATSON & Co 12 12 LONDON
1,287.	1,288.	1,289.	1,290.
JAS.R.WATSON & Co No 12 LONDON	JAS.R.WATSON & Co COOPPAL No 2 LONDON No 12	J.R.WATSON & Co LONDON MADE IN BELGIUM 12	JAS.R.WATSON & Co MADE IN 12 BELGIUM 12 LONDON
1,291.	1,292.	1,293.	1,294.

Central Fire 137

J.B.HADDON. PENZANCE No 12	J.BLANCH&SON No 12 KYNOCH LONDON	J.BLANCH & SON KYNOCH PATENT GROUSE No 2090 12 LONDON	J.BLANCH & SON KYNOCH'S PATENT No 1 GROUSE EJECTOR 12 LONDON
1,295.	1,296.	1,297.	1,298.
JC 12 12 JC	J.CONYERS & SONS No 12 KYNOCH DRIFFIELD	J.COSTAS 12 12 BARCELONA	J.D.DOUGALL & SONS. GLASGOW No 12 ELEY
1,299.	1,300.	1,301.	1,302.
J.E.COOKE No 12 BROMYARD	JEFFERY No 12 GUILDFORD	JEFFERY No 12 PLYMOUTH	JENVEY & TITE No 12 GRANTHAM
1,303.	1,304.	1,305.	1,306.
JESSE.P.HODGSON No 12 KYNOCH LOUTH	J.BURROW KYNOCH'S PATENT No 1 12 GROUSE EJECTOR PRESTON	J.BURROW No 12 NOBELS PRESTON & CARLISLE	J.F.LAYCOCK.WISETON No 12 ELEY
1,307.	1,308.	1,309.	1,310.
J.F.MASON.EYNSHAM HALL No 12 ELEY	J.GRAYHAM & Co No 12 ELEY INVERNESS	J.H.COOK & Co. CIRENCESTER ELEY	J.H.MARTIN & Co. ST.JOHNS No 12 ELEY
1,311.	1,312.	1,313.	1,314.
J.HOBSON No 12 LEAMINGTON	J.HOBSON No 12 KYNOCH LEAMINGTON	J.H.R 12 12 FRANCE	JIALING 12 12 CHINA
1,315.	1,316.	1,317.	1,318.

Central Fire 138

J.B. 12 KYNOCH 12 WALSRODE	J.B. WARRILLOW TRADE MARK No 12 ACCURATE CHIPPENHAM	J.LANG & SON No 12 KYNOCH LONDON	J.LANG & SON KYNOCH PATENT No 12 GROUSE EJECTOR LONDON
1,319.	1,320.	1,321.	1,322.
J.L.WOOD No 12 STAMFORD	J.McCRIRICK & SONS No 12 AYR	JMP 12	J.MUES 12 12 MELBOURNE
1,323.	1,324.	1,325.	1,326.
J.MUES SHELL 12 12 MADE IN BELGIUM MELBOURNE	JOHN FRASER No 12 ELEY EDINBURGH	JOHN FRY No 12 DERBY	JOHNSON & REID DARLINGTON No 12 ELEY
1,327.	1,328.	1,329.	1,330.
JOHNSON & REID DARLINGTON No 12 ELEY	JOHNSON & WRIGHT LTD KYNOCH NORTHAMPTON No 12	JOHN WARRICK READING No 12	JOYCE No 12 LONDON
1,331.	1,332.	1,333.	1,334.
JOYCE No 12 LONDON	JOYCE No 12 LONDON	JOYCE No 12 LONDON	JOYCE No 12 LONDON
1,335.	1,336.	1,337.	1,338.
JOYCE No 12 LONDON	JOYCE No 12 LONDON	JOYCE No 12 LONDON	JOYCE No 12 LONDON
1,339.	1,340.	1,341.	1,342.

Central Fire 139

JOYCE LIMITED Nº 12 EJECTOR LONDON	JOYCE LIMITED Nº 12 GASTIGHT LONDON	JOYCE LIMITED Nº 12 GASTIGHT LONDON	JOYCE LIMITED Nº 12 GASTIGHT LONDON
1,343.	1,344.	1,345.	1,346.
JOYCE & Cº LONDON BAILEY'S GAS CHECK PATENT Nº 12	J.PURDEY & SONS Nº 12 ELEY'S EJECTOR	J.PURDEY & SONS Nº 12 ELEY EJECTOR	J.RIGBY & Cº Nº 12 KYNOCH LONDON
1,347.	1,348.	1,349.	1,350.
(design) Believe to be canceled.	J.RIGBY & Cº LONDON KYNOCH'S PATENT GROOVE Nº 2090 Nº 12	J.R.WATSON & Cº LONDON MADE IN BELGIUM 12	JSS 12 GAUGE
1,351.	1,352.	1,353.	1,354.
J.S.WILLIAMS Nº 12 PONTYPRIDD	JULIAN Nº 12 BASINGSTOKE	JULIAN Nº 12 BASINGSTOKE	JULIAN BASINGSTOKE Nº 12 ELEY
1,355.	1,356.	1,357.	1,358.
J.V.NEEDHAM 12	J.W.WILLCOCKS.STAMFORD Nº 12 ELEY	J.WOODWARD & SONS 12	J.WOODWARD & SONS ELEY 12
1,359.	1,360.	1,361.	1.362.
J.WOODWARD & SONS KYNOCH 12	J.WOODWARD & SONS KYNOCH 12	J.WOODWARD & SONS PATENT Nº 2090 Nº 12	JWP 12
1,363.	1,364.	1,365.	1,366.

Central Fire 140

J.W.WILLCOCKS.STAMFORD No 12 ELEY	KALCO 12 12 EUROPE	KAVANAGH & SON No 12 DUBLIN	K.D.RADCLIFFE No 12 COLCHESTER
1,367.	1,368.	1,369.	1,370.
KENT 12 12 KENT	KENT 12 12 KENT	KENT No 12 WANTAGE	KENT & SON No 12 WANTAGE
1,371.	1,372.	1,373.	1,374.
KENT & SON No 12 WANTAGE	KENT & SON WANTAGE No 12 ELEY	KERRIDGE 12 12 YARMOUTH	K.F. 12 12 SPECIAL
1,375.	1,376.	1,377.	1,378.
KINGDON No 12 BASINGSTOKE	KINGDON. BASINGSTOKE No 12 ELEY	KINGDON No 12 KYNOCH BASINGSTOKE	KOLN-ROTTWEIL 12 12 AKTIENGESELLSCHAFT
1,379.	1,380.	1,381.	1,382.
KOLN-ROTTWEIL 12 K R A R 12 AKTIENGESELLSCHAFT	K.RIDER. PHILA. No 12 ELEY	KROMSON 12 12 ESPAÑA	KYNOCH 12
1,383.	1,384.	1,385.	1,386.
KYNOCH ★ ★ No 12 BALL	KYNOCH. BIRMINGHAM No 12	KYNOCH. BIRMINGHAM No 12	KYNOCH No 12 BIRMINGHAM
1,387.	1,388.	1,389.	1,390.

KYNOCH No 12 BIRMINGHAM	KYNOCH No 12 BIRMINGHAM	KYNOCH No 12 BIRMINGHAM	KYNOCH No 12 BIRMINGHAM
1,391.	1,392.	1,393.	1,394.
KYNOCH No 12 BIRMINGHAM	KYNOCH No 12 BIRMINGHAM	KYNOCH 12 12 BIRMINGHAM	KYNOCH N.I. 12 12 BIRMINGHAM
1,395.	1,396.	1,397.	1,398.
KYNOCH A.HOLLIS&SON No 12 BOMBAY BIRMINGHAM	KYNOCH MADE IN No 12 GREAT BRITAIN BIRMINGHAM	KYNOCH WITTON No 12 CARTRIDGE BIRMINGHAM	KYNOCH No 12 BLACK
1,399.	1,400.	1,401.	1,402.
KYNOCH E.T.L. 12 12 BONAX	KYNOCH No 12 ENGLAND	KYNOCH No 12 GASTIGHT	KYNOCH No 12 GASTIGHT
1,403.	1,404.	1,405.	1,406.
KYNOCH No 12 GROUSE	KYNOCH No 12 GROUSE	KYNOCH PATENT No 12 No 2090 GROUSE EJECTOR	KYNOCH 12 12 NITROBALL
1,407.	1,408.	1,409.	1,410.
KYNOCH 12 12 NITRO-BALL	KYNOCH 12 12 NOBEL	KYNOCH 12 12 NOBEL	KYNOCH 12 12 NOBEL
1,411.	1,412.	1,413.	1,414.

KYNOCH PATENT No 12 "OPEX"	KYNOCH PATENT No 12 "OPEX"	KYNOCH 12 12 PARADOX	KYNOCH No 12 PERFECT
1,415.	1,416.	1,417.	1,418.
KYNOCH E.T.L. 12 12 PRIMAX	KYNOCH WATERPROOF No 12	KYNOCH No 12 WATERPROOF	KYNOCK & Co. BIRMINGHAM
1,419.	1,420.	1,421.	1,422.
KYNOCH & Co. 12 12 BIRMINGHAM	KYNOCH'S No 12 PATENT	KYNOCH'S PIEPER No H·LIEGE 12 PATENT	KYNOCH'S No U.M.T.&C.MFG Co. 12 PATENT
1,423.	1,424.	1,425.	1,426.
KYNOCH'S S.D.&G No 12 PATENT	KYNOCH'S No TRULOCK & HARRIS 12 DUBLIN PATENT	KYNOCH W.BITTE No COELN 12 PATENT	KYNOCH'S No W.GREENER 12 BIRMINGHAM PATENT
1,427.	1,428.	1,429.	1,430.
KYNOCH'S PATENT No 12 EXPERT SHELL SQUIRES.N.Y.	KYNOCH'S PATENT No 12 No 2090 GROUSE EJECTOR	No KYNOCH'S PATENT PERFECTLY 12 GASTIGHT LONDON	LACHAUSSEE LIEGE
1,431.	1,432.	1,433.	1,434.
LA GAULOISE 12 GEVELOT 12 GEVELOT	LAMBRO 12 12 ITALY	LAMBRO 12 12 ITALY	LANCASTER'S "PYGMY" No 12 ELEY
1,435.	1,436.	1,437.	1,438.

Central Fire 143

LANGLEY No 12 LUTON	LANGLEY No 12 KYNOCH LUTON & HITCHIN	LANGLEY & LEWIS CASE MADE No SPM 12 IN FRANCE LUTON	LANG LONDON No 12 ELEY
1,439.	1,440.	1,441.	1,442.
LAPORTE 12 12 INT'L	LATENIT 12 12 FRANCE	1901 No 12 LEADER	LEATHAM 12 12 DURHAM
1,443.	1,444.	1,445.	1,466.
LEECH & SONS CHELMSFORD No 12	LEECH & SONS No 12 KYNOCH CHELMSFORD	LEECH & SON CHELMSFORD KYNOCH'S PATENT GROUSE No 2090 No 12	LEON BEAUX 12 12 MILANO
1,447.	1,448.	1,449.	1,450.
12 LEON BEAUX & C 12 MILANO	LEON BEAUX & C 12 MILANO 12	12 LEON BEAUX & C MILANO 12	LEON BEAUX & C 12 MILANO 12
1,451.	1,452.	1,453.	1,454.
L-EXPRESS 12	LIBERTY No 12 BULK	LIGHTNING No 12 U.M.C.CO.	LINNINGTON NEWPORT I.W. No 12 ELEY
1,455.	1,456.	1,457.	1,458.
LINSLEY BROS No 12 KYNOCH LEEDS	LINSLEY BROS No 12 LEEDS & BRADFORD	LINSLEY BROS LEEDS & BRADFORD ELEY No 12	LINSLEY BROS KYNOCH'S PATENT No 12 GROUSE EJECTOR LEEDS & BRADFORD
1,459.	1,460.	1,461.	1,462.

Central Fire 144

LISLE No 12 DERBY	LISLE CASE MADE IN FRANCE No 12 DERBY	LISLE CASE MADE IN FRANCE No 12 DERBY	LITTLEFORD No 12 KYNOCH CIRENCESTER
1,463.	1,464.	1,465.	1,466.
L.KEEGAN 12 12 DUBLIN	LLOYD LEWES 12 12 case made in GERMANY	LLOYD & SONS No CHAMPION 12 LEWES	L.M.I.-12-MAIONCHI
1,467.	1,468.	1,469.	1,470.
LOADED IN 12 SHELL MADE IN GERMANY 12 AUSTRALIA	LOADED IN LONDON FOR A.W.GAMAGE Co CASE MADE IN GERMANY No 12 HOLBORN E.C.	LOCKSLEY CARTRIDGE Co 12 SYDNEY 12	LOCKSLEY CARTRIDGE Co 12 SYDNEY 12
1,471.	1,472.	1,473.	1,474.
LONG BRASS 12 12 LONDON	LOWRANCE & SON No 12 BARNSLEY	L.P.M. 12 12 PORTUGAL	LUCK'S EXPLOSIVES 12 12 LONDON
1,475.	1,476.	1,477.	1,478.
LUX ✱ ✱ 12	LYALVALE 12	LYALVALE ★ ☆ 12	LYON & LYON LTD MADE IN 12 12 GERMANY CALCUTTA
1,479.	1,480.	1,481.	1,482.
MACNAUGHTON No 12 KYNOCH EDINBURGH	MACPHERSON No 12 INVERNESS	MACPHERSON No 12 INVERNESS	MADD ◇ ◇ 12
1,483.	1,484.	1,485.	1,486.

Central Fire 145

MADD / 12 / 12 / MADD 1,487.	MADD / 12 / 12 / FRANCE 1,488.	MADE IN / 12 / 12 / BELGIUM 1,489.	MADE IN / 12 / 12 / ENGLAND 1,490.
MADE IN / 12 / 12 / ENGLAND 1,491.	N° MADE IN 12 / FRANCE 1,492.	Made in Germany / 12 ORRO SNS 12 / SCHONEBECK 1,493.	MADE IN / 12 / 12 / GREAT BRITAIN 1,494.
MADE IN GT BRITAIN / 12 1,495.	MADE IN / 12 / 12 / GT. BRITAIN 1,496.	12 / 12 / MADE HOLLAND 1,497.	Made in Hungary / * 12 * 1,498.
Made in Hungary / * 12 * 1,499.	MADE IN USSR / 12 / 69 / 65 mm 1,500.	12 / 70 / MADE IN USSR 1,501.	MADE IN USSR / 12 / 70 1,502.
MADE IN USSR / 12 / 70 / 65 mm 1,503.	12 / 71 / MADE IN USSR 1,504.	MAIONCHI / 12 / 12 / CHED 1,505.	MAIONCHI / 12 / 12 / GF ITALY 1,506.
MAIONCHI 12 / 12 / ITALY 1,507.	MAIONCHI / 12 / 12 / ITALY 1,508.	MAIONCHI / 12 / 12 / ITALY 1,509.	MAIONCHI / L.M.I.-12 1,510.

Central Fire 146

1,511. MAIONCHI 12 12 L.M.I.	1,512. MAIONCHI 12 12 L.M.I.	1,513. MAIONCHI L.M.I. 12	1,514. M.AITKEN&SONS No 12 KYNOCH PATENT GROUSE EJECTOR CRIEFF
1,515. MAJOR 12 12 B.P.Co	1,516. MALCOMSON&Co No 12 LURGAN	1,517. MALEHAM SHEFFIELD & LONDON ELEY No 12	1,518. MALLARD 12 GA C.C.Co.
1,519. MALLARD 12 12 C.C.Co.	1,520. MANUFRANCE 12 12 SAINT-ETIENNE	1,521. MARCEL GAUPILLAT & Cie 12 12	1,522. MARRIAGE & Co No 12 REIGATE
1,523. MARTIGNONI 12 12 GENOVA	1,524. MARTIGNONI 12 12 GENOVA	1,525. MARTIGNONI 12 12 GENOVA	1,526. MARTIGNONI 12 GENOVA
1,527. MARTIN.GLASGOW&ABERDEEN No12 W.ELEY	1,528. MARTIN.GLASGOW&ABERDEEN No12 W.ELEY	1,529. No MARTIN 12 GLASGOW,EDINBURGH&ABERDEEN	1,530. MARY-ARM ☆ 12 ☆
1,531. MARY 12 12 Bergerac	1,532. MASTER 12	1,533. MAVRULIS 12 12 HELLAS	1,534. M B 12 12 ITALY

Central Fire 147

ME.CA 12 12 ITALY	melior 12 12 CIC	MELIOR 12 12 MELIOR	METAL BREVETE CAL 12 N° 6 GEVELOT S.G.D.G.
1,535.	1,536.	1,537.	1,538.
METEOR 12	M.GAUPILLAT 12 PARIS 12	MGM 12 12 VALENCE	MIDLAND 12 12 CARTRIDGE
1,539.	1,540.	1,541.	1,542.
MIDLAND GUN Co N° 12 BIRMINGHAM	MIDLAND GUN Co N° 1 12 KYNOCH BRIGG	MILBURN & SON N° 12 KYNOCH BRAMPTON	MILBURN KYNOCH'S PATENT N° 12 GROUSE EJECTOR BRAMPTON
1,543.	1,544.	1,545.	1,546.
MIRITA 12 12 C	MOHAWK 12 GA BY REMINGTON	MOLE. HEMEL HEMPSTEAD N°12 ELEY	MONARCH GUN WORKS L'POOL N°12 ELEY
1,547.	1,548.	1,549.	1,550.
MONK N° 12 KYNOCH CHESTER	MONK N° 12 KYNOCH CHESTER	MOORE & GREY KYNOCH'S PATENT N° 12 GROUSE LONDON	MORTIMER N°12 H EDINBURGH
1,551.	1,552.	1,553.	1,554.
MULLERITE 12	MUNICAR 12 12 FRANCE	MUNICAR 12 12 FRANCE	MUNICAR 12 12 VIERZON
1,555.	1,556.	1,557.	1,558.

Central Fire 148

MUNICAR-12 VIERZON — 1,559.	MUNICAR 12 VIERZON — 1,560.	MUNICOES DE MOCAMBIQUE LDA 12 — 1,561.	MUNITIONS 12 MGM 12 — 1,562.
MUNITIONS 12 MGM 12 — 1,563.	MUNIZIONI ESTE-ITALY — 1,564.	MUNYSUR 12 ESPANA 12 — 1,565.	NEGRELLO 12 ESTE-ITALY 12 — 1,566.
NEWLAND & STIDOLPH No 12 ELEY — 1,567.	NEWMAN & SON No 12 HAVERHILL — 1,568.	NEWNHAM No 12 LANDPORT — 1,569.	1901 No 12 NEW RIVAL — 1,570.
NEWTON.MANCHESTER No 12 ELEY — 1,571.	NIMROD 12 — 1,572.	NITEDAL 12 — 1,573.	NITEDALS 12 KRUDTVÆRK 12 — 1,574.
NITEDALS 12 KRUDTVÆRK 12 — 1,575.	NITRO 12 GA EXPRESS — 1,576.	NITROKOL No 12 LONDON — 1,577.	N M T No 12 — 1,578.
NOBBS 12 LINCOLN MADE IN BELGIUM 12 — 1,579.	NOBEL No 12 GLASGOW — 1,580.	NOBEL No 12 GLASGOW — 1,581.	NOBEL No 12 GLASGOW — 1,582.

Central Fire 149

NOBEL GLASGOW No 12	NOBEL N.I. GLASGOW No 12	NOBEL GLASGOW 12 12	NOBEL-GLASGOW 12 12 N
1,583.	1,584.	1,585.	1,586.
NOBEL LONDON No 12	NOBEL REY FRANCE 12 12	NOBEL SPORT 12 12	NOBEL'S BALLISTITE No 12
1,587.	1,588.	1,589.	1,590.
NOBEL'S ELEY BALLISTITE No 12	NOBEL'S ELEY BALLISTITE No 12	NOBEL'S BALLISTITE No 12 N	NOBEL'S U.M.C.Co. BALLISTITE No 12
1,591.	1,592.	1593.	1,594.
NOBEL'S U.M.C.Co. BALLISTITE No 12	NOBEL'S BALLISTITE 12 12 N	NOBEL'S EMPIRE No 12	NOBEL'S EMPIRE No 12 ELEY
1,595.	1,596.	1,597.	1,598.
NOBEL'S EMPIRE 12 12 N	NON-CORROSIVE 12	NON CORROSIVE RUSTLESS 12 12	NORMAL HENDON No 12
1,599.	1,600.	1,601.	1,602.
NORMAL HENDON MADE IN BRISTOL No 12	NORMAL HENDON MADE IN FRANCE 12 12	NORMAL LONDON No 12	NORMAL NIMROD No 12
1,603.	1,604.	1,605.	1,606.

Central Fire 150

NORMAL No 12 POWDER	NORMAL KYNOCH'S PATENT No 12 GROUSE EJECTOR POWDER Cº	No 12 NORMAL WATERPROOF	NORMAL No 12 W.R.A.Cº
1,607.	1,608.	1,609.	1,610.
NORAMCO 12	NORWESTERN NOX 12	N.S.W. AUST 12 12 A.D.I. P/L	Olin 12 GA 100 YEARS
1,611.	1,612.	1,613.	1,614.
ORBEA 12 12 SPAIN	ORBEA 12 12 VITORIA	ORBEA 12 12 VITORIA	ORIGINALE NOBEL'S No 12 O.N
1,615.	1,616.	1,617.	1,618.
Pachmayr LOS ANGELES 15 CALIF.	PAGE WOOD BATH 12	PAGE WOOD BRISTOL Nº 12	PAPE NEWCASTLE & SUNDERLAND KYNOCH Nº 12
1,619.	1,620.	1,621.	1,622.
12 P 12 12 12	PARKINSON Nº 12 ULVERSTON	PARSONS Nº 12 NUNEATON	PARSONS SHERWIN & Co Lo NUNEATON Nº 12
1,623.	1,624.	1,625.	1,626.
12 PATARCA 12 ANCONA	12 PATARCA 12 ANCONA	12 PATARCA 12 ANCONA	12 PATARCA 12 ANCONA
1,627.	1,628.	1,629.	1,630.

Central Fire 151

PATSTONE.SOUTHAMPTON No12 ELEY	PAWAM 12 12 PIONKI	PAWAM 12 12 PIONKI	PB 12 12 PB
1,631.	1,632.	1,633.	1,634.
PB 12 12 PB	PB 12 12 PB	P.C.C. No 12 LEAGUE	PERAZZI 12 12 BRESCIA
1,635.	1,636.	1,637.	1,638.
PETERS No 12 IDEAL	PETERS 12 12 IDEAL	PETERS 12 H.V.	PETERS 12 VICTOR
1,639.	1,640.	1,641.	1,642.
PHILLIPS BROS No 12 MARLBOROUGH	C.PINDER&Co No 12 BASINGSTOKE	P.J.CLARKE No 12 BOURNE	PLUMBERS LD 12 12 GT.YARMOUTH
1,643.	1,644.	1,645.	1,646.
P.MORRIS&SON No 12 KYNOCH HEREFORD	PNEUMATIC CARTRIDGE Co EDINBURGH No 12	PNEUMATIC CARTRIDGE CO LTD EDINBURGH ELEY No 12	POINTER 12 12 C.C.Co.
1,647.	1,648.	1,649.	1,650.
P.POULSEN No KYNOCH PATENT 12 CROSS EJECTOR KJØBENHAVN	PURDEY No 12	PURDEY No 12	PURDEY&SONS No 12 LONDON
1,651.	1,652/R.	1,653/R.	1,654.

Central Fire 152

PURDEY&SONS PATENT No 2090 LONDON No 12	PURDY No 12 THIRSK	RAKER 12 12 RAKER	RAMSBOTTOM MANCHESTER No12 ELEY
1,655.	1,656.	1,657.	1,658.
RANDELL'S FOREIGN 12 12 MADE CASE SPECIAL SMOKELESS	R A 12 GA TRACER	R C 12 12 ITALY	R.CAMPBELL&SONS No 12 KYNOCH LEYBURN
1,659.	1,660.	1,661.	1,662.
.RED. No 12 .DEVIL.	RED No 12 DEVIL	REMINGTON 12 GA	REMINGTON 12 GA
1,663.	1,664.	1,665.	1,666.
REMINGTON 12 GA EXPRESS	REMINGTON 12 GA PETERS	REMINGTON 12 GA PETERS	REMINGTON 12 GA PETERS
1,667.	1,668.	1,669.	1,670.
REMINGTON 12 GA R X P	REMINGTON UMC No 12 ARROW	REMINGTON UMC No 12 CLUB	REM-UMC CASE MADE No 12 IN U.S.A. ECONOMY
1,671.	1,672.	1,673.	1,674.
REMINGTON UMC No 12 LIGHTNING	REMINGTON UMC No 12 NITROCLUB	REMINGTON UMC No 12 REMILION	REMINGTON UMC No 12 REMILION
1,675.	1,676.	1,677.	1,678.

Central Fire 153

REM-UMC No 12 ARROW	REM-UMC CASE MADE No 12 IN U.S.A. ARROW	REM-UMC No 12 BEST	REM-UMC No 12 Remington
1,679.	1,680.	1,681.	1,682.
REM-UMC CASE MADE No 12 IN U.S.A. Remington	REM-UMC No 12 ECONOMY	REM-UMC CASE MADE No 12 IN U.S.A. ECONOMY	REM-UMC No 12 NEW CLUB
1,683.	1,684.	1,685.	1,686.
REM-UMC No 12 NITRO CLUB	REM-UMC CASE MADE No 12 IN U.S.A. NITRO CLUB	REM-UMC No 12 REMILION	REM-UMC No 12 SHURSHOT
1,687.	1,688.	1,689.	1,690.
1901 No 12 REPEATER	REY FRERES NIMES 12	REY FRERES FRANCE 12 12	Believe to be canceled.
1,691.	1,692.	1,693.	1,694.
R.L.CAPELL 12 12 NORTHAMPTON	R.M 12 12 ROMA	R*M*C 12 12	ROBERTSON & SON.WICK. No12 ELEY
1,695.	1,696.	1,697.	1,698.
No ROBIN HOOD 12 1903	ROBIN HOOD 12 12 R.H.P. CO	ROBINSON No 12 HULL	ROSSON DERBY No12 ELEY
1,699.	1,700.	1,701.	1,702.

Central Fire 154

1,703. ROSSON DERBY 12 NORWICH ELEY	1,704. ROSSON No 12 KYNOCH'S PATENT GROUSE EJECTOR DERBY	1,705. ROSSON & Co No 12 ELEY NORWICH	1,706. ROTTWEIL MADE IN GERMANY METAL — Printed shot size.
1,707. ROTTWEIL 12 67 CLUB 32	1,708. ROTTWEIL 12 12 RAUCHLOS SINOXID	1,709. ROTTWEIL 12G 12G ROTTWEIL	1,710. ROWLATT No 12 WELLINGBORO'
1,711. R-P 12 GA 3-1-B	1,712. R.PINTO 12 12 ESTE	1,713. R.PINTO 12 12 ESTE	1,714. R.RAINE.CARLISLE KYNOCH No 12
1,715. R.ROBINSON No 12 KYNOCH HULL	1,716. R.T.HODGSON No 12 KYNOCH HARROGATE	1,717. RUDD No 12 NORWICH	1,718. RUSTLESS 12
1,719. RUSTLESS 12 12 SINOXID WATERPROOF	1,720. R.WISE.KIDDERMINSTER No 12	1,721. R.W.S. 12 12 NURNBERG	1,722. RWS 12 12 NURNBERG
1,723. RWS 12 12 SINOXID RAUCHLOS	1,724. RWS/GECO 12 12 SINOXID ROTTWEIL	1,725. RWS/GECO 12 12 ROTTWEIL	1,726. RWS/GECO 12 12 ROTTWEIL

Central Fire 155

SAGA 12 12 LERIDA	SAGA 12 12 LERIDA	SAGA 12 12 SAGA	SAGA 12 12 SAGA
1,727.	1,728.	1,729.	1,730.
SALVO * * 12	SALVO ✦ ✦ 12	SARSON'S No 12 AYLESBURY	SAVAGE No 12 HI-POWER
1,731.	1,732.	1,733.	1,734.
SAVAGE No 12 SUPERIOR	SAVAGE No 12 SUPERIOR	SBP 12 12 MADE IN CZECHOSLOVAKIA	SBP 12 12 MADE IN CZECHOSLOVAKIA
1,735.	1,736.	1,737.	1,738.
SBP 12 12 MADE IN CZECHOSLOVAKIA	S.C.Co No 12 STAR	SCHÖNEBECK 12	SCHÖNEBECK 12
1,739.	1,740.	1,741.	1,742.
SCHULTZE No 12	No SCHULTZE 12 C.H.M.C LONDON	SCORPIO 12	SCOTCHER No 12 BURY ST EDMUNDS
1,743.	1,744.	1,745.	1,746.
SCOTCHER & SON No 12 KYNOCH BURY ST EDMUNDS	SEARS 12 GA	SEARS 12 GA SPORTLOAD	SEARS 12 GA TED WILLIAMS
1,747.	1,748.	1,749.	1,750.

Central Fire 156

SEARS 12 GA XTRA-RANGE	SECURA 12 12 SPORCOLIEGE	Nº SELBY ELECTRIC 12 W.R.A.CO.	SELLIER & BELLOT 12
1,751.	1,752.	1,753.	1,754.
SELLIER & BELLOT 12	Sellier & Bellot 12	SELLIER BELLOT MADE IN CZECHOSLOVAKIA 12	SELLIER BELLOT MADE IN CZECHOSLOVAKIA 12
1,755.	1,756.	1,757.	1,758.
SELLIER & BELLOT 12 S.B. 12 MADE IN GERMANY SCHOENEBECK	S.F.M 12 12 GEVELOT	S.G.Co Nº 12 E.B. YEOMAN	S. GRANT Nº 12 LONDON
1,759.	1,760.	1,761.	1,762.
S.GRANT & SON KYNOCH'S PATENT Nº 12 GROUSE EJECTOR LONDON	S.GRANT & SONS. LONDON Nº 12 ELEY	S.GRANT & SONS Nº 12 KYNOCH LONDON	Believe to be canceled.
1,763.	1,764.	1,765.	1,766.
S.JACKSON Nº 12 KYNOCH NOTTINGHAM	SKELTONS.L&.WARRINGTON Nº12 ELEY	SLINGSBY BROS Nº 12 BOSTON.	SMALL Nº 12 KYNOCH NEWCASTLE
1,767.	1,768.	1,769.	1,770.
SMALL KYNOCH'S PATENT Nº 12 GROUSE EJECTOR NEWCASTLE	SMALLWOOD.SHREWSBURY Nº12	SMI 12 12 ITALY	SMI 12 12 ITALY
1,771.	1,772.	1,773.	1,774.

SMI 12 12 MADE IN ITALY 1,775.	SMITH & SONS. NEWARK No 12 1,776.	SMITH & SONS. NEWARK KYNOCH No 12 1,777.	SMOKELESS 12 1,778.
SMOKELESS ✶12✶ 1,779.	SMOKELESS ✶12✶ 1,780.	SMOKELESS ☆12☆ 1,781.	SMOKELESS ☆12☆ 1,782.
SMOKE ✶12✶ 1,783.	SMOKELESS No 12 1,784.	SMOKELESS 12 12 GASTIGHT 1,785.	SMOKELESS 12 12 GASTIGHT 1,786.
SMOKELESS 12 12 GASTIGHT 1,787.	SMOKELESS 12 12 GASTIGHT 1,788.	SMOKELESS FOREIGN 12 12 MADE CASE GASTIGHT 1,789.	SMOKELESS MADE IN 12 12 GERMANY GASTIGHT 1,790.
SMOKELESS R.W.S. 12 12 NUREMBERG GASTIGHT 1,791.	SMOKELESS 12 12 MADE IN ENGLAND 1,792.	SMOKELESS 12 12 MADE IN GREAT BRITAIN 1,793.	SMOKELESS 12 12 NON CORROSIVE 1,794.
SMOKELESS 12 12 NON CORROSIVE 1,795.	SMYTHE No 12 KYNOCH DARLINGTON 1,796.	SMOKELESS MADE IN 12 12 GERMANY GASTIGHT 1,797.	SMYTHE 12 DARLINGTON STOCKTON-ON-TEES 1,798.

Central Fire 158

SMYTHE.DARLINGTON&STOCKTON No.12 ELEY	SMYTHE No 12 GROUSE EJECTOR KYNOCH'S PATENT DARLINGTON & STOCKTON	SNIA 12 12 ITALY	SNIA BPD 12 12 ITALY
1,799.	1,800.	1,801.	1,802.
SOFIM 12 ITALY 12	SOFIM 12 12	SOLOGNAC ☆ ☆ 12	S*P 12 12
1,803.	1,804.	1,805.	1,806.
S.P.&A. No 12 Co	E S.P.&A.Co B No 12	SPARTAN 12 12 FRANCE	SPEC.12 No 12 COMPETITION
1,807.	1,808.	1,809.	1,810.
SPECIAL 12 12 GASTIGHT	SPECIAL 12 12 GASTIGHT	SPECIAL 12 12 GASTIGHT	SPECIAL 12 12 GASTIGHT
1,811.	1,812.	1,813.	1,814.
SPECIAL 12 12 SMOKELESS	SPECIAL 12 12 SMOKELESS	SPECIAL 12 12 SMOKELESS	SPECIAL 12 12 SMOKELESS
1,815.	1,816.	1,817.	1,818.
SPECIAL 12 12 SMOKELESS	SPECIAL 12 12 SMOKELESS	SPECIAL 12 12 SMOKELESS	SPECIAL 12 12 SMOKELESS
1,819.	1,820.	1,821.	1,822.

Central Fire 159

SPECIAL 12 12 SMOKELESS	SPECIAL FOREIGN 12 12 MADE USA SMOKELESS	SPECIAL FOREIGN 12 12 MADE CASE SMOKELESS	12 12 SPEED
1,823.	1,824.	1,825.	1,826.
SPENCER No 12 KYNOCH NEWPORT I.W.	SQUIRES. N.Y. No 12	SSM 12 12 ENGLAND	STANDARD 12 12 TYPE CHAMPIONNAT
1,827.	1,828.	1,829.	1,830.
STAR MADE IN USA 12 BRAND	STAR 12 12 S.C. CO.	STAR 12 12 SHOT	STEEL 12 GA LINED
1,831.	1,832.	1,833.	1,834.
STEEL 12 GA LINED	Ste Fse DES MUNITIONS PARIS SFM 12 12	STENSBY. MANCHESTER No 12 ELEY	STENSBY. MANCHESTER No 12 ELEY
1,835.	1,836.	1,837.	1,838.
STEPHENS No 12 HORSHAM	STOVIN No 12 GRANTHAM	SUPER 12 12 ALL METAL	SUPER DD 12 12 MADE IN HOLAND
1,839.	1,840.	1,841.	1,842.
SUPER 12 12 STAR	SUPER STAR 12 12 SWEDEN	SUPER 12 12 SUPER	SUPER 12 12 SUPER
1,843.	1,844.	1,845.	1,846.

Central Fire 160

SUPERIOR No 12 GUARANTEED	SUPERIOR No 12 MOGUL	SUPERTUNET 12	SUPERTUNET 12
1,847.	1,848.	1,849.	1,850.
S&W 12 12 USA	SWARTKLIP 12	S W F 12 12 USA	SYKES & SONS No 12 OLDHAM
1,851.	1,852.	1,853.	1,854.
SYKES & SONS No 12 OLDHAM	TAITAL SUDAN 12	TARGET 12G. 12G. N.Z.	TARRANT No 12 CAMBRIDGE
1,855.	1,856.	1,857.	1,858.
TAYLOR & SONS No 12 PENZANCE	T.BLAND & SONS LONDON No 12	T. DAINTITH No 12 ELEY WARRINGTON	TEMA 12 12 TEMA
1,859.	1,860.	1,861.	1,862.
TEMA 12 12 TEMA	TEMPLE & Co No 12 BASINGSTOKE	T. HEATHMAN No 12 CREDITON	THE CLUB No 12 CARTRIDGE
1,863.	1,864.	1,865.	1,866.
T.HEPPLESTONE KYNOCH'S PATENT No 12 GROUSE EJECTOR MANCHESTER	THE ROCKETER ELEY No 12 PALMER SON & Co	THOs JACKSON & SON LONDON	TISDALL No 12 CHICHESTER
1,867.	1,868.	1,869/R.	1,870.

Central Fire 161

TISDALL, CHICHESTER No 12 ELEY 1,871.	T.J.EVANS No 12 WELSHPOOL 1,872.	T.PAGE-WOOD No 12 BRISTOL 1,873.	T.P.WOOD & Co. BRISTOL & CARDIFF No 12 1,874.
TRENT 12 12 GRIMSBY 1,875.	TRENT 12 12 GRIMSBY 1,876.	TRENT 12 12 GRIMSBY 1,877.	TRENT MADE IN ENGLAND 12 12 1,878.
TRENT 12 12 MADE IN ENGLAND 1,879.	TRENT MADE IN BELGIUM 12 12 FAIRFIELD-GRIMSBY 1,880.	TRENT FOREIGN MADE 12 12 TRENT-GRIMSBY 1,881.	TRENT FOREIGN MADE 12 12 TRENT-GRIMSBY 1,882.
TRENT FOREIGN MADE 12 12 LOADED IN ENGLAND TRENT-GRIMSBY 1,883.	TRENT FOREIGN MADE 12 12 LOADED IN ENGLAND TRENT-GRIMSBY 1,884.	TRENT MADE IN BELGIUM 12 12 TRENT-GRIMSBY 1,885.	TREPČA 12 12 TU 1,886.
TRULOCK & HARRISS, DUBLIN No 12 1,887.	TRULOCK & HARRISS, DUBLIN KYNOCH No 12 1,888.	TRULOCK & HARRISS, DUBLIN KYNOCH PATENT GROUSE EJECTOR No 12 1,889.	TRUST CAL 12 EIBAR 1,890.
TUNET 12 1,891.	TUNET 12 12 TUNET 1,892.	TUNET 12 12 TUNET 1,893.	TURNER CASE MADE 12 12 IN FRANCE READING 1,894.

Central Fire 162

TURNER CASE MADE 12 IN FRANCE 12 READING	TURNER. READING & NEWBURY No 12	TURNER. READING & NEWBURY. No 12.	TURNER. READING & NEWBURY. No 12 T. ELEY.
1,895.	1,896.	1,897.	1,898.
TURNER.READING&NEWBURY No 12 T.ELEY.	TURNER. READING & NEWBURY KYNOCH No 12	TURNER.READING&NEWBURY KYNOCH'S PATENT GROOVE PATY.No 2090.55. No 12.	T-WARNOCK 12 12 BENALLA
1,899.	1,900.	1,901.	1,902.
T.W.MURRAY&Co ESTABLISHED No 12 1828 CORK	T.W.MURRAY&Co ESTABLISHED 12 1828 12 CORK	No TYLER 12 HIGHBRIDGE	U.E.E 12 12 ✧ ✧
1,903.	1,904.	1,905.	1,906.
U.E.E. 12 12 ESPAÑA	No UGLOW 12 THORVERTON	U.M.C.Co No 12 ACME	U.M.C.Co. No 12 ARROW
1,907.	1,908.	1,909.	1,910.
U.M.C.Co No 12 BLACK CLUB	U.M.C.Co BRIDGPORT.CONN 12 B	U.M.C.Co No 12 CHALLENGE	U.M.C.Co No 12 CHALLENGE
1,911.	1,912.	1,913.	1,914.
U.M.C.Co No 12 HIGH-BASE	U.M.C.Co No 12 MAGIC	U.M.C.Co No 12 MAJESTIC	U.M.C.Co No 12 MONARCH
1,915.	1,916.	1,917.	1,918.

U.M.C.CO. No 12 NEW CLUB	U.M.C.CO. No 12 NEW CLUB	U.M.C.CO. No 12 NITRO	U.M.C.CO. No 12 NITRO CLUB
1,919.	1,920.	1,921.	1,922.
U.M.C.CO. No 12 PRIMROSE CLUB	U.M.C.CO. No 12 SMOKELESS	U.M.C.CO No 12 UNION	UNIFRANCE 12 12 CHEDDITE
1,923.	1,924.	1,925.	1,926.
No.12 U S AJAX	No.12 U S CLIMAX	No.12 U S CLIMAX	No.12 U S CLIMAX
1,927.	1,928.	1,929.	1,930.
No.12 U S ROMAX	VENABLES & SON OXFORD No 12	VENABLES & SON CASE MADE No 12 IN FRANCE OXFORD	VENABLES & SON No 12 KYNOCH OXFORD
1,931.	1,932.	1,933.	1,934.
VEREINIGTE KOLN-ROTTWEILER 12 12 PULVEREABRUKEN	VICTORY 12 12 VICTORY	VIHTAVUORI 12	VIHTAVUORI -12-
1,935.	1,936.	1,937.	1,938.
VIKING 12 12 HUNTER	VIRI CAL.12	VIRI 12 12 FRANCE	VOUZELA 12 12 12 BROU
1,939.	1,940.	1,941.	1,942.

VOUZELAUD BROU 12 12	VOUZELAUD BROU 12 12	VULKAN G.G.&Co 12 12	WALLIS BROS. LINCOLN No 12 ELEY
1,943.	1,944.	1,945.	1,946.
WALSRODE 12	PAT. WANDA PEND 12	WANLESS No 12 SUNDERLAND	WANLESS SUNDERLAND No 12 ELEY
1,947.	1,948.	1,949.	1,950.
W. WANLESS KYNOCHS PATENT No 12 GROUSE EJECTOR SUNDERLAND	WARD & SON KYNOCH PATENT No 12 GROUSE EJECTOR WORCESTER	WARD THOMPSON 12 STOCKTON 12	WATKINS & Co BANBURY No 12 ELEY
1,951.	1,952.	1,953.	1,954.
WATSON BROs No 12 OLD BOND STREET	WATSON BROS. OLD BOND STREET KYNOCH'S PATENT GROUSE EJECTOR No 12	WATSON BROS OLD BOND STREET KYNOCH'S PATENT GROUSE EJECTOR No 12	W. CAMERON No 12 KYNOCH BALLYMENA
1,955.	1,956.	1,957.	1,958.
W.C CO. No 12 SURE SHOT	W. COOMBS No 12 FROME	W. COTON No 12 KYNOCH COVENTRY	W. COULTAS No 12 GRANTHAM
1,959.	1,960.	1,961.	1,962.
W. DARLOW No 12 BEDFORD	W.E. BAKER No 12 TAVISTOCK	WEST. CAN. 12 12	WESTERN No 12 AA
1,963.	1,964.	1,965.	1,966.

WESTERN FIELD Nº 12	WESTERN RECORD Nº 12	WESTERN MADE IN AUSTRALIA SUPER-X Nº 12	WESTERN MADE IN U.S.A. SUPER-X Nº 12
1,967.	1,968.	1,969.	1,970.
WESTERN MADE IN AUSTRALIA XPERT Nº 12	WESTERN MADE IN U.S.A. XPERT Nº 12	WESTERN MADE IN U.S.A. XPERT Nº 12	WESTLEY RICHARDS 12 12
1,971.	1,972.	1,973.	1,974.
WESTLEY RICHARDS EXPLORA Nº 12	WESTLEY RICHARDS SUPER MAGNUM EXPLORA Nº 12	WESTLEY RICHARDS & Co Ltd · 12 ·	WESTLEY RICHARDS & Co KYNOCH PATENT GROUSE Nº 12 Ltd
1,975.	1,976.	1,977.	1,978.
WESTLEY RICHARDS & Co KYNOCHS LONDON PATENT GROUSE Nº 12	W. EVANS. LONDON Nº 12	W. EVANS LONDON Nº 12	W. EVANS. LONDON Nº 12 ELEY
1,979.	1,980.	1,981.	1,982.
W. EVANS. LONDON Nº 12 CASTIGHT	W. EVANS. LONDON Nº 12 · KYNOCH ·	W. EVANS LONDON Nº 12 KYNOCH	W. GARDEN Nº 12 KYNOCH ABERDEEN
1,983.	1,984.	1,985.	1,986.
W. GOLDEN Nº 12 HUDDERSFIELD	W. GOLDEN Nº 12 HUDDERSFIELD	W. GRIFFITHS KYNOCH PATENT Nº 12 GROUSE EJECTOR MANCHESTER	W M 12 12 FABRIK BISCHWEILER
1,987.	1,988.	1,989.	1,990.

Central Fire 166

WOLFF & Co 12 12 WALSRODE	WOLFF & Co 12 12 WALSRODE	WOOLLISCROFT·LEEK No 12 ELEY	W.P.JONES No 12 BIRMINGHAM
1,991.	1,992.	1,993.	1,994.
W.P. JONES. BIRMᵐ No 12 ELEY	W. POWELL & SON. BIRMᵐ ·12·	W. POWELL & SON No 12 KYNOCH BIRMINGHAM	W.R.A.Co. No 1 12 XX
1,995.	1,996.	1,997.	1,998.
WREN No 12 HUNGERFORD	W. RICHARDS No 12 LIVERPOOL	W. RICHARDS No 12 KYNOCH'S PATENT GROUSE EJECTOR LIVERPOOL	W. RICHARDS No 12 KYNOCH LIVERPOOL
1,999.	2,000.	2,001.	2,002.
W. RICHARDS No 12 PRESTON	W.R. LEESON No 12 ASHFORD	W.R. PAPE No 12 ELEY NEWCASTLE	W.R. PAPE No 12 KYNOCH NEWCASTLE ON TYNE
2,003.	2,004.	2,005.	2,006.
W.T. HANCOCK No 12 308 HIGH HOLBORN	W. HAYNES No 12 READING	WHITE. NORTHAMPTON & PARIS No 12	WHITNEY CARTRIDGE Co 12
2,007.	2,008.	2,009.	2,010.
W. HODGSON No 12 RIPON	W. HOOTON SLEAFORD No 12	W.H. POLLARD No 12 LONDON	WILKINSON No 12 PALL MALL
2,011.	2,012.	2,013.	2,014.

Central Fire 167

WIGGLESWORTH No 12 THIRSK 2,015.	WILKINSON'S No 12 KYNOCH DURHAM 2,016.	WILKINSON'S No 12 KYNOCH DURHAM 2,017.	WILLIAMS & POWELL No 12 LIVERPOOL 2,018.
WILLIAMS & POWELL KYNOCH'S PATENT 12 SCROUSE EJECTOR LIVERPOOL 2,019.	WINCHESTER 12 GA 2,020.	WINCHESTER 12 GA 1866-1991 2,021.	WINCHESTER 12 GA AA 2,022.
WINCHESTER 12 GA AA 2,023.	WINCHESTER 12 GA AUSTRALIA 2,024.	WINCHESTER 12 GA AUSTRALIA 2,025.	WINCHESTER 12 GA F.G.C. 2,026.
No WINCHESTER 12 W LEADER 2,027.	No WINCHESTER 12 RANGER MADE IN USA 2,028.	WINCHESTER MADE IN USA No 12 RANGER 2,029.	No WINCHESTER 12 REPEATER 2,030.
No WINCHESTER 12 SUPER SPEED 2,031.	No WINCHESTER 12 SUPER SPEED 2,032.	WINCHESTER MADE IN ITALY No 12 SUPER SPEED 2,033.	WINCHESTER MADE IN USA No 12 SUPER SPEED 2,034.
WINCHESTER 12 GA WESTERN 2,035.	WINCHESTER 12 12 WINCHESTER 2,036.	WINCHESTER MADE IN ITALY 12 12 WINCHESTER 2,037.	WINCHESTER No 12 XPERT II 2,038.

WITTON No 12 BIRMINGHAM	WITTON No 12 BIRMINGHAM	W.J.FELL No 12 WARRACKNABEAL	W.J.JEFFERY & Co No 12 LONDON
2,039.	2,040.	2,041.	2,042.
W.J.JEFFERY & Co No 12 LONDON	W.J.JEFFERY & Co No 12 E LONDON	W.J.JEFFERY & Co LTD 12 12 MADE IN BAVARIA LONDON	W.J.JEFFERY & Co LTD LONDON No 12
2,043.	2,044.	2,045.	2,046.
W.J.JEFFERY & Co LTD No 12 K LONDON	W.J.JEFFERY & Co LTD No 12 K LONDON	W.J.POWELL No 12 LEISTON	W.KAVANAGH&SON 12 12 DUBLIN
2,047.	2,048.	2,049.	2,050.
W.KAVANAGH&SON No 12 KYNOCH DUBLIN	WOOLLISCROFT·LEEK No12 ELEY	W-W 12 GAUGE	W-W 12 GA AA
2,051.	2,052.	2,053.	2,054.
W.WALLAS.WIGTON No12 ELEY	W.WANLESS KYNOCHS PATENT No 12 GROUSE EJECTOR SUNDERLAND	W.W.GREENER LONDON No 12 AND BIRMINGHAM	W.W.GREENER No 12 LONDON & BIRMINGHAM
2,055.	2,056.	2,057.	2,058.
W.W.GREENER'S DWARF No12 ELEY	XTRA-RANGE No 12 J C HIGGINS	ZENITH 12 12 G.G.&Co	ZIGOR 12 12 ZIGOR
2,059.	2,060.	2,061.	2,062.

Central Fire 169

2,063. ZIGOR 12	2,064. ELEY 10 12 LONDON	2,065. GREENER E K POLICE GUN	2,066. W GREENER E K 1940
2,067. W GREENER E K 1941	2,068. W GREENER E K POLICE GUN	2,069. W GREENER E K POLICE GUN	2,070. BOSS No 10
2,071. DICKSON & SON EDINBURGH H. No 10	2,072/R. E No 10 LONDON	2,073/R. ELEY BROS No 10 LONDON	2,074. ELEY No 10 CANADA
2,075. ELEY'S "EXPRESS" 10	2,076. ELEY-KYNOCH 10	2,077. ELEY-KYNOCH 10 10	2,078. ELEY LONDON No 10 H.C.S. N.Y.
2,079. I.X.L. No 10	2,080. JOYCE & Co No 10 LONDON	2,081. KYNOCH 10	2,082. KYNOCH L 10
2,083. KYNOCH & Co 10 10 BIRMINGHAM	2,084. KYNOCH No 10 BIRMINGHAM	2,085. KYNOCH No 10 BIRMINGHAM	2,086. KYNOCH'S PATENT No 2090 GROUSE CARTRIDGE

Central Fire 170

2,087. KYNOCH WITTON No 10 CARTRIDGE BIRMINGHAM	2,088. 1901 No 10 LEADER	2,089. 1901 No 10 LEADER	2,090. 10 GA MADE IN U.S.A.
2,091. MANTON No 10 CALCUTTA	2,092. 1901 No 10 NEW RIVAL	2,093. P.C.C. 10 G LEAGUE	2,094. REMINGTON 10 GA PETERS
2,095. W.R.G.&M.Co. LIMITED	2,096. REMINGTON ELECTRIC 2MM SEISMIC	2,097. No 8	2,098. CHARLES·OSBORNE & CO. BIRMINGHAM
2,099. U.M.C.Co No 10 A	2,100. U.M.C.CO. No 10 SMOKELESS	2,101. U.M.C.CO. No 10 UNION	2,102. USE BERDAN PRIMER No 1
2,103. V.L.&D. NEW YORK No 10 KYNOCH	2,104. WINCHESTER No 10 LEADER	2,105. ZULU * *	2,106. ELEY·LONDON No 8 GASTIGHT
2,107. ELEY'S No 8 EJECTOR LONDON	2,108. HOLLAND & HOLLAND ELEY No 8 H.H. PARADOX	2,109. KYNOCH * 8 *	2,110. NOBELS No 8 ELEY BALLISTITE

Central Fire 171

V.L.&D. NEW YORK No 8 KYNOCH 2,111.	No WESTERN SUPER-X 8 INDUSTRIAL 2,112.	No WESTERN SUPER-X 8 INDUSTRIAL 2,113.	2,114. Engine Starter
DYER & ROBSON No LONDON 4 2,115.	No ELEY BROS 4 LONDON 2,116.	ELEY-KYNOCH 4 4 ICI 2,117.	ELEY 4 4 NOBEL 2,118.
GEVELOT 4 4 PARIS 2,119.	K LTD 27 2,120.	KYNOCH 4 2,121.	KYNOCH & Co No 4 BIRMINGHAM 2,122/R.
KYNOCH No 4 BIRMINGHAM 2,123.	KYNOCH PATENT No 4 PERFECT BIRMINGHAM 2,124.	KYNOCH PATENT No 4 PERFECT BIRMINGHAM 2,125.	KYNOCH 4 4 NOBEL 2,126.
No ELEY 2 LONDON 2,127.	HOLLAND & HOLLAND No 2 2,128.		

Central Fire 172

POWDER TRANSPORTATION

These two are by Sellior & Bellot. It was cheaper to ship powders in cases as cartridges than in bulk.

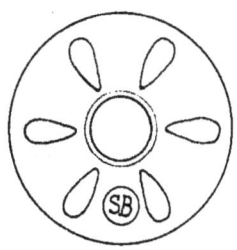
2,129.

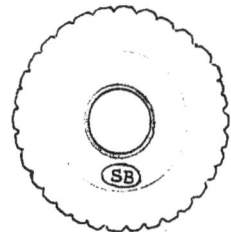
2,130.

PUNT GUN CARTRIDGES

2,131. 2,132.

PYROTECHNIC CARTRIDGE

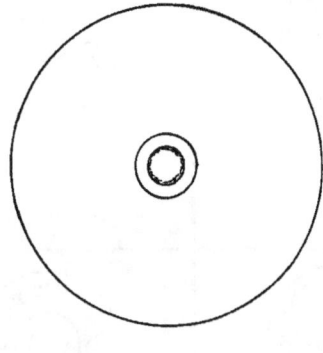
2,133.

2,134.

YACHT CANNON

2,135.

Central Fire 173

BELATED EDITIONS

Due to various reasons, a few headstampings have missed their alphabetical placing in the main listing. Sod's law if you like, but having completed the headstamping list I have then found a box of drawings that have never been added to my headstamp bank. Perhaps I should have left them all out, but that is not me. They are here shown under the above heading. Four blank pages then follow. Should you start drawing, then you may like to fill these up for yourself.

2,136. 12mm	2,137. 14mm	2.138. .360	2,139.
2,140. 28g	2,141.	2,142.	2,143.
2,144.	2,145.	2,146. 18g	2,147.
2,148.	2,149.	2,150.	2,151.
2,152. 15g	2,153/R. 14g	2,154.	2,155.

Central Fire Extra 174

A HILL / Nº 12 / KYNOCH / HORNCASTLE	AMERICAN / 12 GA / EAGLE	A & N.C.S.LD / Nº 12 / KARACHI	ATKIN. 2. JERMYN ST. S.W. / Nº 12 / ELEY
2,156.	2,157.	2,158.	2,159.
AURE LE PAGE / F. DUMOND Succʳ / 12 PARIS 12	AUSTIN'S / Nº 12 / EXTRA SPECIAL	BEESLEY LONDON / Nº 12 / ELEY	BOND THETFORD / Nº 12 / ELEY
2,160.	2,161.	2,162.	2,163.
BOSS & Cº LONDON / Nº 12 / ELEY	B.P.D. / 12 12 / ROMA	C.A. BOGARDUS / Nº 12 / CHAMPION	C.A.C. / Nº 12 / ELEVEN FIFTY
2,164.	2,165.	2,166.	2,167.
C.A.C / 12 12 / GAUGE	C.A.C. / Nº 12 / GUN CLUB	C.A.C. / Nº 12 / LONG RANGE	C.A.C / 12 12 / N.Z
2,168.	2,169.	2,170.	2,171.
C.A.C. / 12 12 / ☆ ☆ / N.Z	C.A.C. / Nº 12 / STANDARD	C.A.C. / Nº 12 / STANDARD HEAVY	C.A.H.& CO / 12
2,172.	2,173.	2,174.	2,175.
CARLSBAD / Nº 12 / AMMO CO	CARR BROˢ / Nº 12 / ELEY / HUDDERSFIELD	CARR & Cº / Nº 12 / KYNOCH / NOTTINGHAM	CARTRIDGE / Nº 12 / GASTIGHT
2,176.	2,177.	2,178.	2,179.

Central Fire Extra 175

C.B / N°12 / KYNOCH	CHEDDITE 12 / 12 / ITALIA	C.&H. OMAHA / 12 GA / 12 GA PAT PEND	C.H.&S. / N°12
2,180.	2,181.	2,182.	2,183.
CASE MADE IN GERMANY / N°12	DICKSON & SONS / N° 12 / ELEY EDINBURGH	E.B / N° 12 / LONDON	F.E.STOCKER. S⸵ AUSTELL / N°12 / ELEY
2,184.	2,185.	2,186.	2,187.
F.N. / 12 12 / MADE IN BELGIUM / HERSTAL	12 / Gauge	N° G.E.BOND / 12 / THETFORD	N° G.H.DAW'S / 12 / PATENT
2,188.	2,189.	2,190.	2,191.
GIBBS BRISTOL & LONDON / N°12 / ELEY	HENRY ATKIN / N° 12 / N / LONDON	JAMES. B. WARRILOW / TRADE MARK / N° 12 / ACCURATE CHIPPENHAM	J.B. / 12 12 / WALSRODE
2,192.	2,193.	2,194.	2,195.
J. PURDEY & SONS / N° 12 / ELEY EJECTOR	LANGLEY / N° 12 / LUTON & HITCHIN	LAPUA / 12	L. BACHMANN / 12 12 / BREVETE
2,196.	2,197.	2,198.	2,199.
LEPUS / ☆ ☆ / 12	SPORTING PARK LTD / 60. NEW BOND. ST / LONDON / ELEY N°12	LYON & LYON / N° 12 / CALCUTTA	MACNAUGHTON EDINBURGH · 12 ·
2,200.	2,201.	2,202.	2,203.

Central Fire Extra 176

MADE IN ENGLAND 12 12	MADE IN GREAT BRITAIN 12 12	MADE IN JAPAN 12 GA	MANTON CALCUTTA Nº 12
2,204.	2,205.	2,206.	2,207.
MILBURN BRAMPTON Nº 12	Mref.SE D'ARMES & DE CYCLES ST ETIENNE 12 12	PETERS TARGET Nº 12	RED DEVIL Nº 12
2,208.	2,209.	2,210.	2,211.
Remington 12 GA MADE IN USA DUPONT	REMINGTON EXPRESS 12 GA MADE IN USA 3¼ - 1¼ - 6	SCHULTZE LONDON Nº 12	S.G.Co YEOMAN Nº 12
2,212.	2,213.	2,214.	2,215.
Ste FSE DES MUNITIONS PARIS 12 12	T. POWELL & Cº LTD SALISBURY Nº 12	TRENT MADE IN ENGLAND 12 12	U.M.C.CO. EXPERT Nº 12
2,216.	2,217.	2,218.	2,219.
U.M.C.CO. UNION Nº 12	NO.12 MADE IN USA U S DEFIANCE	NO.12 U S FIRST	WEEKES PATENT 12
2,220.	2,221.	2,222.	2,223.
WESTERN NEW CHIEF MADE IN USA Nº 12	WESTERN PEERLESS Nº 12	WESTERN RECORD Nº 12	WINCHESTER BLUE RIVAL Nº 12
2,224.	2,225.	2,226.	2,227.

Central Fire Extra 177

WINCHESTER 12 GA WONDER 2,228.	W.R.A.Co. No 12 RIVAL 2,229.	W.R.A.Co. No 12 S.Q 2,230.	W.R.A.Co. No 12 STAR 2,231.
ELEY.LONDON No 10 GASTIGHT 2,232.	ELEY NOBEL 2,233. 10g	PETERS No 10 TARGET 2,234.	R.G.&M.F.C.Co. LIMITED 2,235. 10g
W.R.A.Co. No 10 S.Q 2,236.	The squares below are for your personal additions.		W.R.A.Co. No 10 STAR 2,237.

The squares below are for your personal additions.

For Personal Drawings

For Personal Drawings

For Personal Drawings

THE
SIDE ELEVATIONS

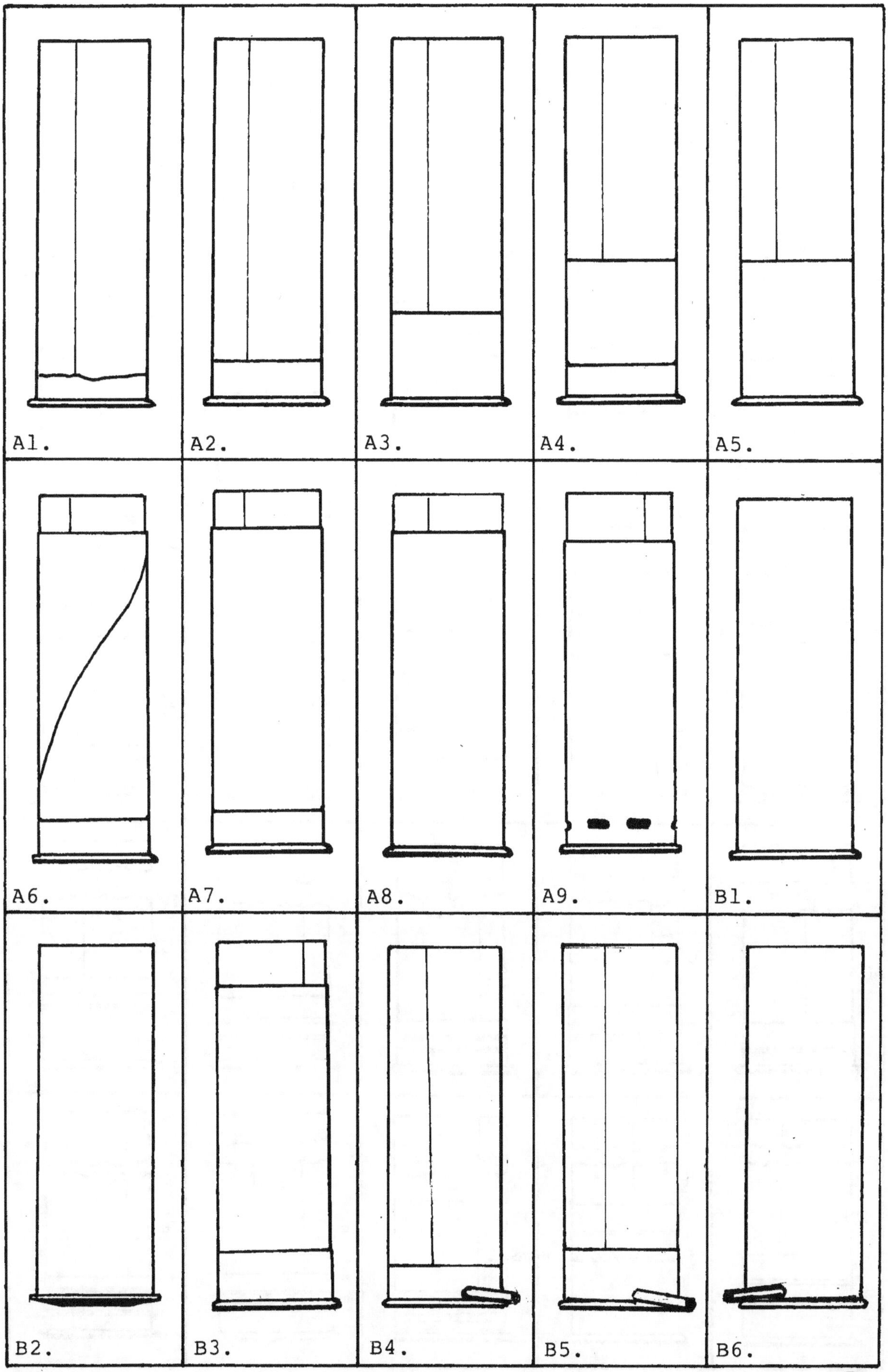

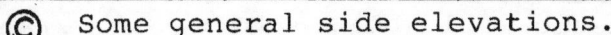
Some general side elevations.

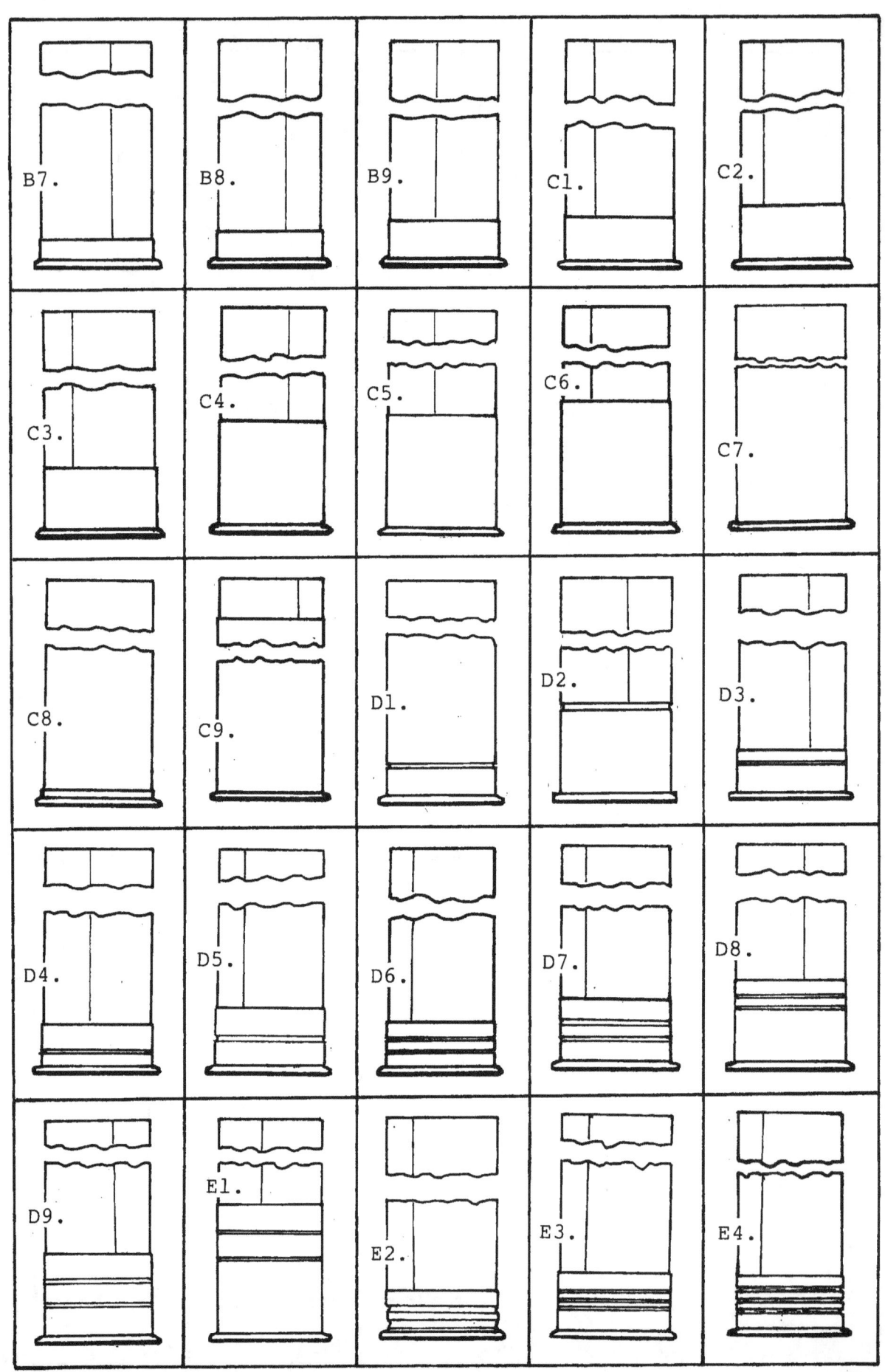

Drawn as paper tubed. Plastic would be seamless.

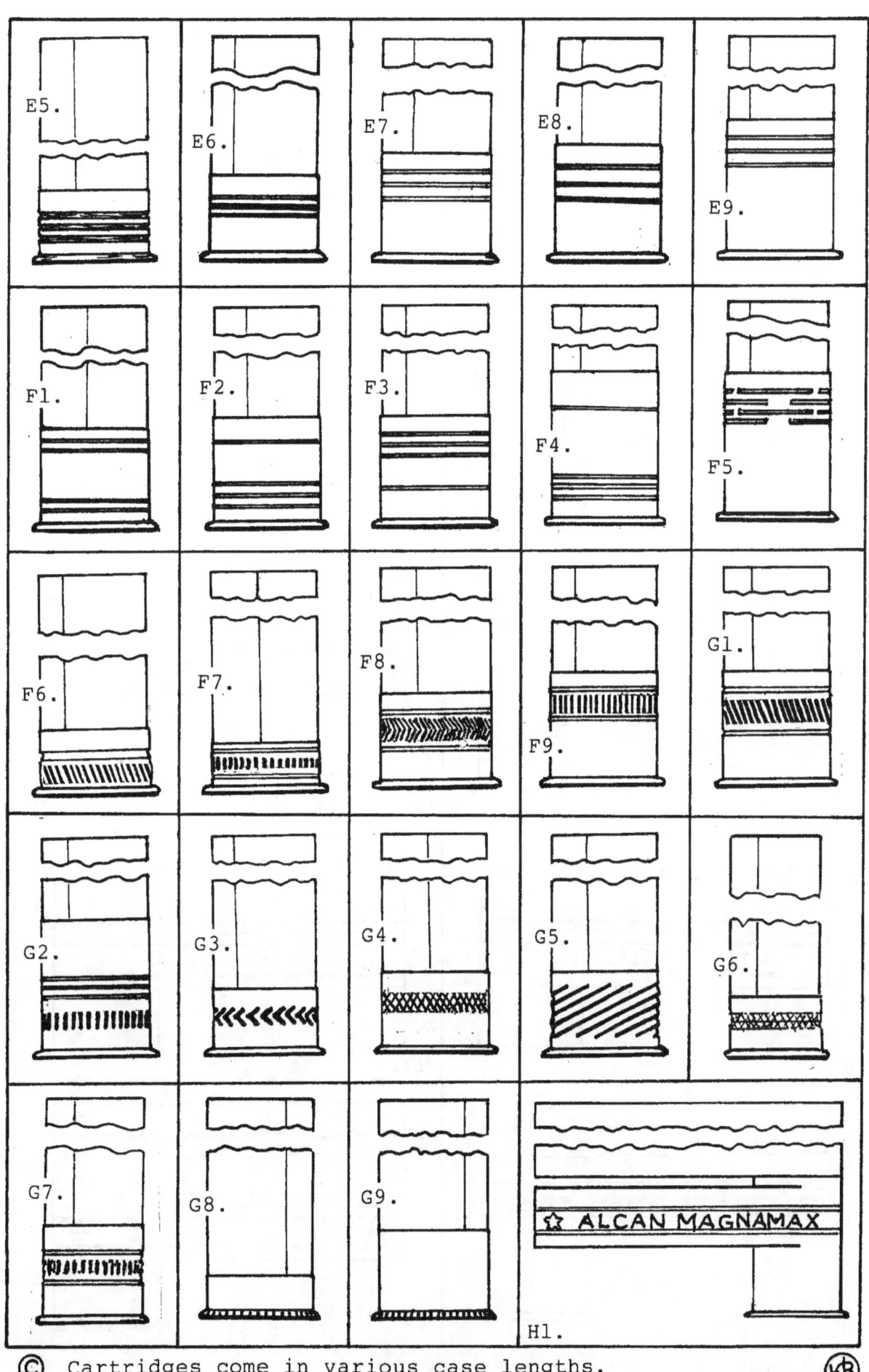

© Cartridges come in various case lengths.

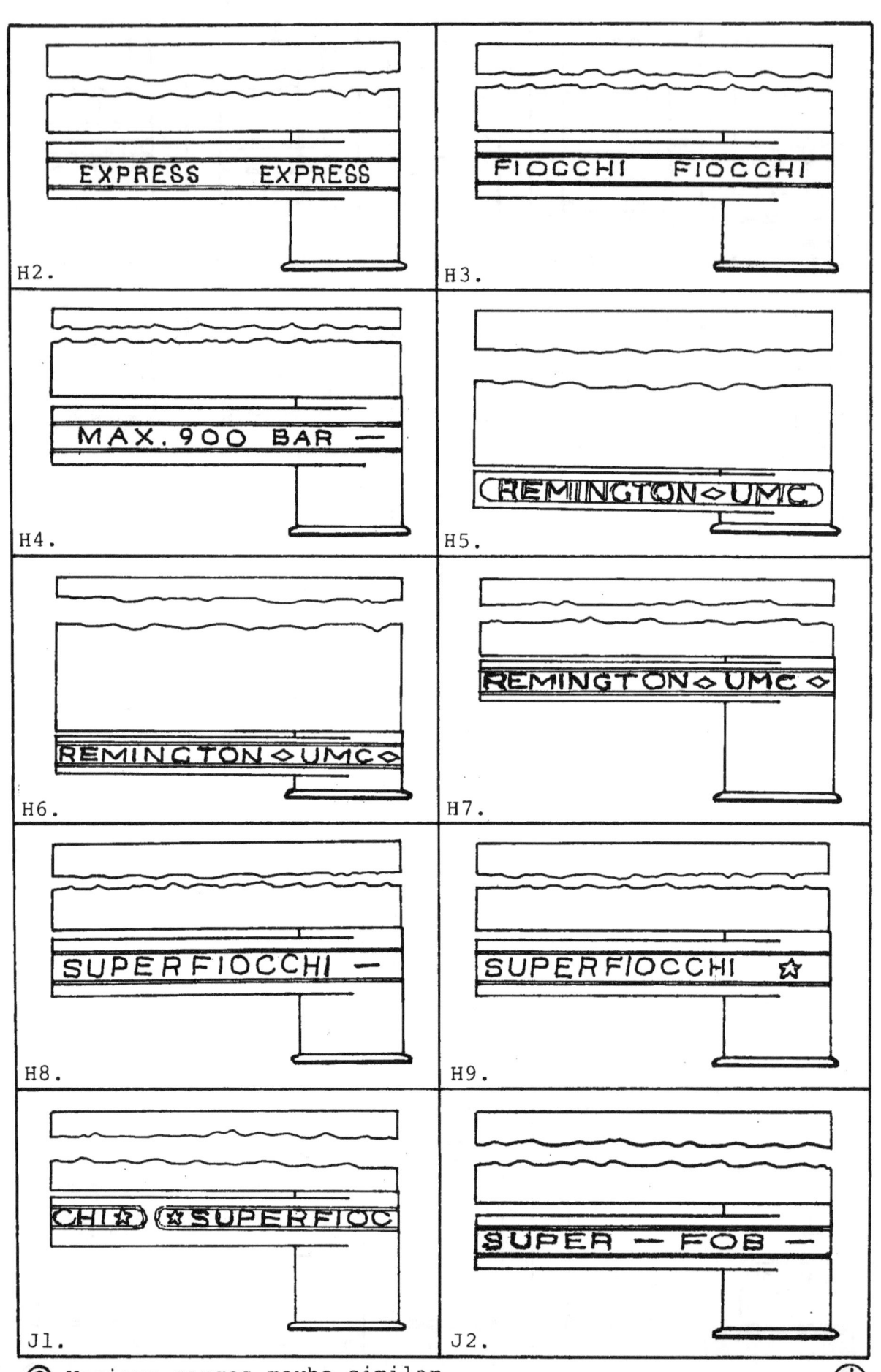

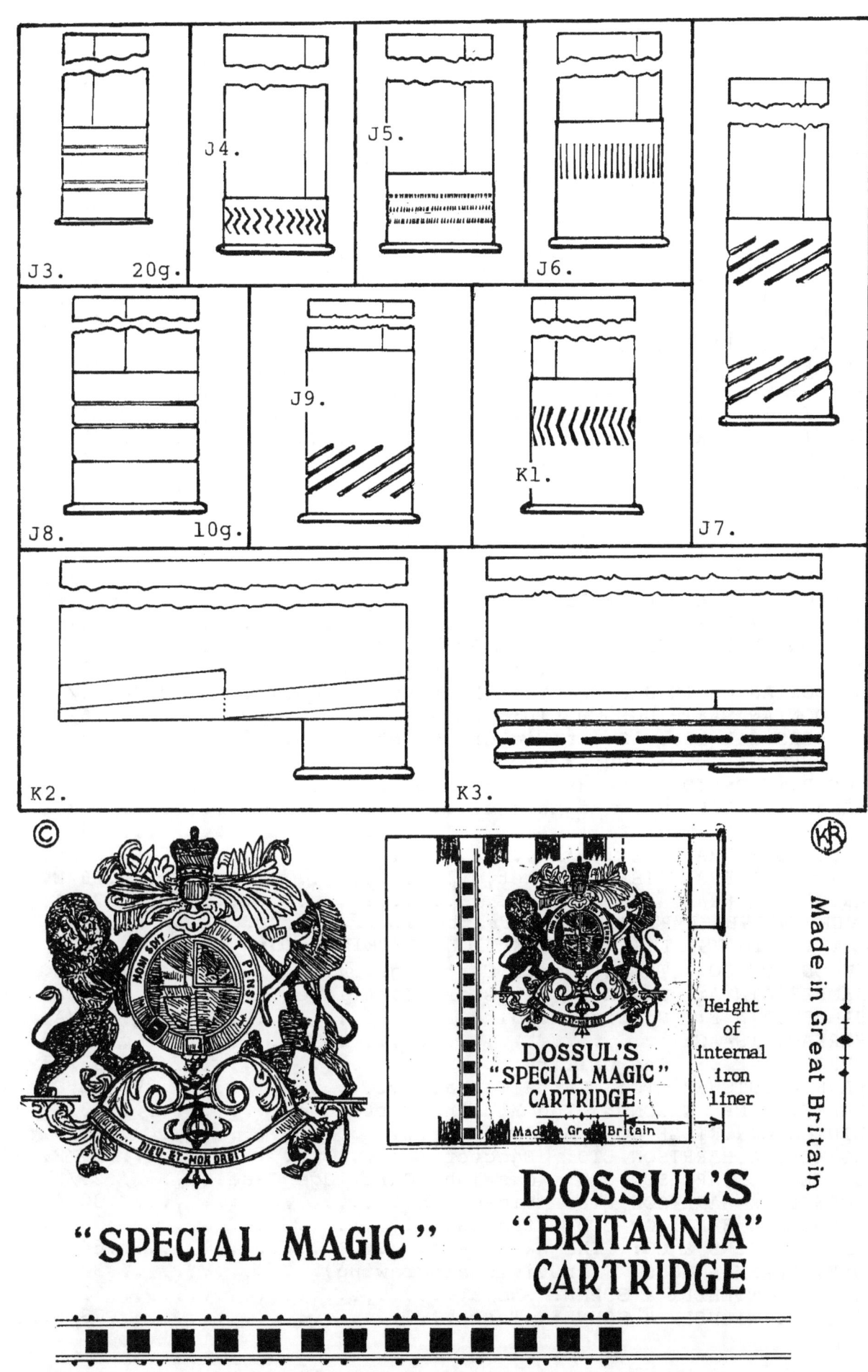

INDEX TO PLATES

```
ALCOCK & PIERCE PTY LTD:  Smokeless Kilos Cartridge.......22/B.
ALDER MARKE:..............................................21/C.
ALDERSONS LTD:  Algame Express...........................22/C,D.
ALLWELL & PHIPPS:.........................................22/E.
AMERICAN AMMUNITION CO:  Al Smokeless.....................22/F.
AMERICAN AMMUNITION CO:  (Hellis).........................23/A.
ANDERSON F A:  The Sacville Cartridge.....................36/A.
ARMY & NAVY CO-OP SOC:  Eley Gas-tight Case...............23/D.
ARMY & NAVY CO-OP SOC:  Eureka............................23/E.
ARMY & NAVY CO-OP SOC:  A & NCS,Ltd (Bombay)..............23/F.
ARMY & NAVY STORES:  The Ancos Cartridge..................24/A.
ATKIN, HENRY LTD:  Pegamoid Paper.........................42/F.
BAILEY, CHARLES A:........................................27/C.
BAMFORD, J C LTD:  50th Anniversary 1945-1995.............49/A.
BARKE P W:................................................60/E.
BASCHIERI & PELLAGRI. S P A:  MB..........................24/B.
BEAULIEU MANOR ESTATE:....................................51/D.
BONETT P A:  The Mallard..................................58/A.
BOSS & CO LTD:  .........................................24/C.
BOYNE ESTATE:  The Alec Morris............................24/D.
BRAUN & BLOEM:  BB........................................24/E.
BRITISH ASSOCIATION FOR SHOOTING & CONSERVATION:  1908....24/F.
BSA GUNS UK LTD:  High Velocity Field Load................25/A.
BUCHHOLZ DIANA PULVERFABRIKEN:  18 gauge..................25/B.
BUCKINGHAMSHIRE OTTER HOUNDS:.............................25/C.
CALEDONIAN CARTRIDGE CO LTD:  Brit CPX B.32...............25/F.
CALEDONIAN CARTRIDGE CO LTD:  Brit The Ounce..............25/E.
CALEDONIAN CARTRIDGE CO LTD:  Brit Velox 285.........25/D,26/A.
CALEDONIAN CARTRIDGE CO LTD:  XL's........................26/B.
CALIBERS G&L LTD:  Super Victory Skeet....................38/B.
CALIBERS G&L LTD:  Super Victory Trap.....................38/C.
CAMBER, N B LTD:  The Harley Hornet.......................55/F.
CARNARVON, EARL OF:  Highclere............................43/F.
CARTOUCHIE FRANCAISE:  ...................................26/D.
CARTOUCHIE FRANCAISE:  'K'................................26/F.
CARTOUCHIE FRANCAISE:  Rocket, Eley.......................26/E.
CARTOUCHIE FRANCAISE:  'T'................................27/A.
CAVER (WOLVERHAMPTON) LTD:  Trotters......................27/B.
CAWADIAN INDUSTRIES LTD. DOMINION CARTRIDGE CO:  Imperial.26/C.
CAWOOD GUN CO:  The Woodcock Cartridge....................27/C.
CHAMBERLAIN A:  The A.C. Wiltshire Cartridge..............21/A.
CHAMBERLAIN E:  Special Loading E.C.......................33/A.
CHEREAU, ISAAC:  .........................................48/E.
CHURCHILL E J:  The Utility...............................33/B.
CLARK & BUTCHER LTD:  Carta Carna......................29/A,B,C.
CLARKE, HENRY & SONS:  The Midland Cartridge..............43/A.
CLINTON CARTRIDGE CO:  Mallard............................29/D.
COGSWELL & HARRISON LTD:  Ejector.........................29/E.
COGSWELL & HARRISON LTD:  Gastight Cartridge Case.........29/F.
COGSWELL & HARRISON LTD:  Victoroid.......................30/A.
COGSWELL & HARRISON LTD:  (Paris).........................30/B.
COHEN, S SONS & CO:  The Ak-U-Rate........................64/C.
COLE, FRANK & SONS:  (Provisional drawing)................37/F.
COLLATH, WILHELM & SOHNE:  No,5...........................73/F.
COLLATH, WILHELM & SOHNE:  Tesco..........................73/E.
```

```
COLONIAL AMMUNITION CO LTD:  Gastight Cartridge Case......30/C.
COLONIAL AMMUNITION CO LTD:  Standard Heavy...............30/D.
COMMONWEALTH CARTRIDGE CO:  C.C.C..........................30/E.
COONEY, GEORGE:  ..............................................39/A.
CORDES, H G:  .................................................43/C.
CORDING, J C & CO LTD:  Beater................................49/B.
CORDING, J C & CO LTD:  Fillbag...............................49/C.
CORDING, J C & CO LTD:  Turnax..............................49/D,E.
COTON, WALTER:  ..............................................71/B,C.
COTSWOLD GAME FARM LTD:  The Cotswold.......................30/F.
CROWE, RONNIE:  The Chelmer....................................63/D.
CROWE, RONNIE:  The Crow.......................................63/E.
CRUDGINGTON, I M LTD:  The Crudgington Cartridge...........46/F.
CRUDGINGTON, I M LTD:  SPA....................................46/E.
DANSK PATRON INDUSTRI:  DPI...................................31/A.
DAW & CO:  Nursing Chunder.....................................31/B.
DE LAMBERT, A:  Eley Gas-tight Cartridge Case.............21/B.
DELORME, A:  Clamecy 'T'......................................31/C.
DICKSON, J & SON LTD:  The Caledonian.......................50/A.
DICKSON, J & SON LTD:  The Waverley.........................49/F.
DODD, D D:  ...................................................31/D.
DOMINION CARTRIDGE CO LTD:  Imperial.........................26/C.
DOUILLES EN ACIER ARMCO:......................................32/A.
DOUILLES A BROUCHE SOC IE TU:  (Pin-fire)...................31/E.
DOUILLES A BROUCHE SOC IE TU:  (Central-fire)...............31/F.
DRESTE & COLLINSBUSCH:  ......................................32/B.
DUMOND:.......................................................32/C.
DUNMORE SHOOTING CENTRE:  The Dunmore Royal.................32/D.
DYKE, FRANK & CO LTD:  Yellow Wizard Rustless...............32/E.
DYMOND, MARTIN:  The Kit-Hill.................................54/D.
EBRALL BROS:  Countryman......................................32/F.
EICHEL:  .....................................................33/C.
ELAHEE BUKSH & COY:  Kynoch Unlined Nitro Quality..........33/E.
ELAHEE BUKSH & COY:  Smokeless Cartridge....................33/D.
ELEY BROS LTD:  ..............................................33/F.
ELEY BROS LTD:  The Pigeon....................................34/A.
ELEY BROS LTD:  Smokeless Cartridge..........................34/B.
ELEY IMI AMMUNITION DIV:  Black 32g..........................34/D.
ELEY IMI AMMUNITION DIV:  (Engine start)....................34/C.
ELEY IMI AMMUNITION DIV:  Grand Prix.........................34/E.
ELEY LTD:  North American Skeet 28g................34/F,35/A.
ELEY HAWK LTD:  Eley Classic Game............................35/B.
ELEY HAWK LTD:  Eley & Shooting Times Game Gun Comp'......35/C.
ELVEDEN ESTATE GUN CLUB:  ....................................35/D.
ERRE:  High Speed.............................................35/E.
EVANS, WILLIAM:  Mark-Over...................................74/B,C.
EVILL, ALAN & CO:  The Express 73...........................22/A.
EXPLOSIFS DE CLERMONT MULLER & CIE:  Mullerite.............35/F.
FABRIQUE NADIONALE d'ARMES:  2 inch.........................36/B.
FIOCCHI USA/LMCS:  Lousie Mandrell 1996 Shoot..............36/F.
FIRLE SHOOT:  The Ram Cartridge..............................37/A.
FIRMS NOT KNOWN:  77/A;  77/B;  77/D Aster;  77/C Falk;

                 77/E Clay Birds;  77/F Exposition;  78/A 'T';

                 78/B Loda;  78/C Lux;  78/D Spitfire;

                 78/E Ringer;  78/F Wanker:
```

FLOBERT: 'T'	37/B,C,D,E.
FREENEY'S: The Atom	36/E.
FRERES REY:	62/D.
GAMEBORE CARTRIDGE CO: Tin Shot	38/D.
GATES OF BALDOCK: Ford	38/E.
GATES TRACTORS: Ford	38/F.
GAUPILLAT M:	55/A.
GEORGE G: Velox	39/C.
GEVELOT: 'T'	39/E.
GIBBS, GEORGE LTD: Kynoch 5/8" Brass	39/B.
GILMAN, J & SON LTD:	50/B.
GIULIO FIOCCHI: Lecco	39/F, 40/A.
GORDON CARTRIDGE CO: Smokeless Powder	40/C.
GORDON, FRANK A:	36/C.
GRANT & LANG: Instanter	66/A.
GREENFIELD OF SALISBURY LTD: The Wessex	40/D,E.
GUINARD A:	21/D.
GUNNERSIDE SHOOT:	40/F, 41/A.
HAERNS KRUDTVAERK:	41/B.
HAJI DOSSUL, A & SONS: Britannia Cartridge	21/E.
HAJI DOSSUL, A & SONS: Special Magic	21/F.
HALFZ GHOUSE & CO: Smokeless Field Cartridge	41/C.
HANDY, G J & CO LTD: Handy	40/B.
HARRIS SCARFE LTD: The Speedite	41/D.
HARRIS SCARFE LTD: Unicorn	41/E.
HARTLEY'S SPORTS STORE: Hartsport	41/F.
HARVEY SHAW SUCCESSORS: Rhenwest	42/B,C.
HASHIM S HASHIM:	42/A.
HAWKES BROS: Barwon	42/D.
HAWKES BROS: Corio	42/E.
HAYGARTH, C H & SONS: Economax	28/B.
HAYGARTH, C H & SONS: The Mallard Cartridge	28/C.
HELLIS, CHAS & SONS:	23/A.
HELLIS, CHAS & SONS: (Bird)	28/D,E.
HELLIS, CHAS & SONS: The Economist	28/F.
HEYER, CHARLES A & CO: Eley Gas-tight for Schultze	27/E.
HEYER, CHARLES A & CO: Simba	27/F.
H H THE RULER OF QATAR:	43/E.
HIBBARD W G; SPENCER F F; & BARTLETT A L: Star Brand	72/E.
HIGHCLERE ESTATE: Highclere	44/A,B.
HIRTENBERG:	44/C.
HOLLAND & HOLLAND LTD: 150th Anniversary	45/D.
HOPKINS, H G & SONS:	43/D.
HORDENS, ANTHONY: Tree Brand	23/B.
HOULIER BLANCHARD:	45/E.
HULL CARTRIDGE CO LTD: Three Crowns	46/B.
HUNGERFORD PARK ESTATE: 1oz Game Load	46/C.
HUTCHINSON: Nobel's Sporting Ballistite	46/D.
ICI OF AUSTRALIA & NZ: 20 Gauge Case	47/B.
ICI OF AUSTRALIA & NZ: Curtiss &Harvey's	47/A.
ICI OF AUSTRALIA & NZ: Empire GR	48/A.
ICI OF AUSTRALIA & NZ: Empress	47/C.
ICI OF AUSTRALIA & NZ: Rex	47/E.
ICI OF AUSTRALIA & NZ: Rocket, Eley	47/F.
ICI OF AUSTRALIA & NZ: Scarebird	47/D.
IMI AUSTRALIA LTD: Duck Load	48/D.
IMI KYNOCH LTD: Grand Prix, Eley	48/B.
IMI KYNOCH LTD: Tracer, Eley	48/C.
ISAAC CHEREAU:	48/E.

```
JAKTKLUBB:  1863-1988........................................48/F.
JARRY P:  ....................................................59/A.
JEFFERY, W & SON:  ...........................................76/A.
JEFFERY, W & SON:  The Sky High...............................76/B.
JONES, ROBERT:  The Liver Cartridge...........................63/B.
KENT CARTRIDGE CO LTD:  ......................................50/C.
KINGSTONE LISLE SHOOT:  ......................................50/D.
KIRKEE FACTORY:  KF Special...................................50/E.
KNIGHT, PETER:  Invincible....................................58/F.
KOLN-ROTTWEILER AG:  .........................................50/F.
KRUKCL:  Boxford 1990 (Berks).................................51/A.
LANCASTER, CHARLES & CO:  Generally Useful..............,,,,,,28/A.
LIBERTY CARTRIDGE CO:  .......................................51/B.
LILAND WINGSHOOTING:  ........................................51/C.
LOCKE, WALTER & CO:  Locke Special............................71/D.
LOUISE MANDRELL:  1996 Shoot..................................36/F.
LUCKING ?:  Swing Don't Poke..................................51/E.
LYAVALE LTD:  Express Supreme.................................51/F.
LYAVALE LTD:  World Cup.....................................52/A,B.
LYON & LYON LTD:  Gamester....................................52/C.
MAHILLON H:  Eley Cases................44/D,E,F. 45/A,B,C.
MALLOCH P D:  The Red Grouse..................................56/D.
MANTON & CO:  Special Express.................................52/D.
MANUFACTURE FRANCAISE d'ARMES:  (All brass pin-fire)..........52/E.
MANUFACTURE GENERALE DE MUNITIONS:  (14 m/m).................52/F.
MANUFACTURE GENERALE DE MUNITIONS:  'T'......................53/A.
MARATOS, N & SON:  ...........................................56/B.
MARLBOROUGH GUN SHOP:  Marlborough Cartridge..................53/B.
MARLBOROUGH GUN SHOP:  The Marlborough........................53/C.
MARLBOROUGH GUN SHOP:  Moonraker..............................53/D.
MARSDEN, T & SONS LTD:  Globe.................................68/E.
MARSHALL, SONS & CO:  (Tractor start).......................53/E,F.
MARTIGNONI:  (Dogs)...........................................54/B.
MARTIGNONI:  (Ducks)..........................................54/A.
MARTIGNONI:  (Rabbit).........................................54/C.
MELBOURNE SPORTS DEPOT:  Meteor...............................54/E.
METROPOLE:  ..................................................54/F.
MONTAGU, LORD:  Beaulieu Manor Estate.........................51/D.
MOOR END GAME FARM:...........................................55/C.
MULTI-SPORTS:  The Multi-Shot.................................55/D.
MUNITIONSWERKE:  Waldheil.....................................55/E.
NAUGHTON, T & SONS LTD:  The Blazer...........................68/F.
NEW ZEALAND CARTRIDGE COLLECTORS CLUB:  1961-1986.........56/A.
NOBEL EXPLOSIVES CO LTD:  Gas-tight Waterproof Case.....56/D,E.
NOBEL EXPLOSIVES CO LTD:  Noneka..............................56/C.
NOBEL EXPLOSIVES CO LTD:  Sporting Ballistite Special.....56/F.
NOBEL INDUSTRIES LTD:  Duxbac, Eley...........................57/C.
NOBEL INDUSTRIES LTD:  Grand Prix, Eley.......................57/A.
NOBEL INDUSTRIES LTD:  Sporting Ballistite....................57/B.
OAKES BROS:  The Oakes Cartridge..............................57/E.
OAKES & CO LTD:  Premier......................................57/D.
ORBEA:  Trust.................................................57/F.
ORMSBY GAME SERVICES:  .......................................58/A.
ORR, P & SONS:  Challenge.....................................59/E.
ORR, P & SONS:  Grand Prix, Eley..............................59/F.
PACHMAYR GUN WORKS:  (Cruet set)..............................58/C.
PARKER, HUGH:  Special........................................45/F.
PEARSON & CO:  Nobel's Sporting Ballistite Special........58/E.
```

```
PNEUMATIC CARTRIDGE CO LTD:  Pneuma........................59/B.
PNEUMATIC CARTRIDGE CO LTD:  Pneumatic Special.............59/C.
POLISH STATE AMMUNITION:  Eagle Trap........................59/D.
POUDERIES REUINES DE BELGIQUE:  Clermonite..............60/A,B.
PULVERFABRIK POwDER FACTORY:  Olympia........................60/C.
PULVERFABRIK POWDER FACTORY:  (Pheasant).....................60/D.
RAF LAKENHEATH ROD & GUN CLUB:  ..............................60/F.
RAKER:  Bang Bang Bugger.............................................61/A.
RANDALL WRIGHT:  Amberite Cartridge............................61/B.
RAUFOSS AMMUNITIONS FABRIKKER:  ..............................61/C.
REMINGTON UMC ARMS CO INC:  (No,2)............................62/A.
REMINGTON UMC ARMS CO INC:  (No,3)............................61/D.
REMINGTON UMC ARMS CO INC:  (12 m/m)..........................61/F.
REMINGTON UMC ARMS CO INC:  Hand Loaded......................61/E.
REMINGTON UMC ARMS CO INC:  Kleanbore (8 gauge)............62/B.
REMINGTON UMC ARMS CO INC:  (Message sender)...............62/C.
REY FRERES:  ......................................................62/D.
RHEINISCHE WESTFALISCHE SPRINGSTOFF:  De Zwaluw Pin-fire..62/E.
RHEINISCHE WESTFALISCHE SPRINGSTOFF:  De Zwaluw (Central).62/F.
RHEINISCHE WESTFALISCHE SPRINGSTOFF:  Marke Einhorn........63/A.
ROBIN HOOD AMMUNITION CO:  ..................................63/C.
SANDRINGHAM RABBIT CLEARANCE SOC LTD:......................63/F.
SAYER'S:  Bulzi....................................................64/A.
SCHULTZE CO LTD:  The Captain (20 gauge)...................64/B.
SELLIER & BELLOT:  Hubertus....................................64/E.
SELLIER & BELLOT:  Meteor......................................64/D.
SHIMWELL BROTHERD (PTY) LTD:  Unity..........................64/F.
SIMMONS, MICK LTD:  The Lightning.............................55/B.
SIR RICHARD SUTTON'S SETTLED ESTATES:  Benham Estate....65/A,B.
SIX MILE BOTTOM:  ................................................65/C.
SMItHS GORE:  ....................................................65/D.
SOCIETY FRANCAISE DES MUNITIONS (SFM):....................65/E,F.
SQUIRES, HENRY C:  Tournament Shell..........................43/B.
STYPE ESTATE:  ..................................................66/B.
SUPER CARTRIDGE CO PTY LTD:  All Metal...................66/C,D.
TARDEY FRERES:  (Pin-fire punt gun)..........................66/E.
TEIKOKU E' YAKKYOSEIZA:  T.Y.K...............................66/F.
TESCHNER-COLLATH:  ..............................................73/D.
THE CARTRIDGE:  ...............................................67/A,B.
THE GUN COUNTER:  .............................................67/C,D.
THE HINGSTON-SMITH ARMS CO LTD:  ...........................67/E.
THE MEMBURY ESTATE:  .........................................67/F.
THE MULLERITE CARTRIDGE WORKS. PULVeRMANN, MARTIN LTD:  ..68/A.
THE NETTLEBED SHOOT:  ........................................68/B.
THE TULCHAN ESTATE:  ..........................................68/C.
THUMPERS:  Express Special.....................................68/D.
TISDALL, W H LTD:  Perfection..................................73/A.
TISDALL, W H LTD:  The Retriever............................73/B,C.
TRYON CO:  Buffalo Brand.........................................69/E.
TURNER, THOS & SONS LTD:  Turnax............................69/A,B.
TURNER, THOS & SONS (READING) LTD:  Blue Rapid............69/C.
TURNER, THOS & SONS (READING) LTD:  Hornet.................69/D.
UNITED KINGDOM CARTRIDGE CLUB. UKCC:  First Anniversary...70/B.
UNION METALLIC CARTRIDGE CO. UMC:  Nitro....................69/F.
UNITED STATES CARTRIDGE CO:  Defiance.......................70/C.
VALE IRONMONGERS:  The Vale...................................70/D.
VODAFONE LTD:  Vodafone........................................70/E.
```

```
VON-DREYES, FREDERICK:  (0·70)...............................36/D.
VOR ROUSSEAUX:  ..............................................70/F.
WALSHE A P:  Walshe's Special Cartridge.......................23/C.
WELCH W A:  ..................................................71/E.
WESTERN CARTRIDGE CO:  Super'X' Industrial....................71/F.
WESTERN CARTRIDGE CO:  Western Xpert..........................72/A.
WESTLEY RICHARDS & CO LTD:  game load.......................72/B,C.
W.F.S LTD:  Reach Me Downs....................................72/D.
WHITBY & CO:  (Cartridge pocket knife)........................72/F.
WILKINSON'S:  The Beacon....................................74/A,E.
WILLIAMSON & SON:  ...........................................74/D.
WILTSHIRE ROD & GUN CO:  .....................................74/F.
WINCHESTER (AUSTRALIA) PTY LTD:  21 years in Australia....75/C.
WINCHESTER (AUSTRALIA) PTY LTD:  Quail Load................75/B.
WINCHESTER (AUSTRALIA) PTY LTD:  Rabbit Load...............75/A.
WINCHESTER REPEATING ARMS CO:  Leader.....................75/D,E.
WINCHESTER-WESTERN DIV:  .....................................75/F.
WINDER, GEORGE:  The New Century..............................39/D.
WOBURN RABBIT CLEARANCE SOC LTD:  ............................76/C.
WOLF & CO:  ..................................................76/E.
WOLF & CO:  Cymax Standard....................................76/D.
WOLF & CO:  Wolf-Marke........................................76/F.
WRIGHT, RANDALL:  ............................................61/B.
WYMAN & ABBOTT:  .............................................71/A.
```

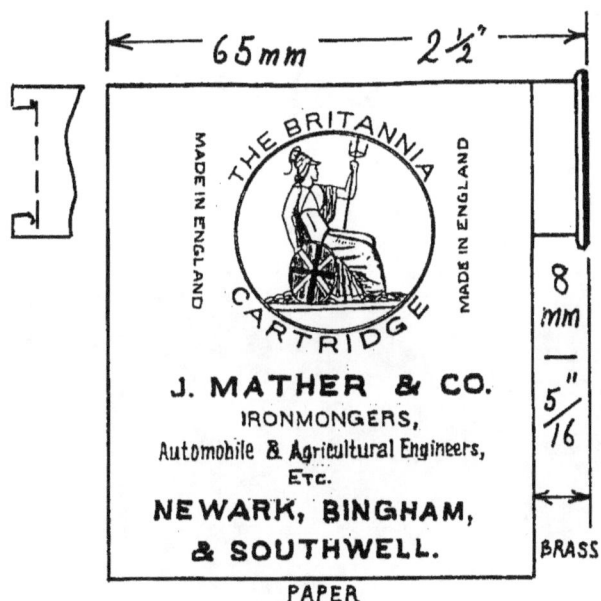

One of my early drawings.

www.ingramcontent.com/pod-product-compliance
Lightning Source LLC
Chambersburg PA
CBHW080915230426
43667CB00015B/2686